Introduction to Christian Counseling

PASTOR DAVID CASTLEMAN

FOREWARD

When I was asked to read Pastor Dave's book "Introduction to Christain Counseling" I was honored. I remember thinking "I've been a professional counselor for eleven years, I should have some valuable input to share."

Additionally, having been in the ministry for quite some time, I have also had the pleasure of working next to amazing pastors. Some of these pastors I have watched struggle with counseling their sheep. The problems being beyond their training. To get the opportunity to read this much needed guide for helping Christians in the counseling settings, especially pastors, was beyond exciting. Putting it succinctly, I could not wait to get started and "help". I was going to make lots of notes.

As a professional counselor, who is a Christian, I considered myself to be a Christian counselor working in the secular world, bringing the love of Christ to my clients as I could...and then I began reading the book. Can I tell you that my whole practice has been turned upside down? Everything I had learned and thought I knew was blown out the window. This book made me reevaluate how I have been counseling for the past eleven years.

Please understand that as a licensed counselor, taking insurance and abiding by the ethical guidelines of the licensing board there are certain things I have to take into consideration. With that being said, my conscience was telling me that I had to find a new balance, where my faith and profession collided. After reading the book a lot of prayer and study went into how I viewed and functioned in my chosen career.

I remember in the middle of reading "Introduction to Christian Counseling" and sitting across from a client thinking about everything we had ever done in our sessions. This happened more and more as I continued to read "Introduction to Christian Counseling". Suddenly, I found myself reassessing all of my therapy sessions. Was I really counseling from a Christian perspective.

Having gone to a major secular university, we studied all of the major theories and therapy based styles on the different theories we had learned. I have spent eleven years trying to fit the theories I had learned, the ones I had been told work best, the ones we were taught "you had to use in order to have an effective counseling model," into my personal belief system. After reading this book, the theories I have learned and been told to use, no longer seemed to fit anywhere in my preferred counseling style.

Since reading "Introduction to Christian Counseling" the Lord has worked beyond my wildest imaginations. I find my case load being filled with more and more clients who want to receive counseling from a true Christian perspective. I have had so many opportunities to speak to clients about Christ and I have been able to witness true transformation in several of my clients.

I am excited that you are being afforded the opportunity to read "Introduction to Christian Counseling" for yourself. You will find so much helpful information in the following pages. It is such a great introduction for those who truly desire to help others with an accurate and authentic Christain based counseling model. Helping others the way we, as believers, are supposed to help them, from a Biblical perspective.

Whether you are a novice or a veteran in helping others, I pray that "Introduction to Christian Counseling" exposes you to new and powerful counseling techniques and styles that will result in greater results for every person you counsel.

Brandy Peoples
Brandy Peoples, LPC-S
Founder Peoples' Family Counseling

Contents

Introduction

Over twenty years ago God put in my heart a desire to see believers raised up who love the Lord and have a desire to serve others with a compassion and dedication that matched Jesus' ministry while He walked on the earth in the form of a man. After all, Jesus declared in the gospel of John, chapter 14, verse 12 the following:

"I tell you the truth, anyone who believes in me will do the same works I have done, and even greater works, because I am going to be with the Father." (NLT)

I had been serving in my local church on various levels, had graduated from my first bible school, and subsequently earned a Bachelor's Degree in Theology. Included with this desire, God called my wife and I to plant a church. After counseling with our Pastor and my "Father" in the faith they both confirmed what God had put in our hearts. Within a few months we had moved, started a church, and was seeing uncommon growth, both numerically as well as spiritually. Things were going great.

That is, until Mary and John (names have been changed to maintain their privacy), who had been attending our church for a short while contacted me and asked if we could talk. "Sure" I said, and we met.

In a very short time I realized that Mary and John had serious marital issues and that we would have to meet on a regular basis to get things ironed out. However, as things progressed I learned that their marriage was in worse shape than either one wanted to admit in front of the other so I began meeting with them individually, hoping to get the bedrock issues resolved.

It didn't take long, in fact, during the first individual session with each one they both admitted that, on their wedding day the Holy Spirit had spoken to each one of them separately, not to marry the other one. When I asked, why they proceeded with the ceremonies, both replied that they didn't want to hurt the other one and that all their guests were already present for the wedding. So they went through with it.

We continued to meet, I assigned homework and, even though both were making feeble attempts at completion, neither one took the assignments very serious. I began to realize how unprepared I was to handle issues at this depth. Even after nearly a decade of serving as a head usher, as an Adult Christian Education program director, and standing beside my Pastor watching and learning from him, similar to how the disciples stood beside Jesus, learning something new every day. On top of that, I had received two years of bible school learning how to be a Pastor and four years of "higher" education learning how to be a Theologian.

From the outset I truly believed that I was prepared, both naturally and spiritually, to be used by God in the process of helping others. Unfortunately, this first attempt continued to deteriorate until one evening I received a phone call from John asking for me to come and bail him out of jail, which we did.

As the story of what happened unfolded, I learned that Mary and John had been driving on a major four-lane highway when an argument ensued and they continued to denigrate each other. Then, at some point in the dispute, Mary decided that she was immediately getting out of the car while it was traveling over fifty-five miles per hour. Mary was so resolute in her decision that she opened the door of the car and attempted to jump. Fortunately, John had grabbed ahold of her to prevent her exit while at the same time hitting the brakes and getting the car onto the shoulder of the highway.

During the incident passers-by had witnessed what appeared to them to be a man attempting to "push" a woman out of a moving vehicle and called 911. Police responded, John was arrested, taken to jail, processed, and bail was set, which resulted in the phone call that we received.

I would like to say that Mary and John worked things out and were happily reunited, but I cannot do so. John ended up having the charges against him dismissed, and they resolved their conflict by getting divorced. I learned several things from this single experience:

- When the Holy Spirit tells you to do (or to not do) something, even if it seems to be a hard thing, listen.

- That serving beside someone, even for extended periods of time, does not necessarily prepare you to perform every task that may arise.

• Formal education, by itself, will not always be sufficient preparation for a person to effectively fulfill the rigorous requirements essential to a given position.

• Even special training in biblical studies and theology had not prepared me for what laid ahead, if I were to continue to be a Pastor.

• Finally, that I needed to obtain further education specific to helping others with their individual issues and concerns.

So, it was with great tenacity and passion that I enrolled in the American Association of Christian Counselor's courses through Light University. And after completing one hundred sixty-five classes ranging from helping marriages, youths, sexual dysfunctions, general issues, and numerous others, I was awarded a Honorary Master of Divinity degree through Global Theological University of Tampa, Florida.

Consequently, Dr. Leon van Rooyen, the founder of Global Theological University, asked me if I would be interested in writing this treatise: Introduction to Christian Counseling. I have obviously agreed, and the following work is a result of many hours of prayer, research and determination.

I sincerely hope and pray that this work greatly aids you in furthering both your desires to help others as well fulfilling your God-given gifts and calling.

Chapter 1: Choosing a Technique

Jesus came that we might have an abundant life (cf. John 10:10); this act of love was planned even before God created the heavens and the earth. Nonetheless, God gave each of us the choice of right and wrong: He gave us free will. Today, the philosophy of determinism declares that *all acts of the will result from causes which determine either in such manner that man has no alternative modes of action or that* **the will is still free in the sense of being uncompelled**.[1] Scripturally, I have concluded the later to be true; that all men have free moral agency: *free in the sense of being uncompelled* as to our everyday decisions and choices.

Before He ever spoke, God, in His infinite omniscience, understood how things would turn out with His creation. He is never caught "off-guard" and He is never surprised by what transpires either in the world or in our lives, personally. This should give us a reason to rejoice; knowing that our loving Father, even in the planning stages, had our redemption already in mind.

Counseling, in its basic sense has been around since the Garden of Eden. God, Himself told - or counseled - Adam and Eve to leave the fruit of a specific tree within the garden alone. Did they listen to that wise counsel? Well, we all know they didn't. This resulted in mankind falling from grace and being forced out of the Garden. In short order, we learn that Adam and Eve gave birth to two brothers, Cain and Abel. As these two boys grew each one, as an act of free will, decided their direction in life: Abel became a shepherd while Cain became a farmer.

When it was time for the harvest, Cain presented some of his crops as a gift to the Lord. Abel also brought a gift—the best portions of the firstborn lambs from his flock. The Lord accepted Abel and his gift, but he did not accept Cain and his gift. This made Cain very angry, and he looked dejected. "Why are you so angry?" the Lord asked Cain. "Why do you look so dejected? You will be accepted if you do what is right. But if

---

[1] Philip Babcock Gove (Editor in Chief); (Webster's Third New International Dictionary of the English Language: Unabridged; Springfield, Massachusetts; Merriam-Webster Inc., Publishers; 1993); Page 616

you refuse to do what is right, then watch out! Sin is crouching at the door, eager to control you. But you must subdue it and be its master." One day Cain suggested to his brother, "Let's go out into the fields." And while they were in the field, Cain attacked his brother, Abel, and killed him. (Genesis 4:3-8 NLT)

Obviously their mother and father (Adam and Eve) had taught these two young men certain things about how to honor God. We know this because at harvest-time they both brought gifts before God. Apparently Abel decided to listen to their wise counsel, Cain did not. Their choices resulted in Abel and his offering being accepted by God while Cain's was not. Again, we see a man's choices determine his direction; and still, the loving Creator is not caught unaware.

We can learn a wide variety of theological truths from this account, relating to the fallen nature of humanity, but what else can we learn from these early acts of sin, as it pertains to our current subject? This is a question that everyone must answer if they are involved in helping others: you can give wise godly counsel; counsel that is true to Scripture and perfectly sound concerning a precise set of circumstances, but you cannot force the hearers to follow your recommendations any more than God could force Adam and Eve or Cain to follow the wise counsel they had received.

However, not being able to force our suggestions and counsel upon another should in no way discourage us from gaining knowledge about the counseling process. Realizing that God created us as free moral agents; that is, having the ability to choose between right and wrong, should not deter us from increasing our experiences and skills; nor should our inability to impose godly counsel upon another cause us to simply throw up our hands in surrender; giving up on ever helping anyone.

As we proceed you will be required to ask yourself several questions. Questions such as:

- Is this what God wants me to do?

- What personal traits do I have that are considered positive or negative to the counseling process?

- Am I willing to work on changing the negatives and resist the propensity for pride regarding the positives?

- Can I properly handle people refusing my advise?

- Do I have the ability to stand firm in the face of controversy and criticism?

- Am I capable of empathizing with others?

- Am I willing to walk in love with the unlovable?

- Can I look beyond, without dismissing, the sin in order to help the sinner?

There are an infinite number of questions that I could pose at this point, but most of them you would not be able to answer honestly until you have found yourself in the specific set of circumstances; and yet, the questions I have already eluded to should be answered with as much introspection and honesty as possible prior to embarking upon this journey.

Any counseling can be extremely challenging but Christian based counseling has its own set of additional challenges - most of which arise from differing beliefs and doctrinal persuasions of the counselee. Even within the Christian counseling community there are wide chasms of beliefs as to the best way of helping people. For example, Jay E. Adams, widely recognized as the organizer of the well known, biblically based method of counseling known as *Nouthetics*, soundly discounts eclecticism and integrationism as it pertains to counseling. Adams makes it exceedingly clear that he believes the Bible should be a Christian counselor's sole source when he says:

The Christian's basis for counseling, and the basis for a Christian's counseling, is **nothing other than the Scriptures of the Old and New Testament. The Bible is his counseling textbook.**

"Why?" you ask, "After all, the Christian doesn't use the Bible as his basis for...engineering, architecture, music, - so why should he insist that the Scriptures are the basis for counseling?

The answer to that question is at once both simple and profound... The Bible was given to help men come to saving faith in Christ and then to transform believers into His image (2 Timothy 3:15-17)... God assigns this life calling of transforming lives by the Word to the man of God, (and) the Holy Spirit strongly declares that the Bible

fully equips *him for this work...*

> *As future ministers of the Word, be just that - only that, and nothing else but that - ministers of the Word! Do not forsake the Fountain of living water for the* **cracked cisterns of modern counseling systems.**[2]

Multitudes of other Christian counselors have disagreed with Adams believing that it is proper to learn from other counseling models as long as *any contribution of extrabiblical sources* (are) *distinctly subordinate and secondary to the givens of a biblical model. Other sources may be informative and provocative: we may learn from and be challenged by our own experience, popular fiction, history, the mass media, psychology* (etc.)... But the truth of all these things must be judged by Scripture and reinterpreted according to the Spirit's wisdom. [3]

With this thought in mind we will begin with a short overview of modern psychoanalysis, which will include a brief discussion of various approaches to counseling and the individual commonly accredited with the extrapolation of each model.

Sigmund Freud (Freudianism)

Sigmund Freud is considered by most to be the father of modern psychoanalysis. He believed that the mind is a complex energy-system that consists of three parts: The Id; the Ego; and the Superego.

Listen, to what the "The Internet Encyclopedia of Philosophy" reveals on this very subject: *The theory Id termed "tripartite" simply because...Freud distinguished three structural elements of the mind, which he called Id, Ego, and the Superego. The Id is that part in which are situated the instinctual sexual drives which require satisfaction; the Superego is that part which contains the "conscience", namely, socially-acquired control mechanisms (usually imparted in the first instance by the parents) which have been internalized; while the Ego is the conscious self created by the dynamic tensions and interactions between the Id and the Superego, which has the task of reconciling their conflicting demands with the requirements of the external reality. It is in the sense that the mind is to be understood as a dynamic energy-system.*[4]

---

[2] Dr. Timothy Clinton and Dr. George Ohlschlager, Competent Christian Counseling Volume 1, (Colorado Springs, Colorado, Waterbrook Press; 2002); Page 45, emphasis added.

[3] Dr. Timothy Clinton and Dr. George Ohlschlager, Competent Christian Counseling Volume 1, (Colorado Springs, Colorado, Waterbrook Press; 2002); Page 46.

[4] http://www.iep.utm.edu/freud (November 15, 2012)

In other words all of humanity has an innate set of wants and needs which must be satisfied (the Id). However, once we are born the world influences us by imposing on us an arbitrary set of rules to live by that are contrary to our instinctual drives (the Superego). Then, when inconsistencies and conflicts arise between our instincts and society's expectations the Ego kicks in to reconcile that conflict.

According to Freud, man's primary issue is poor socialization. The counseled, once evaluated will be shown to have been the helpless victim of an over-bearing society. A society where external pressures may have been either perpetuated or reinforced by parents, older siblings, grandparents, church, or any other aspect of society where, as a child, they were influenced. Consequently, individuals are no longer considered responsible for their actions. Instead of accepting responsibility for personal actions, society is blamed. This philosophy has permeated and become so engrained into our culture that the one who speaks of personal accountability and responsibility is archaic and considered to be close minded.

Jay E. Adams sums this process up quite well when he writes:

*The Superego is the culprit in the Freudian system. According to Freud, the problem with the mentally ill is an over-socialization of the Superego. An over-socialized conscience is overly severe and overly strict. The mentally ill are victims of the Superego. The Ego, the third unit in man, is the arbiter, or the conscious self. A conflict arises when the Id desires to be expressed but is frustrated by the Superego. The primitive wants to seek expression, but the overly severe Superego standing at the threshold hinders the Id from expressing itself in the conscious life of the individual. This battle, which takes place on the subconscious level, is the source of one's difficulties... The Ego functions on the level of responsibility whereas the Id and Superego function on the level of irresponsibility. When the Id is repressed by the Superego, the person in conflict experiences what Freud called "guilt feelings". Guilt feelings, however, are not feelings that stem from real guilt. Since his feelings of guilt is false, **one does not need to confess his sin**...but rather what he needs to do is to rid himself of falsehood. **So, naturally enough, the therapy consists of making one FEEL RIGHT by dispelling false guilt.**[5]*

The individual who believes in personal responsibility and

---

[5] Jay E. Adams, Competent To Counsel (Grand Rapids, Michigan, Zondervan; 1970); Page 10, emphasis added.

accountability must critically question Freudianism because it tears down all notions of individual responsibility.

Since our focus here is Christian based counseling there is one final element of Freudianism I must address. Yet, I am also a great proponent of not trying to re-invent the wheel every time I need one; so, once again I will draw from Adams' wealth of knowledge and simply quote him:

> *Freud hung out his shingle on Easter Sunday. For someone to whom every action had significance, however, covert or inconsequential it may seem to be, surely such a overt act must be viewed as symbolical. The fact that Freud thought little of religion in general and less of Christianity in particular is an historical fact. He called himself "a complete godless Jew" and a "hopeless pagan"... For him, Christianity was an illusion that had to be dispelled. Like all other religions, it was a sign of neurosis... He calls the biblical accounts "fairly tales". Religion was invented, he claimed, to fulfill man's needs... Before adopting Freudian principles, Christians should know these basic Freudian presuppositions which underlie all he wrote.*[6]

Freudianism falls within the category commonly referred to as Expert Knowledge counseling, which requires extensive education and very specialized training prior to being able to actually help anyone. Another common issue with the Expert Knowledge counseling type of assistance is that it usually requires an extended number of sessions with large amounts of time and money spent in the process.

A second style of analysis common to the Expert Knowledge category of counseling techniques is B.F. Skinner's *Behavioral Modification*, which we will review next.

B.F. Skinner (Behavioral Modification i.e Operant Behavior or Operant Conditioning).

Burrhus Frederic Skinner (commonly known as BF Skinner) was one of the most distinguished individuals involved with Behavioral Modification/Operant Conditioning analysis systems of the early to mid twentieth century. The primary functions of this form of psychoanalysis is that it seeks to understand and control behavior apart from *mythical concepts*

---

[6] Jay E. Adams, Competent To Counsel (Grand Rapids, Michigan, Zondervan; 1970); Pages 15-16.

like mind, attitudes, freedom, dignity, etc.[7]

According to the "Foundation for Truth in Reality" *as with all behaviorists he* (Skinner) *assumes Man is incapable of responsibility, self-disciple, self-determined morality and even autonomous achievement because there is no self in the first place. To him you simply "react" and "behave" to external forces, and thought and awareness are nothing more than annoying, meaningless by-products. The results of this is that the concepts of consciousness, awareness, self-control, will, self-determination, and personal responsibility cannot and do not exist within their ideological frameworks. These are considered minor things and of no meaningful significance. At best all internal subjective states, including feelings, are nothing more than chemical reactions in the brain or stimulus-response reactions to evolutionary and immediate environmental forces.[8]*

So, what does all of this mean? Skinner believed that man is the highest form of animal in existence: but an animal none-the-less. He alleges that mankind evolved organically through the natural process of selection and a strong desire to survive. When one boils it all down, according to Skinner, man is simply the product of his environment.

One of the methods of research Skinner used to support his theory was "Operant Behavior" wherein he initiated rats into an environment where their food was dispensed to them as they pressed on or pushed a bar in a specific manner. As the rats became accustomed to the results of their actions the number of times they operated the bar increased.

After various experiments he *extended the principles of operant behavior to a consideration of verbal behavior. Skinner used his data to argue that behavior is controlled, and* **the critical role of the psychologist is to define the parameters of effective control for appropriate social implications.**[9]

Note the comment, *the critical role of the psychologist is to define the parameters of effective control for appropriate social implications.* My question is, "How can the psychologist determine exactly what is appropriate if mankind evolved organically?" Who sets the moral, social, and psychological guidelines, if there are no fixed guidelines to be followed?"

Jay E. Adams apparently had similar concerns when he wrote his

---

[7] Finis Jennings Dake, God's Plan For Man (Lawrenceville, Georgia, Dake Publishing, 1977); Page 81.
[8] http://www.sntp.net (November 15, 2012).
[9] http://www.newworldencyclopedia.org (November 15, 2012) emphasis added.

"sausage" analogy: *Ask any four Skinnerians, "Is it true that you can make any kind of sausage you want?" And the answer will come back, "Yes, we can." Skinnerians agree that out of the other end of the meat grinder - the behaviorist process, they can produce any sort of person a human being is physiological capable of becoming. Given the proper contingencies plus an adequate reward and "aversive control schedule" ...they can train the human animal... to do whatever they wish. "I see" you say, "but now; tell me what kind of sausage should we grind?" One answers, "Polish sausage." Another counters, No, I think Italian sausage would be better." The third insists, "Give me celery sage every time." And a fourth chimes in, "It doesn't matter to me, I like them all." Do you see the problem" ...You could never get them to agree on what that human being should look like. Pressed hard enough, their ideas of the ideal human being would differ according to each man's likes and dislikes, code of ethics, and whims... Skinnerians lack adequate standards.*[10]

Additionally, with all of his research Skinner never advocated the use of punishment as an effective means of controlling behavior, arguing that punishing stimuli only led to short-term changes in behavior and usually resulted in the punished individual learning new ways to avoid detection while actively pursuing the adverse behavior. But his resolve in the belief that positive and negative (not to be confused with punitive) stimuli, proved to be effective in bringing about permanent change was absolute.

However, according to Adams; *all this may be translated into Freudian terms and amounts to saying about the same thing. Whereas Freud sees the counslee as not responsible but holds **others** responsible (poor socialization is the problem). Skinner would say that man is not responsible because a determined animal cannot be held accountable (the **environment** is the cause of human behavior).*[11]

So, where does this leave us in our quest for finding a proper biblically based counseling method? As for me, I have to seriously question every aspect of the Expert Knowledge style of helping people. Does this automatically require me to discount every facet of these psychotherapies? No, but it does compel me to critically evaluate them in any Christian counseling course of action I would take.

---

[10] Jay E. Adams, How To Help People Change (Grand Rapids, Michigan, Zondervan, 1986); Pages 58-59.

[11] Jay E. Adams, The Christian Counselor's Manual (Grand Rapids, Michigan, Zondervan; 1970); Page 81, emphasis added.

As we proceed along our journey we will cross over from the "Expert Knowledge" category of psychoanalysis to what has been classified as the "Common Knowledge" style, with our first method being known as Rogerianism.

Carl Rogers (Rogerianism or non-directive or client-centered counseling)

Rogerianism or "Rogerian Therapy" may also be referred to as "non-directive" or "client-centered" counseling. As you learn of these various name tags remember that they all have the same foundation. For example; as you climb a stairway there is always one thing that each step has in common with all the other steps - they are all interrelated and that without the foundation the entire stairway could not exist.

Carl Rogers, the patriarch of Rogerianism, was raised with strong Christian beliefs and was actually taking religion classes in preparation for the ministry when he took advantage of an opportunity to go to Beijing with nine other students to attend a Christian conference. Rogers remained in China for six months and upon returning he spoke about how his experiences there had broadened his thinking so much that he began to doubt some of his own religious views. Rogers ended up changing his course of study from religion to a clinical psychology program and eventually obtained a Ph.D. in that field.

Rogers basically viewed people as good and that mental health was the normal progression of life. He also believed that mental illness, criminality, among other human problems were distortions of this normal progression.

Contrary to Freud's and Skinner's theories, Rogers' theory was simple. According to Dr. C. George Boerer, *The entire theory is built on a single "force of life" he calls* **the actualizing tendency**. *It can be defined as the built-in motivation present in every life-form to develop its potential to the fullest extent possible. We're not talking just about survival: Rogers believed that all creatures strive to make the very best of their existence. If they fail to do so, it is not for a lack of desire...* **Keep in mind...that Rogers applies it to ALL living creatures**. *Some of his earliest examples... include seaweed and mushrooms.*[12]

---

[12] http://www.webspace.ship.edu (November 15,2012) emphasis added.

Rogers also believed that humanity, as a result of the actualizing tendency created society and culture. Unfortunately, due to an innate need to develop to our fullest potential, we as human beings as well as our culture will continue to become more and more complex. In fact, this instinctive force will ultimately cause our culture to become so complex that it will eventually assume a virtual life of its own. This drive to develop could become so strong and powerful that the culture, which was created by and for human beings, could possibly even destroy humankind.

While Rogerian Therapy has some specialized terms that one should be familiar with in order to avoid confusion, Rogers himself would argue that there is no need for an expert psychologist at all. He believed that all men have within themselves the ability to deal with all of their problems. In response to this specific subject Adams writes that the... *Rogerian theory (and therapy) is based upon the idea that* **all men** *have adequate knowledge and resources to handle their problems. That, naturally, offers an optimistic outlook for counselors. Even the counselee himself has such knowledge. The basic assumption is that persons with unresolved problems simply have not been living up to their potential. Latent within them lie the solutions to all their problems. They have the potential to do right. As a matter of fact, (as I already stated) Rogers believes that* **at his core man is good, not evil.**[13]

Let's review what he just said; *at his core man is good, not evil.* This is a basic misconception of the liberal humanistic thinking; man is autonomous; he stands alone; he is independent of any Creator and as such is only responsible to himself - not God.

Once again Adams responds to these concepts when he says; *the Rogerian system confirms sinful man's belief that he is autonomous and has no need of God... According to Rogers, men in sin must be "accepted," not admonished: "The counselor accepts, recognizes, and clarifies these negative feelings"...* (and) *genuine responsibility is undermined by the idea of acceptance.*[14]

As we progress through our review of some of the more common methods of analysis and counseling techniques we must regularly return to our previous statement that *any contribution of extrabiblical sources* must be

---

[13] Jay E. Adams, The Christian Counselor's Manual (Grand Rapids, Michigan, Zondervan; 1970); Page 83, emphasis added

[14] Jay E. Adams, Competent To Counsel (Grand Rapids, Michigan, Zondervan; 1970); Pages 82-83.

subordinate and secondary to the givens of a biblical model. This requirement alone should cause some serious issues to arise within any Christian since we do, or at least should have, a personal relationship with the very Creator that Rogerian Therapy alleges is uninvolved and unnecessary.

Sadly, adaptations of Carl Rogers' so-called "client-centered counseling" dominate the field of Pastoral Counseling and form the basis of most liberal and much conservative. (William) *Hume wrote: Some of the leaders in pastoral counseling consider the client-centered therapy of Rogers extreme and have modified it to fit into their particular concept of the pastoral role, while others have taken it as it is and given it a religious setting.*[15]

In closing this discussion I feel compelled to tell you that you must be extremely careful if you choose to use any portion of the Rogerian model of counseling. There is, if truth be told, no way that, being theologically sound, you can use this model intact. Yet, there may be some informative and provocative elements, which, if critically modified might be useful even within a Christian counseling setting.

I previously stated that we would briefly discuss two methods common to the Expert Knowledge category of psychoanalysis and two with the Common Knowledge category. As promised, we have discussed Freud and Skinner under the first; and so far, Rogers under the second category. Now, we will turn our focus to Mowrer.

O. Hobart Mowrer (Behavioral Therapy and Integrity Therapy/Groups)

Orval Hobart Mowrer is well known for his research surrounding Behavioral Therapy. Born in the early 1900's Mowrer suffered with bouts of depression for most of his life. With the first episodes of depression occurring when he was around 14 years old, probably brought on by the loss of a family member.

With depression continuing its assault on Mowrer throughout his high school years he decided on psychology as a career by the time he entered college. However, after nearly four years in college and being

---

[15] Jay E. Adams, Competent To Counsel (Grand Rapids, Michigan, Zondervan; 1970); Pages 80-81.

instrumental in a scandal over an unofficial, unapproved survey that he had distributed throughout the school's campus, wherein two professors lost their jobs Mowrer left school without a degree. He was, nevertheless, not dissuaded from his desires and ended up earning his doctorate in 1932.

During the late 1930's Mowrer began experimenting with electric shock because he suspected that fear was a conditioned response, which was contrary to the, then, commonly held belief that fear was an instinctual response. Subsequent to receiving unusually generous funding for his research Mowrer was able to use human subjects, as opposed to animals, for the first time. During these experiments Mowrer proved his theory to be correct, which became crucial in his later work.

Throughout this time Mowrer's faith in Freud's psychoanalysis theories were being greatly diminished. This was partially due to the fact that, after repeated attempts by his own psychoanalyst's attempts to cure his problems. But, *most importantly, Harry Stark Sullivan* (a contemporary of Mowrer's) *had persuaded him that the key to mental health lay in healthy, scrupulously honest human relationships, not in intrapsychic factors.*[16]

Mowrer took this newfound belief and applied it to his personal life, confessing to his wife secrets that ranged from his adolescence all the way into their married years: after which he experienced several years of relief from the symptoms of depression.

As a result of Mowrer's work and life experiences he had arrived at some personal convictions concerning his perceptions of guilt and sin. Regrettably, he had no interest in traditional religion even though he knew that these same concepts were readily recognized and accepted within the Christian community.

It wasn't until the mid 1950's when Mowrer read a Christian novel that caused him to really focus on the pathological potential of secret misdeeds and, as a result, he eventually joined the Presbyterian Church in search of someone who would call sin what it is and deal with it as a destructive force in people's lives. Nevertheless, it didn't take long for him to become disillusioned because of the churches soft stance on sin. Furthermore, there were also other areas of doctrine that he fiercely objected to within his denomination so he left the church.

---

[16] http://en.wikipedia.org/wiki/Orval_Hobart_Mowrer (November 15, 2012)

Some have called Mowrer an atheist, which he may have been. However, even in his disillusionment with the church he made an effort to restore the doctrine of personnel sin to the consciousness of the church. Eventually he was able to obtain the funding to develop a program where he was able to teach seminary students his counseling and group therapy models.

During this time group therapy, known at the time as "Integrity Therapy", had emerged and was growing. Mowrer, however, rejected the psychotherapeutic ideals that dominated most of the groups he studied. In this case it is interesting to note that Mowrer did consider these groups as an opportunity for confession and emotional involvement. Within these group meetings virtually everything was allowed and even encouraged, with one exception: violence or the threat of violence. This freedom would often lead to vulgar and aggressive language, physical expressions, affections, and intimate details of members' lives and their misdeeds.

In unison with the three previous counseling models of non-biblical techniques Mowrer's conclusions involve a distortion of the truth as we know it to be according to Scripture. In order to address Mowrer's Integrity Groups from a biblical perspective I will, once again, quote Adams at length:

He (Mowrer) *thinks that man's problems stem from bad behavior. Bad behavior for Mowrer means behavior that hurts other people, the kind of behavior that brings one into head-on clashes with other persons in society... When Mowrer talks about bad behavior, for instance, he does not mean behavior that violates the law of God. He has no concept of rebellion against a holy God or sin against Him. Bad behavior means merely, "I've hurt another individual"...Guilt may be removed by confessing one's wrong to the offended person and engaging in restitution for atonement. Confession, restitution, and atonement, remember, are strictly horizontal; they have dimensions only on the level of man to man. Atonement is not through Christ... it is achieved by the suffering of confession and restitution... He needs forgiveness from others; they need forgiveness from him.* [17]

Adams and Mowrer were contemporaries who not only knew each other from afar but spent time working together attempting to help others

---

[17] Jay E. Adams, The Christian Counselor's Manual (Grand Rapids, Michigan, Zondervan; 1970); Pages 86-87.

through counseling. Referring to one such occasion Adams writes:

> *I worked under Mowrer during the summer session. That was an unforgettable experience for which I shall always be grateful... During the summer of 1965...we conducted group therapy with Mowrer for seven hours a day. Along with five others, I flew with him, drove with him, ate with him, counseled together with him and argued with him five days a week. I learned much during that time, and while today I certainly would not classify myself as a member of Mowrer's school, I feel that summer program was the turning point in my thinking. There in those mental institutions, under Mowrer's methods, we began to see people...helped by confessing deviant behavior and assuming personal responsibility for it. Mowrer's emphasis upon responsibility was central. Mowrer urged people to "confess" their wrongs (not to God, but) to others they had wronged and to make restitution wherever possible. Mowrer is not a Christian. He is not even a theist, and we debated the issue of humanism all summer.[18]*

Having briefly dealt with Mowrer and his Behavioral Modification/Integrity Group Therapy models of helping counselees overcome disorders associated to the psyche let's move on to one final style of therapeutic methodology. The system that I'm referring to has been dubbed "Nouthetic Counseling," which began in 1968 with the establishment of the Christian Counseling and Education Foundation at Westminster Theological Seminary[19] and flourished under Jay E. Adams' writings in the 1970's. Because Adams has been the primary proponent of Nouthetics he is commonly considered to be the originator of these techniques, which are still being widely used today.

Jay E. Adams (Nouthetic Counseling)

Jay E. Adams was born in 1929 and accepted God's free gift of salvation when he was fifteen years old. Adams was passionate about his relationship with God and desired to see His will done. He was diligent in his studies; ordained and pastored several churches; and taught counseling at Westminster Seminary. Then, after the summer that he spent Mowrer, Adams opted for clearing out all of the psycho-rubble he had previously learned and replace it all with a viable Bible based alternative. Sadly enough, what Adams found was a vacuum.

---

[18] Jay E. Adams, Competent To Counsel (Grand Rapids, Michigan, Zondervan; 1970); Page XV.

[19] Dr. Timothy Clinton and Dr. George Ohlschlager (Competent Christian Counseling Volume One; Colorado Springs, Colorado; Waterbrook Press; 2002); Page 40.

He began to build a competent biblically-based counseling method and after years of counseling, preaching, teaching, and intense study he developed foundational techniques for counseling that use Scripture to confront believers about their sin, with the goal of helping to restore them to usefulness.[20]

While we wouldn't have to do much searching to find opposition to Adams' model we also must remember that Adams himself said that his work was foundational in nature, which meant he had developed some firm planks in the bridge for a believer to crossover to mental, social, economic, and biological wellbeing. He also expressed concern that some of the planks may not have been installed, some have not yet been uncovered, while others would need more work. Adams was acutely aware the he did not have it all figured out; he even expressed a strong desire to have other believers come on-board and help in the development of a legitimate, biblically based counseling model. While none of the methods he had studied were biblically based, Adams also learned that none of them had been critically evaluated in light of God's Word. In an attempt to develop an all encompassing nouthetic model Adams wrote:

Constructing a biblical methodology takes critical care; it is going to take much time and effort to build that foundation adequately. No one has a foundation and methodology that is totally scriptural. Such work has only begun. My foundation surely has planks that are rotten and some that are missing. The reader must watch where he walks. There may have been planks that have been nailed in backwards or upside down. But of one thing I am certain: there are a number of biblical planks that are soundly nailed down. At present I am measuring and sawing others. But in order to get them nailed all of the way across, other Christians must also lay hold of the hammer and nails and help.[21]

The development of the nouthethic style of counseling comes directly from Scriptures and is derived from the *words nouthesis and noutheteo* (which) *are the noun and verb forms in the New Testament from which the term nouthetic comes.* [22] The Greek *nouthesia, (**noo-thes-ee'-ah**...calling attentions to i.e.*

---

[20] http://www.nanc.org (November 15, 2012).

[21] Jay E. Adams, The Christian Counselor's Manual (Grand Rapids, Michigan, Zondervan; 1970); Page 92.

[22] Jay E. Adams (Competent To Counsel; Grand Rapids, Michigan; Zondervan; 1970); Page 41.

(by impl.) mild rebuke or warning: admonition: 3559)²³ is used regularly in the New Testament, especially in the Pauline epistles, and carried with it the meaning of change, out of concern, through confrontation. In some aspects it may be considered to be the forerunner to our modern-day "intervention". However, unlike most intervention methods, which are rarely scripturally based; nouthetic confrontation is solely based on scripture. It also endeavors to reconcile an individual back to a right relationship with their Creator; along with all of the other elements provided by Christ via spiritual regeneration and the renewal/transformation of the mind.

Nouthetic counseling consists primarily of at least three elements, which when combined form the original rationale of this method - *to bring about change in a counselees personality or behavior - or both*. Nouthetic confrontation always:

- Implies that there is a problem needing to be dealt with;

- Presupposes an obstacle that must be conquered; and

- Something is wrong with the individual being confronted.

In tackling these issues directly, Adams makes the following comment:

> *Nouthetic confrontation, then, necessarily suggests first of all there is something wrong with the person who is to be confronted nouthetically. The idea of something wrong; some sin; some obstacle; some problem; some difficulty; some need that has to be acknowledged and dealt with, is central. In short, nouthetic confrontation arises out of a condition in the counselee that God wants changed.*²⁴

So, how does one know when God wants something changed? The answer: when there is an attitude; active thought life; and/or activity in a person's life that is contrary to Scripture. Unfortunately, answering the question is far easier than effecting the needed changes. Far too often the initial obstacle needing to be hurdled is simply getting the counselee to recognize that there truly is a problem in a given area. Then, if progress is made and you are able to move forward, another, very common obstacle

---

²³ James Strong (Strong's Exhaustive Concordance of the Bible; Nashville, Tennessee; Thomas Nelson Publishers; 1990); Page 50, Greek Dictionary.

²⁴ Jay E. Adams, Competent To Counsel (Grand Rapids, Michigan, Zondervan; 1970); Page 45.

that arises is excuse making. Making excuses, especially when dealing with Christians, will likely include the use of misinterpreted Scripture.

Just getting beyond these initial obstacles can, at times, be extremely daunting and disheartening. This is why we should have already dealt with some of the previous questions, i.e. "Do I have the ability to stand firm in the face of controversy?" "Am I willing to walk in love with the unlovable?" "Can I look beyond the sin in order to help the sinner?" - Remember those questions from the beginning?

In attempting to get past the first obstacle of recognizing the problem even exists Adams vehemently declares that the primary problem with all of mankind is sin, which is absolutely correct in accordance with Scripture. However, because Adams so staunchly believes in that fact, his first requirement for anyone seeking help, is to confirm or establish their salvation by faith in Christ. In fact, his position is such that counseling cannot even start until the counselee has been evangelized and born again.

Why would Adams be so insensitive about this? Remember his earlier statement, *the basis for a Christian's counseling, is nothing other than the Scriptures of the Old and New Testament.* [25] In order for Scripture to be effective in biblically based counseling the counselee must have a belief in the God of the Bible. He or she must believe that the Word is *theopneustos* (#2315)[26] - the inspired or God-breathed word to all who will believe - and is good for teaching, reproof, correction, and instruction in righteousness (2 Timothy 3:15-17). Supporting this belief Adams says:

> *The whole process of... structuring a person by disciplined training to walk in the path of righteousness is preceded by three important counseling activities, all of which involves the use of the Holy Scriptures. To begin with, Paul asserts that the Scriptures are holy (or unique)... They possess a unique power... to lead unconverted sinners to salvation through faith in Christ.* **Then for those who have experienced this salvation** *they have the power to do four things: (1)* **teach** *(i.e. set the norms for faith and life); (2)* **reprove** *(i.e. rebuke erring Christians effectively so that the rebuke brings conviction of wrong); (3)* **correct** *(...to "set straight again." After knocking us down, the Scriptures set us up again to walk in the path of righteousness...); (4)* **discipline**

---

[25] Dr. Timothy Clinton and Dr. George Ohlschlager (Competent Christian Counseling Volume One; Colorado Springs, Colorado; Waterbrook Press; 2002); Page 45.

[26] James Strong (Strong's Exhaustive Concordance of the Bible; Nashville, Tennessee; Thomas Nelson Publishers; 1990); Page 36, Greek Dictionary.

(structured training) in righteousness (the Scriptures continue to work with us structuring our lives in a daily discipline toward godliness...)[27]

Adams himself is right on the money concerning his scriptural principals and we agree, fundamentally. However, I have, unfortunately counseled with some individuals that were introduced to nouthetic confrontation by previous counselors who, either had lost (for whatever reasons) their ability to lovingly confront others; or where the counselee, possibly due to an under developed relationship with their counselor, had grossly misinterpreted the previous counselors' actions. For this reason I am compelled to reiterate and stress the necessity of walking in love with the unlovable.

Failure to express the love of God in difficult situations can result in a counselee walking away from help, never to be freed from the burden that caused them to come forward seeking help. Or, worse yet, it could drive a wedge so deep in their relationship with God that they opt to abandon Him forever.

Jesus Himself declared that the first and greatest commandment is, to love God with all your heart, mind, and soul; and the second is, to love your neighbor as yourself (Matthew 22:37-39). These two commandments should be the focus of all counseling and any idea of authoritative confrontation without love is inconsistent with biblically based counseling no matter what methodology it claims to come under.

Love is the goal in all phases of nouthetic counseling - not the distorted view of love being espoused by the world or even some distortions of God's love commonly being touted in some of our current post-modern; culturally and politically correct; purely seeker-sensitive churches that are far too common nowadays. Adams deal directly with this issue when he writes:

A simple biblical definition of love is: The fulfillment of God's commandments. Love is a responsible relationship to God and to man. Love is a relationship conditioned upon responsibility, that is, responsible observance of the commandments of God. The work of preaching and counseling, when blessed by the Holy Spirit, enables men through the gospel and sanctifying word to become pure in heart, to have peaceful consciences, and

---

[27] Jay E. Adams, The Christian Counselor's Manual (Grand Rapids, Michigan, Zondervan; 1970); Pages 94-95, emphasis added.

to trust God sincerely. Thus the goal of nouthetic counseling is set forth plainly in the Scriptures: to bring men into loving conformity to the law of God.[28]

There have been volumes written about Nouthetic Counseling (several of which I have in my personal library) and I could continue to discuss it with you, however, as I said from the outset, my quest here is simply to give you a brief overview of multiple systems in the counseling process. That, I have accomplished.

Up to this point I have introduced you to various methodologies of psychoanalysis and counseling techniques. As we proceed I feel it would benefit you to have a little better understanding of this crucial work that every minister of God will be called upon to perform at some point in time. In closing this section, I am encouraging, indeed challenging, you to choose a specific style of counseling and then, work toward being competent in it, in order to accurately be of assistance to others in their time of need.

The Uniqueness of Christian Counseling

You may be asking yourself right now, "Why would I have to decide which style or technique of counseling I should adopt?" To answer this question and many others like it, we would be required to set down individually and discuss a virtually unlimited number of variables. However, there are some reasons that remain constant in all situations. One of which is of paramount concern, involves your personal convictions and beliefs.

Failure to pin down a specific style in the beginning will ultimately result in less than competent abilities on your behalf to be effective in helping others. Stop and think for a moment, if you will, of someone whom you have been witnessing to for a time, attempting to evangelize them with the Gospel of Christ. Yet, every time an opportunity arises for them to make a commitment they reply, "I'm just not sure yet"; or "I'm still looking into Christianity, but I'm also considering this other religion"; or maybe they are attempting to live a Christian life without spiritual regeneration. In this case, how effective would their life be when it comes to living in the righteousness of Christ? Or maybe they ask, "What if something better comes along after I choose?" Personally, I have never been satisfied with

---

[28] Jay E. Adams, Competent To Counsel (Grand Rapids, Michigan, Zondervan; 1970); Page 55.

half-baked responses or excuses and neither should you: and anyone seeking help from a counselor should not be satisfied with inadequate responses either.

Remember that, after deciding on a primary style, you can learn from other models and, if you have already got a solid foundation to draw from, judge what you have learned and then, if necessary, reinterpret it according to Scripture. Only after judging every step in your process with properly interpreted Scripture should you include it into your own counseling model. However, if you have no foundation to draw from; no Scriptural understanding for judging techniques; you will be tossed to and fro by every technique that crosses your path.

In order to assist you in your decision I have included five crucial areas where Christian counseling is uniquely different from secular models:

1.   **Goals**: Maturity in Christ versus happiness and self-fulfillment. Maturity in Christ is a foreign, even offensive, concept to secular counseling, which targets human satisfaction as the primary, if not the sole, goal of therapy. While happiness to contentment is a desired by-product of following Christ, sometimes Christian maturity follows a painful road that must be traveled for maturity to develop...

2.   **Ground**: God revealed in the Scripture versus human wisdom and imagination. We do not dispute the value and use of human wisdom and imagination. However, unless these powers are submitted to the lordship of Christ, the results are often vain and temporal and lead to either human debasement or pride and self-exaltation. All Christian counseling must be grounded in and evaluated against the revelation of God in the Old and New Testaments.

3.   **Process**: Transformation versus adjustment. Christ transforms us from the inside out through the operation of the Holy Spirit in our lives and relationships... An adjustment model inherently presumes the greater power of external forces and serves to help others adjust to them without reference to Christ. Transformation of the inner person empowers people to complete

the work of sanctification in two dimensions: internal change and external adjustment.

4.   **Means**: Working out our salvation versus pragmatism (whatever works)... The means by which we grow comes either from God or from our own efforts divorced from God. No doubt human efforts effect change, but change can be easily directed toward evil or ineffective ends...for there are many ways that seems right to all of us (Proverbs 4:12). Working out our salvation is a functional process for making life work well by applying biblical principles, but it always points to a deeper relationship with Christ.

5.   **Values**: Absolute and eternal versus situational and temporal. In this post-modern, post-Christian age, it is easy to get caught up in the situational and relativistic values of some clients, which challenge our own values at times. Sometimes it is difficult to uphold and advocate God's standards.[29]

As you can easily see Christian counseling techniques are unique in a variety of areas. As ministers for Christ, these are not areas where we can even consider violating. For example: Does the means actually justify the end? Or, "Can the wisdom of man, legitimately stand up against the wisdom of God?" If you can honestly answer "yes" to **both** of these queries, please conduct a firm and thorough examination of your beliefs to see whether or not you are actually operating in the faith (2 Corinthians 13:5).

Before moving on we should not assume there are no similarities between Christian counseling models and secular models. There are. To name a few we should consider the three D's:

1.   **Direction**: Both Christian and secular models give direction; direction that is unique to each one - but it is direction nonetheless.

2.   **Development**: Both styles usually work toward a better quality of life for the counselee, which usually involves personal development on behalf of the counselee.

---

[29] Dr. Timothy Clinton and Dr. George Ohlschlager, (Competent Christian Counseling Volume 1; Colorado Springs, Colorado, Waterbrook Press; 2002); Pages 77-78, emphasis added.

3.   **Diversity**: Whether you choose Christian or secular each model has great diversity within their respective techniques.

The potential variables in Christian counseling models versus secular models are, quite literally, innumerable. While we have discussed but a single drop of water from the ocean of counseling it is still crucial for you to determine where you stand concerning some specific areas prior to giving advice to someone else on a specific subject. For example: How can you effectively counsel a young lady concerning abortion if you have not already made a determination as to where you stand? Unfortunately, we are taught by secularist not to push our morals and ideals onto the client; that we should conduct counseling in such a manner that their wishes, morals, and ideals are supported. As you have, in all likelihood, already deduced Christian counseling differs greatly from clinical or secular counseling in its theories and ethics. In fact, the counselor may even be hindered from true and pure Christian counseling techniques by the wide variety or regulations and laws issued from state to state.

Counseling Defined

You may find it rather strange that we are just now attempting to establish a legitimate definition for counseling. It was simply easier to briefly deal with the various varieties of methods before attempting to nail down a proper, but useful definition.

Because you have already been introduced to some of the counseling models common to the three primary categories of counseling processes that currently exist; it will be much easier now to develop an accurate definition. According to Webster's dictionary to counsel is defined as: *1) To advise esp. seriously and formally after consultation... 2) To recommend esp. as the best or most expedient act, or policy...*[30]

While these common definitions enhance our comprehension level from a purely generic perspective it does little to provide us with a specific definition as it pertains specifically to Christian based or the various secular styles of counseling. Fortunately, we have available to us two different definitions that have already been set forth; each one is what I would call category specific: the first defines Christian counseling; the second, secular

---

[30] Webster's Third New World Dictionary (Springfield, Massachusetts, Merriam-Webster Inc Publishers, 1993); Page 518.

counseling. Within these two distinct definitions you will notice both differences as well as similarities.

Gary Collins has revealed the unique nature of Christian based counseling when he defines it as:

Jesus...had two goals for individuals: **abundant life on earth and eternal life in heaven.** *The counselor who follows Jesus Christ has the same ultimate goals of showing people how to have abundant lives and of pointing individuals to the eternal life that is promised to believers. If we take the Great Commission seriously we will have a strong desire to see all of our counselees become disciples of Jesus Christ. If we take the words of Jesus seriously we are likely to reach the conclusion that a fully abundant life comes only to those who seek to live in accordance with His teachings.*[31]

Now let's consider Albert Ellis' definition concerning secular counseling:

The main goals in treating psychotherapy clients are simple and concrete: to leave clients, at the end of the psychotherapeutic process, with a **minimum of anxiety, guilt, depression (or self-blame), anger and low frustration tolerance (or blame of others and the world around).** *Just as importantly, to give them a method of self-observation and self-assessment that will ensure that, for the rest of their lives,* **they will continue to make themselves minimally anxious and hostile.**[32]

How about that: one shoots for abundance in this life while other seeks to minimize the effects of this life. One focuses on eternal life; the other, for the rest of their life on earth. (What happens to those individuals after this life?) Fortunately for us we also learn another, absolutely critical difference in the two definitions. The first is other-centered, i.e. Jesus focused; and the second is self-centered, i.e. self-observation and assessment. Finally the last distinction that is readily observed between these two definitions: Christian based counseling will empower the counselee to draw their strength from an external source - God and His grace; while the secular methods tell the counselee that, in essence, there is no external source to draw strength from; all they have is personal willpower.

---

[31] Dr. Timothy Clinton and Dr. George Ohlschlager, Competent Christian Counseling Volume 1, (Colorado Springs, Colorado, Waterbrook Press; 2002); Page 79, emphasis added.
[32] Dr. Timothy Clinton and Dr. George Ohlschlager, Competent Christian Counseling Volume 1, (Colorado Springs, Colorado, Waterbrook Press; 2002); Page 36, emphasis added.

Because it is so difficult to legitimately nail down a competent working definition of counseling in general we have done a comparative analysis of both Collins' and Ellis' individual definitions let's consider the following, all-encompassing definition:

> **From a client's viewpoint** *it is a relationship with a trained and caring counselor directed toward solving problems and reaching goals that he or she is having difficulty attaining.* **From the counselor's perspective** *it is a multidimensional process that targets and works to change thoughts, feelings, behaviors, relationships, and environments by applying knowledge and skill* **to serve a client's best interest in personal growth and maturation.** *Broadly defined, counseling is a multidisciplinary profession with various standards of practice, ethics, training regimens, and identities.*[33]

By developing an adequate and understandable working definition of counseling we can proceed to the next phase of our study; *The Counselor's Task.*

The Counselor's Task

The counselor's task is as multidimensional as it is crucial to the counselee's progress. We must not become log-jammed into being so close-minded that we could not see the answer, to any given issue, if it were written down for us word by word. Our task, as counselors can be summed up into two broad areas: First, to facilitate change in thoughts, emotions, character, and behavior. Second, to instill changes in values, attitudes, and beliefs. For example, suppose that in an initial interview, a potential client says, "Nothing that I've ever tried has worked out. I'm no good for anything, so I might as well give up." We'll, first of all we must deal with the issues of improper and erroneous thinking: not everything has failed and he does have a purpose; he is good for something - he just hasn't found out what that purpose is, yet.

A large portion of counselee issues will involve improper - wrong or bad - thinking about self, others, or both, as well as the circumstances. Often, a simple adjustment in this area will have a huge impact on the subject matter; remember, *for as a man thinks in his heart, so is he...* (Proverbs

---

[33] Dr. Timothy Clinton and Dr. George Ohlschlager, Competent Christian Counseling Volume 1, (Colorado Springs, Colorado, Waterbrook Press; 2002); Page 36, emphasis added.

23:7).

At other times the client may not be exaggerating too much about their life's failings. When this becomes evident it may be something as simple as helping him to figure out what gifts God has already given him and then, encouraging him to develop them.

Unfortunately, in today's world we are pushed and shoved from nearly every direction to conform. Political correctness; act this way; dress that way; drive a certain type of car and live in a specific style of home or neighborhood and refusal or failure to comply results in being ostracized by so-called friends and sometimes, even family. These socialized stigmas over and over again may serve to confirm erroneous thinking and devastate a persons notional well-being and stability.

As counselors we must not push for conformity when it comes to specific non-sinful lifestyles because God-given gifts directly impact each person's lifestyle. If their lifestyle is not in conflict with God's standards; let them be. Listen, a plumber is not going to wear a three-piece suit to unclog a toilet anymore than a CPA is going to carry around his documentation in a toolbox.

Conformity must be replaced with complimentary action, action that is commensurate with an individual's gifts and talents. Because every living person has God-given gifts, that are custom designed for that person, it is essential that every counselor understands their primary tasks: to facilitate change in thoughts, emotions, character, and behavior as well as to instill changes in values, attitudes, and beliefs.

For this to occur we need to understand that nearly each change will require three steps:

Step one: Confrontation: confronting the counselee about bad thinking, bad attitude, bad character, etc... All of which can easily be summed up with one biblical term - sin. This step is impossible if you subscribe to the secular hypothesis of not being able to push our morals and ideals onto the client.

Step two: Assistance: helping the counselee get out from under the burden created by sin.

Step three: Reconciliation: restoring the counselee to a godly perspective of self and an understanding of the situation.

These three steps could be easily encapsulated in the Apostle Paul's statement to the church at Corinth when he writes: *therefore if any man be in Christ, he is a new creature: old things are passed away; behold, all things are become new. And all things are of God, who hath reconciled us to Himself by* **Jesus Christ**, *and* **hath given to us the ministry of reconciliation**; *to wit, that God was in Christ, reconciling the world unto Himself, not imputing their trespasses unto them;* **and hath committed unto us the word of reconciliation**. (2 Corinthians 5:17-19, emphasis added) When we actively pursue the ministry of reconciliation these three steps will be taken virtually every time.

In addition to the ministry of reconciliation most counselors will find that there is more involved than simply following steps 1, 2, and 3 in order to effectively accomplish our task. Because this is true, a simple three phase supplement may need to be employed to each step as an enhancement.

This three phase process *has a beginning, a middle, and an end...*

Phase one: Building trust to help explore and define the problem(s). *The primary goal of phase one is to help clients tell their story - as clearly and accurately as possible - by building and using a trust relationship. Of crucial importance here is the role of the helping relationship in creating a climate of spiritual and social influence.*

Phase two: Developing a vision for transformed living. *This phase...helps clients define and own what they want. We explore with clients the possibilities of "putting on" a new life in Christ, and... "putting off" the old nature... Goals are specified and resources are employed to achieve them.*

Phase three: Taking action for change and living abundantly. *In this final phase, goals are affirmed and various strategies for achieving goals are brainstormed and assessed. The right strategies are linked into a working plan and clients are encouraged to go "do it."*[34]

The Christian based counselor has a very specific task. One that has the potential to transform lives here in this life and influence where the client ends up spending eternity. What is there about those prospects that are not both exhilarating and terrifying at the same time? And yet, if it's what God want you to do, how can you say - no? After all, Christian

---

[34] Dr. Timothy Clinton and Dr. George Ohlschlager, Competent Christian Counseling Volume 1, (Colorado Springs, Colorado, Waterbrook Press; 2002); Page 64, emphasis added.

counseling is a sacred process where God Himself becomes the source of real change in the client's life; while the Christian counselor is the tool or vehicle our loving Creator chooses to employ in the application of the process.

In closing this section and before moving on to the next it is vital that you make a quality decision concerning which style of therapeutic assistance you are going to focus on as your foundation. Prior to advancing you must choose which one is right for you in order to avoid the potential conflict in future endeavors.

Choosing a Foundation

As I have already noted, the foundational style, technique, or model used in your personal counseling process is crucial. It is so important that failure to choose can, and likely will, bring your counseling career to a horrible end, which is to say nothing of the devastation to your client's mental and emotional health. Prior to advancing however, I am obliged to stress that what I am teaching here is not a *"my way is the only way"* style of counseling. What I am saying is *"choose one model that has its roots in biblically sound doctrine; learn it inside and out, forwards and backwards."* Then, when you do branch out and begin to investigate other methodologies you will be less likely to be drawn away by unsound doctrine, post-modernism, and post-Christian psycho-babble. Concerning this very point Adams succinctly sums up the entire question of methodology when he says:

> *On a foundation of biblical presuppositions, there must be built a fuller methodology that grows out of them and that is appropriate to them at every point. The methodology* **must be oriented biblically and remain within the framework of scriptural principles**. *When you have constructed a platform like that, then you are able to stand upon it, look around at what is happening elsewhere, and you can pick and choose and adapt from that perspective whatever nuggets that an unbeliever (in the common grace of God) has unearthed.*[35]

I am reminded of a time when I was a very young believer and in many ways incredibly immature. When my Pastor, after expending excessive amounts of time and grace on me, said: *"David, you need to find two or three authors, focus on their materials, learn a sound base for your beliefs and then expand*

---

[35] Jay E. Adams, The Christian Counselor's Manual (Grand Rapids, Michigan, Zondervan; 1970); Pages 92-93, emphasis added.

from that point."

At the time I had an insatiable desire to study and learn everything I could about the Bible and every doctrine known to mankind. Unfortunately, I had very little knowledge to draw from and, as I would read various books by various authors, there would be a wide range of differences in thoughts - some of which were in direct opposition with each other. With all the conflicting information I was consuming I started to become conflicted myself and, as a result, I was wearing my Pastor out with questions.

The godly wisdom he gave me that day is what I want to pass on to you: choose one method, learn it, critically consume it in correlation with Scripture; and then, start branching out.

In closing this section, I am compelled by the Holy Spirit to tell you that, if you have chosen any other foundation than a biblically based model you should not proceed any further. That is, at least until you review what you have just learned, prayed about it and received further direction and guidance from the Holy Spirit. In other words, as a "Christian" minister, a Christian model must be our foundation. It must be built and it must be solid. Then, and only then, can we draw from and use various parts of other models as long as they are subordinated to and reinterpreted by properly interpreted Scripture; as on old-time minister put it - *we'll be able to eat the hay and spit out the sticks.*

Chapter 2: Counseling and the Ministry

After spending some time discussing the various styles, techniques, and methodologies used in counseling; it is my prayer that, since you are in the ministry - or some day hope to be - you have opted for a foundation based solely upon the Bible. I understand that there are only a few truly biblically based methodologies to be found and I'm also aware of the fact that as you begin your studies you will, in all likelihood, find some differences with each individual authors theology. The reality, however, is that you may never find a Bible based, Christian counseling style that you agree with on every point; but, you must start somewhere.

Christian counseling has, at its core, the work of redemption and reconciliation. Both of which can only be accomplished under the leadership of Christ. Some Nouthetic counselors, such as Adams, believe that effective counseling cannot be accomplished for anyone until they have been regenerated, i.e. saved. However, I do not personally agree with that stance because there are times when an individual's confidence has to be won before they will trust you. So, if we can help alleviate some of their concern it will go a long way toward developing a relationship: and relationship has been shown by numerous studies to be the single most crucial element in effective counseling.

Someone once said that *people don't care how much you know, until they know how much you care.* Because I have found this statement to be true, it would be wise to show counselees how much we care. Then, once the relationship has began, we can actively pursue the evangelistic aspect of the Christian counseling process. At other times a counselee may walk into the process already prepared by the Holy Spirit for evangelism; when that occurs we must be quick to act and introduce them to Jesus as their personal Savior.

With these thoughts we will proceed to our first question in this segment, which on the surface, may sound rhetorical at first, however, it is one that not only must be asked; it should also be answered: "Is a minister a counselor?"

Is a Minister a Counselor?

Allow me to start to answer this question by quoting the Apostle Paul in his letter to the believers at Ephesus. In the fourth chapter he writes:

"And he gave some, apostles; and some, prophets; and some, evangelists; and some, pastors and teachers; For the perfecting of the saints, for the work of the ministry, for the edifying of the body of Christ: Till we all come in the unity of the faith, and of the knowledge of the Son of God, unto a perfect man, unto the measure of the stature of the fulness of Christ: That we henceforth be no more children, tossed to and fro, and carried about with every wind of doctrine, by the sleight of men, and cunning craftiness, whereby they lie in wait to deceive; But speaking the truth in love, may grow up into him in all things, which is the head, even Christ:" (Ephesians 4:11-15)

In these verses, especially in verse 12 Paul speaks of men being endowed with specific gifts by Christ and then, being given to the Church with their responsibility being to equip God's people to do His work. As well as continuing to encourage the Church until we come into unity in the faith and knowledge of God's Son so that we will become fully grown in the Lord: until we measure up to the full stature of Christ. These verses clearly involve times when instruction in righteousness, via the counseling process, would be appropriate and in order. If properly conducted it will help a believer in the process of maturing.

Additionally, we have the Apostle Paul, in his second letter to Timothy saying: *"All scripture is given by inspiration of God, and is profitable for doctrine, for reproof, for correction, for instruction in righteousness: That the man of God may be perfect, thoroughly furnished unto all good works."* (2 Timothy 3:16-17)

All Scripture is completely and totally trustworthy because God was in charge of its writing. Since the God of the Bible is the same God that created all of humanity, the words contained therein are utterly authoritative for our faith and life; as is referred to by Paul. It is not enough to simply have an academic knowledge of the inspirational Scripture; we must know it to be divinely inspired experientially; through personal application. The words that Paul chose *reproof, correction, and instruction in righteousness* could also be translated as : *setting one straight, disciplining* (as a father does his child), and *training by instruction via warning, example, kindness, and chastisements.*

33

Timothy was a young minister, both in age and in years of ministry, and Paul was teaching him that it was proper for him to use Scriptures to effect Christian growth in the lives of those individuals God had placed under his charge. Sometimes this will require sermonizing, at other times it will involve one-on-one counseling sessions.

Central to the work of the ministry is helping hurting people; in this world there is an abundance of them, so there are no shortages of opportunities if we simply keep our eyes and ears open to the Spirit of God. In speaking specifically to shepherds (pastors) Adams says:

Pastoral counseling is a special, not separate, area of pastoral activity; indeed it is close to the heart of shepherding. It involves the extension of help to wandering, torn, defeated, dispirited sheep who need the restoring mentioned in Psalm 23:3. Restoration here means refreshment. It constitutes the work of putting new life into one by convicting and changing, encouraging and strengthening after trial, defeat, failure, and/or discouragement.[36]

As ministers of the Gospel we must be willing to get down into the pits and ditches that people sometimes find themselves in and help them out. This task is sometimes hard and arduous; sometimes it requires us to get our hands dirty (physically, not spiritually); and yes, sometimes it will be painful. It is never an easy thing to see the way out; take someone by the hand; and begin to lead them to a place of safety only to see them stumble and fall right back into the pit. And yet, it's what we do. As ministers - gifts given to the Church by Jesus Himself - it is our duty to express the love of God to the hurt, the lost, and even the unlovable.

Our primary task is to mature believers, i.e. to make disciples. Above all else, our allegiance has to be with Jesus and our responsibility is to fulfill the Father's expectations in our life. To help us meet these expectations God has given to us *every Word that proceeds from His mouth* (Deuteronomy 8:3) and *He never leaves us nor forsakes us* (Hebrews 13:5). Because *the Christian minister must be willing (and be able) to assume the full task to which God has called him: that of ministering to men and women who suffer from the pains and miseries that stem from personal sins* as well as helping them to crawl out from under all the dirt that has been piled upon them by life. Am I

---

[36] Dr. Timothy Clinton and Dr. George Ohlschlager, Competent Christian Counseling Volume 1, (Colorado Springs, Colorado, Waterbrook Press; 2002); Page 407.

transferring personal responsibility onto society as Freud does? No, I am simply saying that there are times when things happen and we need help to get beyond the hurt before we can walk in forgiveness; as ministers we can and should be instrumental in this process. When we truly get a grasp of these realities it will greatly benefit our ability to walk in love with others even though we have been previously hurt ourselves.

Addressing the counseling challenges in the local church can benefit the overall effectiveness of pastoral ministry. As MacArthur and Mack...write, "when a pastor neglects the ministry of counseling others, crucial areas of his ministry suffer. For example, his preaching is dramatically affected. He loses touch with the people's difficulties and the thought processes and habits that lead to problems. Then he is not prepared to provide the spiritual weapons they need to overcome those problems." Counseling provides preachers with real life illustrations. (Never forget that the name and specifics of any particular situation must be changed in order to protect the counselor's integrity and the counselee's confidence.) *Keeps them in touch with the emotions of their people, and makes their preaching more applicable to the challenges their listeners confront in daily life[37].*

From a slightly different perspective I will quote from Pastor David Hansen, someone I have great respect for and maintain some of his books in my personal library, even though we tend to disagree from time to time. He writes, *I could fill up many hours a day with counseling. People believe counseling is a great panacea. Yet many are loath to go to a professional counselor. That costs money, and* **real counselors ask hard questions.** *What I do is a mixture of personal friendship, spiritual direction, and discipleship. I go where people are - yes, I make house calls - visit and listen to them. They like that part: but when it comes to the solution part of my dialogue, they find out that I get real moralistic and even pretty demanding. I tell them what Jesus says about their situation and that they need to repent of their sins and start following Him[38].*

To begin with I agree, at least in part, concerning Pastor Hanson's comment about counseling being *a great panacea;* a great cure-all; a universal remedy, which it obviously is not. I cannot, however, agree with his implication that pastors are not *real counselors.* And I must confess that he

---

[37] Jay E. Adams, The Christian Counselor's Manual (Grand Rapids, Michigan, Zondervan; 1970); Page 11
[38] David Hansen, The Art of Pastoring, (Downers Grove, Illinois, InterVarsity Press,1994); Pages 71-72, emphasis added.

may have been writing that "tongue-in-cheek". Simply saying that, while many do believe that way, he does not. It is true that many pastors and/or ministers lack adequate training and experience in the counseling process. However, this does not, if the minister is truly a gift to the Church, relive them from their God directed responsibility of leading His sheep. If any pastor or minster lacks the necessary skills or experience to be effective let them learn.

Also, the above reference to asking *hard questions*: both professional counselor and minister should be asking hard questions. However, in the majority of cases, who is in a better position to truly know an individual's background, lifestyle, familial issues, and spiritual temperament; their pastor or a professional counselor or psychologist? If we are honest with ourselves and *know them that labor among us* (1 Thessalonians 5:12), this is not a hard question to answer. Especially, when we take into consideration that pastors are, or should be, personally associated with their congregants' lives.

In order to bring our initial question: *is a minister a counselor,* to a clear cut "yes" or "no" answer I will quote Adams once again:

To say that the Christian minister is counselor and preacher, par excellence, means that he **is called to these works as his function or office in the church.**[39]

As we proceed with answering, yet, another question that every minister of God will eventually be required to deal with for their own purposes; especially if he is called into the pastorate. The question: *"Can you be a counselor and not be a minister?"*

Can You Be a Counselor and Not Be a Minister?

"Jesus came and told his disciples, "I have been given all authority in heaven and on earth. Therefore, **go and make disciples** *of all the nations, baptizing them in the name of the Father and the Son and the Holy Spirit.* **Teach these new disciples to obey all the commands I have given you.** *And be sure of this: I am with you always, even to the end of the age.""* (Matthew 28:18-20, emphasis added)

According to Jesus all disciples are commanded to *go and make* (more) *disciples,* which involves many facets. All believers everywhere are

---

[39] Jay E. Adams, The Christian Counselor's Manual (Grand Rapids, Michigan, Zondervan; 1970); Page 12, emphasis added.

instructed to give witness to their faith in Jesus; all are commanded to walk in love and forgiveness; and all are to be led by the Spirit of the living God, also known as the Counselor.

"In his grace, God has given us different gifts for doing certain things well. So if God has given you the ability to prophesy, speak out with as much faith as God has given you. If your gift is serving others, serve them well. If you are a teacher, teach well. If your gift is to encourage others, be encouraging. If it is giving, give generously. If God has given you leadership ability, take the responsibility seriously. And if you have a gift for showing kindness to others, do it gladly. Don't just pretend to love others. Really love them. Hate what is wrong. Hold tightly to what is good. Love each other with genuine affection, and take delight in honoring each other." (Romans 12:6-10)

Under the guidance of the Holy Spirit the Apostle Paul tells us that all believers are gifted by God; we all have what I like to call a "special gift" that has been placed within us, which is very special to Him. While God is extravagant, He is not wasteful and I have to believe that He would be especially pleased if we would take that gift and use it to help others. After all, isn't that what Paul alludes to when, immediately after giving a list of God-given gifts, he states: *Don't just pretend that you love others. Really love them...with genuine affection.*

Are all believers called to be an Apostle, Prophet, Evangelist, Pastor, or Teacher? The obvious answer to this question is - "no". However, all are called to look out for the best interests of others; all are called to lend a hand when they have opportunity and ability; and all are to be a catalyst for the love of Christ to be expressed. Fortunately there is a plethora of chances presented on an everyday basis for the believer who has a desire to help spread the awesome goodness of Christ. We live in a hurting world; a world where multitudes are deceived; a world that simply needs to see the untainted love of God. Because opportunities are plentiful, God will use anyone wishing to be used to ease their pain.

The Church...is the central place for healing, growth, and rich relationships. It means seeing peoples pain as a soul wound... It means being invested in others - making a caring connection with someone - rather then merely engaging in skilled talking.[40] When Larry Crabb made this observation he was, in all honesty, referring to

---

[40] Dr. Timothy Clinton and Dr. George Ohlschlager, Competent Christian Counseling Volume 1, (Colorado Springs, Colorado, Waterbrook Press; 2002); Page 31

Christian counselors, but I find it extremely germane to our current subject.

The Church *IS the central place for healing, growth, and rich relationships* but these are not totally and completely accomplished through leadership within any specific church - it is every believer's responsibility. *Individual contributions to the larger body are rooted in personal giftedness, and they impact others for good. This ability to make an impact validates personal significance and is inherently therapeutic.*[41]

In attempting to bring a little more clarity to this issue Adams contends:

*The important matter of whether Christians may legitimately assume the position of counselors as a life task and calling apart from ordination to the Christian ministry. Just as all Christians may give witness to their faith, which involves an informal proclamation of the Word... so all Christians may (indeed, **must)** do counseling. Yet, not all Christians have been solemnly set aside to the work of "nouthetically confronting every man and teaching every man," as the Christian minister is... There are major differences between the minister and the free lance counselor. The minister has the opportunity to do the preventive work that preaching and regular pastoral care provides. The counselor outside of the church has no opportunity to mold a congregation of people into a harmonious, loving body into which counselees may be assimilated and from which they may receive significant help. And, **perhaps most important of all, the processes of discipline...are not available to the Christian counselor who operates from outside the church... The authority of Christ given to those who have rule...** must not be despised. The un-ordained Christian counselor, working outside the organized church of Christ, has not received and cannot exercise such authority.*[42]

I have personally concluded that, in a general sense it is every believers responsibility to be actively involved in helping others in whatever way and wherever possible; especially at those times when the counseling comprises generalized advice, encouragement, exhortation, or simple guidance. However, when the time arrives where confrontation and

---

[41] Dr. Timothy Clinton and Dr. George Ohlschlager, Competent Christian Counseling Volume 1, (Colorado Springs, Colorado, Waterbrook Press; 2002); Page 404.
[42] Jay E. Adams, The Christian Counselor's Manual (Grand Rapids, Michigan, Zondervan; 1970); Pages 12-13, emphasis added.

correction are necessary any believer not in an ordained leadership role ought to defer. These are the times where a minister, an ordained of God man or woman, should be the one addressing the subject in question; primarily due to the dilemma Adams referred to concerning the lack of "authority in Christ" issues.

For our next topic we will take a look at the ministry of reconciliation as it pertains to man-to-God (the vertical plane) as well as man-to-man (the horizontal plane).

The Ministry of Reconciliation

When Adam and Eve sinned in the Garden of Eden, God would have violated His covenant with them had He simply "fixed" what they had done without some level of personal responsibility. Remember God had already warned them not to eat from the tree of knowledge of good and evil; and, it they chose not to listen to His instructions, they would be held accountable for their actions. God said, *in the day that thou eatest thereof thou shalt surely die* (Genesis 2:17). Spiritually Adam and Eve died that very day; even though physical death did not occur for hundreds of years.

Keep in mind that *God is not a man, that He should lie. He is not human, that He should change His mind. Has He ever spoken and failed to act? Has He ever promised and not carried it through?* (Numbers 23:19) If we truly accept the certainty of God and His Word, then we must also accept what is written therein; and yet Adam and Eve both lived for hundreds of years after they ate from the tree. What did God mean then when He declared that death would happen the very day they ate from the tree? The death God was referencing was a spiritual death. Their spiritual connection to their Creator was severed and they became physically and spiritually separated, alienated from a loving Maker, and that is still the condition of the unbelieving world around us.

In writing to the church at Corinth the Apostle Paul wrote: *"...if any man be in Christ, he is a new creature: old things are passed away; behold, all things are become new. And all things are of* **God, who hath reconciled us to himself by Jesus Christ, and hath given to us the ministry of reconciliation;** *To wit, that God was in Christ, reconciling the world unto himself, not imputing their trespasses unto them;* **and hath committed unto us the word of reconciliation. Now** *then* **we are ambassadors for Christ,** *as though God* *did beseech you by us: we pray you in Christ's stead, be ye reconciled to God."* (2 Corinthians 5:17-20, emphasis added)

Take a moment and consider what the Holy Spirit desires to stress here: the word *reconciliation* is the key, so much so that it was used five times in only three verses.

The *ministry of reconciliation* is a vital function that every believer must be actively pursuing; especially the Christian counselor. In fact the ministry of reconciliation is one of the indispensable duties of faithful ministers. We truly are ambassadors for Christ, sent with a message of peace and reunification to the lost world. We come in the name of God, acting under His authority, doing what Jesus did when He was physically here on earth as well as, what He desires now that He is seated in heaven, at the right hand of the Father.

As we delve into this ministry it may be prudent to deal first with some definitions in order to help alleviate any confusion or misunderstandings. First of all we need to know that the words *atonement* and *reconciliation* are not synonymous - they cannot be interchanged because they have different meanings. While the *atonement* was absolutely crucial to Jesus' work, it is outside the purview of our current discussion. So let's simply say that the *atonement* of Christ is the offering of Himself as a propitiation for the divine judgment upon our sin. We do not receive the *atonement*; we receive the results of it - the *reconciliation*.

Reconciliation on the Vertical Plane: Man-to-God

The word reconciliation takes for granted that a breach in relationship has occurred; this severing was brought about by Adam's actions and affects all of mankind. Sin separated man from God and because of this the unregenerate heart is at odds with Him. All of mankind have been separated from their Creator and are under the devils authority; positionally, this places us at odds with God. And yet, through Jesus' atonement we may be reconciled. To *reconcile* actually means to remove the enmity between two parties and, in the strictest sense, involves a change of mind.

Since God never changes - indeed cannot change - because He is immutable, who must do the changing? Let's read verses 18 and 19 of 2 Corinthians chapter 5 again: *"And all things are of **God, who hath***

reconciled us to himself *by Jesus Christ, and hath given to us the ministry of* *reconciliation; To wit, that God was in Christ, reconciling the world unto himself, not* *imputing their trespasses unto them; and hath committed unto us the word of* *reconciliation"*. Notice that God did the work necessary for reconciliation. He took the first step to right the wrong brought about by the actions of man; He allowed His only begotten Son to take away the sin of all mankind. The price of sin has been taken care of; reconciliation is available to all. No one has to do anything to win God's heart. He is not waiting on our works. He is not angry with us; does not hate us; and does not desire to punish us. God loves us - He loves you! This is the wonderful message that Christian counselors have the glorious opportunity to express; and not in word only, but also, in deed.

As ambassadors for Christ this message of reconciliation should be conveyed to everyone: and since God has already blotted out our sins; making us right with Him, why would we ever refuse to be actively involved with the awesome privilege of reconciling people to their loving Creator; especially, after accepting our call into the ministry and then, being given by Christ to His Church? God's intended purpose of thoroughly removing all impediments to complete unity and peace between Himself and us is to *bring the whole universe, except for the rebellious angels and unbelieving man, into full accord with the mind of God, Ephesians 1:10.*[43]

The relationship between God and man was so broken that man was on his own without any means of restoring it. And, apart from Christ and His work at Calvary, we are still in the same predicament. Because of this reality the minister has been placed in the amazing, yet fearful position as God's spokesman on earth to actively pursue the ministry of reconciliation; this is especially true when engaged in the counseling process.

Thus far we have discussed the ministry of reconciliation as it pertains to the vertical plane: man to God and God to man. However, biblical reconciliation is not simply a "vertical" proposition. It also involves the "horizontal" aspects of brotherhood, fellowship, and mankind being reconciled to each other, which is important. *Reconciliation is a change of relationship between persons (God to man; man to man) that involves at least three*

---

[43] W.E. Vine; Vine's Expository Dictionary of Old and New Testament Words, (Nashville, Tennessee; Thomas Nelson Publishers; 1997); Page 932.

elements: **(1) confession of sin** *to God and* **to any** *others* **who have been offended;** *(2)* **forgiveness** *by God and* **by the one who has been offended;** *(3)* **the establishment of a new relationship** *between the offender and God and* **between the offender and the offended party (parties).** *In reconciliation, enmity and alienation are replaced by peace and fellowship.*[44]

Additionally, Adams writes: *Adam was not fashioned for solitary, isolated living. From the beginning his capacity for language, his walks and talks with God in the cool of the day, and God's expressed concern that he not remain alone (Genesis 2:18) are all explicit evidences of the social side of human nature. This social side could not be satisfied by fellowship either with God alone...or with another human alone. God determined to create a being that would enjoy fellowship on both the vertical and the horizontal planes. Man's capacity for fellowship was wide. He could communicate verbally...and he could give and receive love in relationship to others. He was made to love God and his fellowman.*[45]

Man's vertical plane: the reconciliation of man to God must be dealt with at some point in the counseling process. Remember however, that some, such as Adams, believe that we are obligated to deal with reconciliation first; i.e. evangelism must be accomplished before any counseling can begin: but since we have already addressed this matter, we will turn our focus in the direction of the horizontal plane: man-to-man.

Reconciliation on the Horizontal Plane: Man-to-Man

There is no place in the church for division; it is sanctioned neither by common sense, nor by Scripture: the same God who has committed to us this wonderful *message* of reconciliation (2 Corinthians 5:19) has also given us the *ministry* of reconciliation (2 Corinthians 5:18).

Jesus said, *"The most important commandment is this: 'Listen, O Israel! The LORD our God is the one and only LORD. And you must love the LORD your God with all your heart, all your soul, all your mind, and all your strength.' The second is equally important: 'Love your neighbor as yourself.' No other commandment is greater than these.'"* (Mark 12:29-31)

---

[44] Jay E. Adams, The Christian Counselor's Manual (Grand Rapids, Michigan; Zondervan; 1970); Page 63, emphasis added.
[45] Jay E. Adams; A Theology of Christain Counseling (Grand Rapids, Michigan; Zondervan; 1979); Page 126.

It is simply not enough for us to love the Lord our God with all our heart, and soul, and mind, and strength. We must also be willing to love our neighbors as we love ourselves; but we will never be able to accomplish loving our neighbor as much as we love ourselves without the *message* and the *ministry* of reconciliation.

When dealing with the ministry of reconciliation as it pertains to the horizontal phase (man-to-man) we must understand that the elements of reconciliation are different than they are on the vertical plane (God-to-man). Remember that on the vertical plane, we previously came to the proper conclusion that God does not change; any necessary changes need to be made by man. In cases of broken fellowship on the horizontal plane (man-to-man) there must be what amounts to a mutual confession on both parties' behalf. In a nutshell it simply means that "we make up," as is referenced in Matthew 5:23-24, *"So if you are presenting a sacrifice at the altar in the Temple and you suddenly remember that someone has something against you, leave your sacrifice there at the altar.* **Go and be reconciled** *to that person. Then come and offer your sacrifice to God"* (emphasis added). A perfect example of this is found in the Apostle Paul's letter to Philemon:

"I am appealing to you for my child, Onesimus, whose father I have become during my imprisonment. Formerly he was useless to you, but now he is indeed useful both to you and to me. I am sending him, that is, my own heart, back to you. I wanted to keep him with me, so that he might be of service to me in your place during my imprisonment for the gospel; but I preferred to do nothing without your consent, in order that your good deed might be voluntary and not something forced. Perhaps this is the reason he was separated from you for a while, so that you might have him back forever, no longer as a slave but more than a slave, a beloved brother—especially to me but how much more to you, both in the flesh and in the Lord." (Philemon 1:10-16)

When Jesus completed His work at Calvary, the ministry of reconciliation was established and all barriers between the races, social status, sex, and even personality differences were destroyed. In Christ, every relationship - no matter how dysfunctional - can be reconciled if all parties involved are willing to make the effort.

In the above verses the Apostle Paul is actively employing the ministry of reconciliation strategy when he urges Philemon to make up with his run away slave, Onesimus. Not only did Paul urge him to be reconciled; he went the extra mile and directed him to receive Onesimus as a brother in the Lord.

According to Scripture, we see where the Apostle Paul acted properly in his instructions to Philemon; unfortunately, what all secular counseling techniques and many so-called Christian models overlook is the fact that Onesimus and Philemon both have already been reconciled on the vertical plane (man-to-God). Anyone engaged in the ministry of reconciliation, especially ministers and Christians counselors, must understand that any time the Bible deals with broken relationships and reconciliation the guidelines directly correspond to a breach created as a result of sin. Therefore, there are at least three things that we must be aware of and believe on a day-to-day functional level. Those three things are:

1.   Jesus' instructions were given to believers, not unbelievers;

2.   The instructions were given for sins committed against you and not someone else; and

3.   The conflict resolution is within the context of the Church, not the community at large.

In order to substantiate these claims consider the following: *"If another believer sins against you, go privately and point out the offense. If the other person listens and confesses it, you have won that person back. But if you are unsuccessful, take one or two others with you and go back again, so that everything you say may be confirmed by two or three witnesses. If the person still refuses to listen, take your case to the church. Then if he or she won't accept the church's decision, treat that person as a pagan or a corrupt tax collector. "I tell you the truth, whatever you forbid on earth will be forbidden in heaven, and whatever you permit on earth will be permitted in heaven. "I also tell you this: If two of you agree here on earth concerning anything you ask, my Father in heaven will do it for you. For where two or three gather together as my followers, I am there among them."* (Matthew 18:15-20)

Before we misconstrue what Matthew wrote here something needs to be said; the words of Jesus used here are not a license for a full frontal assault on everyone who hurts us or does us wrong. They are not there to give us *permission* to get involved in gossip or slander, or even the underhanded *"you need to pray for so-and-so because..."* comments. No, these guidelines were established to ensure peace and harmony, through reconciliation, within the Church.

In referring to this very subject Adams says: *Problems between*

Christians should not continue unresolved. When they do, strength is sapped from the congregation and members work at cross-purposes. Unresolved problems hurt everyone and dishonor Christ's name. There is no place, therefore, for such loose ends in the Church. God does not allow for loose ends; rather He insists that every personal difficulty that arises (between believers) *must be settled. Whatever comes between Christians must be removed. Every such difference must be cleared up by reconciliation.*[46]

Being reconciled on the horizontal plane (man-to-man) is pivotal to our relationship with God. In fact, when Jesus said, *"Go and be reconciled"* it was not a recommendation. Reconciliation between the children of God is a command; failure to do so on the horizontal plane constitutes sin, which in turn, amounts to a breach of relationship on the vertical plane. Refusing to be reconciled to either God or a fellow believer will have grave consequences, if not dealt with. Jesus was so adamant about this subject that He placed a higher priority on it than worship. He said, *"You have heard that it was said to those of old, 'You shall not murder, and whoever murders will be in danger of the judgment.' But I say to you that whoever is angry with his brother without a cause shall be in danger of the judgment. And whoever says to his brother, 'Raca!' shall be in danger of the council. But whoever says, 'You fool!' shall be in danger of hell fire. Therefore if you bring your gift to the altar, and there remember that your brother has something against you, leave your gift there before the altar, and go your way. First be reconciled to your brother, and then come and offer your gift. Agree with your adversary quickly, while you are on the way with him, lest your adversary deliver you to the judge, the judge hand you over to the officer, and you be thrown into prison. Assuredly, I say to you, you will by no means get out of there till you have paid the last penny."* (Matthew 5:21-26)

Let's look once again at what Adams has to say on this matter:

*These words clearly indicated that there is an urgency to reconciliation. God says, **"Go first".** Indeed, in Christ's example, reconciliation takes precedence over worship. Surely that must be one of the striking features in the example chosen; by using so bold a contrast as that between worship and reconciliation. Unreconciled relations, therefore, constitute **emergency priorities** that may not be handled casually or at one's leisure.*

In Matthew 18, the other side of the question is handled: if your brother has

---

[46] Jay E. Adams, The Christian Counselor's Manual (Grand Rapids, Michigan; Zondervan; 1970); Page 52.

done something against you, again you must go. It is always your obligation to make the first move (as also it is his); you may never say, "He should have come to me!" Jesus doesn't allow for that. Whether you have done something to him or he has done something to you, in either case (Matthew 5; Matthew 18), you are to go. Christ left no loopholes; He covered all the bases.

Picture two brethren who have had a quarrel and go off in a huff; when they both cool down, ideally they ought to meet one another on the way to each other's house seeking reconciliation. Christ says that both of them are obliged to seek reconciliation; it does not matter who was at fault.[47]

This reconciliation plan ought to provide ministers and Christian counselors both with great hope. As Adams said, *"God does not allow loose ends"* within His Church; and, because of His immense compassion, He has not left us to fend for ourselves. We are not required to figure out how to walk this love walk; He has given us a detailed plan to follow.

In closing this crucial discussion let's not forget that we are called *"ambassadors for Christ"* (2 Corinthians 5:20). As ambassadors we operate on foreign soil, acting as a representative of His own government. Couple this information with what we are told in Philippians 3:20 that, *"We are citizens of heaven, where the Lord Jesus Christ lives"* and things should begin to add up. Our citizenship is in heaven and as such we are Christ's ambassadors working on His behalf, following His rules and guidelines here on earth.

When an ambassador from one government is sent to another government it essentially means that they are on friendly terms. God is still withholding His judgement of the world; we are still living in the dispensation of grace; and we are still here as His ambassadors striving for reconciliation of the entirety of mankind back to their Creator. One day God will call His ambassadors home and His judgment will begin. But until then, as believers, ministers, and Christian counselors, we must be actively pursuing reconciliation on both a vertical and horizontal plane for and with everyone.

Thus far we have dealt with and answered the questions: *"Is a minister a counselor?"* And, *"Can a person be a counselor and not be a minister?"* Then, we addressed the crucial ministry of reconciliation aspects of both

---

[47] Jay E. Adams, The Christian Counselor's Manual (Grand Rapids, Michigan; Zondervan; 1970); Page 53, emphasis added.

ministry and counseling. Now, we will deal specifically with an additional seven positive characteristics of a godly counselor and five destructive ones.

Counselor Characteristics to Consider

Because the destructive characteristics need little elaboration we will tackle them first; and yet, even though they need very little explanation, we must be aware of the fact that they are subjective. Being subjective means that, while these areas can be caustic to the counseling process, they are personal and, as such, each individual counselor and counselee must decide how much is too much and how far is too far. The five most common areas to guard against are:

1. **Being Too Authoritative**: The temptation to become overbearing in the use of authority, for most ministers and Christian counselors will not become an issue, but we must be aware of the fact that it can happen.

2. **Maintaining Dogmatic Beliefs**: Becoming so assertive with the "truth" that it becomes a source of division, arguments, or strife which are anti-constructive to the counseling process. This occurs most often in connection with differing doctrinal beliefs. However, we must keep in mind that there are times when we can simply agree to disagree and get on with the task of counseling.

3. **Being Overly Judgmental**: There are numerous areas where a minister or Christian counselor can quickly arrive at an improper conclusion: one that has been based solely on appearances, preconceived notions, or personal dispositions. For example: only hearing one side of the story; or maybe it can be something as simple as a personal dislike (i.e. tattoos, body piercings, attire, hair style, etc...).

4. **Being Excessively Lenient**: Sympathy in the counseling process is indispensable. Even so, turning out to be too sympathetic toward the couselee's personal justifications, rationalizations, or simply their excuses can result in becoming too softhearted. If this happens it can result in making allowances for them to get away with harmful thinking or activity.

5. **Disproportionate Emotionalism**: When a minister or counselor turns out to be too emotionally involved with a counselee or their case, it is not uncommon for their assessment and conclusions to become clouded, which can end in improper

actions or advise. (We will deal with additional issues that can occur during the counseling process in chapter 10.)

While this is, in no way, a complete list of possible destructive personal characteristics in counseling they are probably the most common. Fortunately, with a little foreknowledge and with the Holy Spirit's guidance we should be able to avoid them. Now let's take some time to discuss the aforementioned seven most common profitable characteristics of Christian counseling.

1.   **Ability of Maintaining Focus**: When we choose to be actively involved in helping others we will be required to cross through valleys of darkness and despair with our counselees. Failure to maintain our focus - to remain focused on Christ will result in our own self-esteem and personal identity being negatively affected. As ministers and Christian counselors we must find and maintain our identity in Christ or we will not, in the long run, be able to remain stable enough to effectively finish the race.

2.   **Being Morally Honorable**: In Romans 15:14 the Apostle Paul writes of his conviction that the brothers were filled with goodness. By definition "goodness" *signifies that moral quality which is used, in the NT, of regenerate persons... It describes that which, being "good" in its character of constitution, is beneficial in its effect; it is used (a) of things physical...; ground...; (b) in a moral sense, frequently of persons and things. God is essentially, absolutely and consummately "good"...* **The neuter of the adjective with the definite article signifies that which is "good", lit., "the good," as being morally honorable, pleasing to God, and therefore beneficial.** *Christians are to prove it...to cleave to it...to do it...to work it...to follow after it... to be zealous of it... to imitate it...* (and) *to overcome evil with it.*[48] In order for ministers and Christian counselors to be effective we must be found morally honorable and pleasing to God.

3.   **Having Personal Confidence**: Personal confidence plays a crucial role in the success of the counseling process. Suppose an individual in your congregation comes to you for help and you act wish-washy, confused, or refuse to make eye contact with them.

---

[48] W.E. Vine; Vine's Expository Dictionary of Old and New Testament Words, (Nashville, Tennessee; Thomas Nelson Publishers; 1997); Pages 493-495, emphasis added.

How well do you think the session will go? Concerning this specific characteristic there are a few questions that we can ask ourselves and contend with in order to boost our personal levels of confidence. They include: *Am I actually called by God into the ministry and, by extension, to conduct counseling? *Do I have adequate training (academic indoctrination) and experience (clinical exposure or practical knowledge) to effectively help others? *Have I been able to successfully work through personal life issues scripturally or am I pursuing this in a quest for my own personal healing? **If any of these questions fall short of what you would personally require of a counselor, then you must make the appropriate changes before more wide-ranging damages are done to the counselee.

4.   **Exhibiting Theological Understanding**: *By virtue of our pivotal ministry...we are often required to transmit theological information to people in desperate need of truth-based thinking.*[49] Again in Romans 15:14 right after the Apostle Paul spoke of being full of goodness he continued by saying that you are "filled with all knowledge". Then, in a companion text, he said to *"let the Word of Christ dwell in you richly in all wisdom..."* (Colossians 3:16). These comments mean more then mere memorization; they involve being able to properly interpret the Word, to be able to explain it, and to correctly apply it to a specific set of circumstances: all this requires a certain level of theological understanding.

5.   **Remaining Ethically Pure**: This is a counseling process entitlement, which must be undeniable in all counseling relationships; by all parties involved; and in all areas. *We must regard the counseling relationship as sacred, to be protected from any and all contaminating influences or behaviors. It must be a safe place...we must prove to* (our counselee) *that we can be trusted, that we...will be honest about our training, our experience, our credentials... Our lives will reveal us to be the persons we say we are. Counselors of integrity exemplify a consistency between what they say and what they do.*[50] We must remain beyond all ethical

---

[49] Dr. Timothy Clinton and Dr. George Ohlschlager, Competent Christian Counseling Volume 1, (Colorado Springs, Colorado, Waterbrook Press; 2002); Page 31.
[50] Dr. Timothy Clinton and Dr. George Ohlschlager, Competent Christian Counseling Volume 1, (Colorado Springs, Colorado, Waterbrook Press; 2002); Page 193.

and questionable practices: staying "squeaky clean" is an absolute must and not just on the surface, but deep down inside. In fact, it must be so deep that only we ourselves and the Holy Spirit are aware of its depth.

6.   **Possessing Wisdom**: James tells us that if we *need wisdom- if* (we) *want to know what God wants* (us) *to do-ask Him, and He will gladly tell* (us). *He will not resent* (our) *asking* (James 1:5). Wisdom might also be referred to as prudence or good sense, which is found only in the Bible. All wisdom found in a biblically based counseling process must have its genesis in God. This is especially true when we consider that God Himself tells us that *"Stupidity brings happiness to senseless fools, but* **everyone with good sense follows the straight path***"* (Proverbs 15:21, emphasis added). As ministers, Christians counselors, and ambassadors for Christ we live in a fallen, hostile world wherein we are required to navigate on a daily basis. This cannot be accomplished without divine wisdom - godly common sense. Possessing wisdom involves having knowledge and understanding of general principles, and then, being able to apply them to everyday life within the covenantal and moral guidelines God has already established in His Word.

7.   **A Capacity for Conveying Compassion**: Compassion must flow from the minister or Christian counselor. If a counselee does not have a caring, compassionate experience they may be lost forever - this is especially true during the relationship building process. We are instructed to clothe ourselves with compassion (Colossians 3:12), which means that we will, at times, need to see beyond the clothes, haircuts, body piercings, tattoos, ticks, and any other thing that is a personal dislike in order to reach out and help someone. By definition compassion involves having sympathy for the suffering of someone and often includes a desire to help. In short, having a capacity for compassion will be the driving force that propels us into the sea of lost and hurting people in hopes that we might be able to help some. Compassion was a crucial aspect of Jesus' life and ministry and it should be crucial to ours.

How are you doing thus far? Are you still interested in progressing to the next phase of our study? If so, proceed. If you are still not sure, proceed with caution. If you have already concluded that this is not for you, then walk away now before you end up causing more harm than good. Go ahead; find out what God actually has for your life. He really does have a plan for your life, if this is not it, then may God bless you on your continued search. Just don't quit too soon for, in our next section we are going to address the construction of Christian cognition in the counseling process.

Chapter 3 : Constructing Christian Cognition in Counseling

The world in which we now live is much different than it was thirty, twenty, even ten years ago and as such we have an entire generation that no longer assumes or even accepts the Bible as the moral foundation for humankind. We have all heard and possibly even agreed with comments such as: *"You can make the Bible say anything you want."* Maybe you have heard or even asked yourself questions like, *"With all the different translations of the Bible, how can you know which one is right?"*

On the surface these and numerous similar statements or questions may have a ring of truth to them; especially to the unbeliever or an immature believer. Lines have even been drawn within the church concerning whether or not the Bible is accurate and error free. Unfortunately, there are segments of the Christian community teaching that parts of the Bible can be trusted and believed, while other parts cannot. Consequently, each person is left to their own sinful, distorted opinions as to which verses are accurate and which ones are wrong.

These thoughts might have some accuracy behind them if the Bible were like any other book in the world, replete with subjective theories, miscalculations, and downright error, but it isn't: it is the Word of God Himself. Within this work of the Holy Spirit we can find God's unfolding plan for man; and, if we will spend enough time in study and prayer He will direct the renewing of our mind (Romans 12:2).

This renewing or transforming of the mind is critical to constructing Christian cognition in counseling. In other words, we need to have the proper perspective when it comes to God and His Holy Word. Building a new way of thinking, while it is not easy, can be accomplished if we choose to obey the commands and instructions found within those same Scriptures and draw from the well of God's grace.

Concerning the accuracy of God's Word and its ability to transform our thoughts and actions Adams writes:

Today the lines have been drawn between conservative, Bible-believing Christians and all others who purport to be Christians precisely on the grounds of their views of the Scriptures. Conservatives believe the Bible is the one inerrant, infallible rule of faith and practice; others do not. Everything rides on this point of contention: has God revealed Himself fully and infallibly in the Scriptures? If you believe the Scriptures are the inerrant, full revelation of God's will to man, you will submit to them, whether you like what they tell you or not.

If you believe in some lesser view of the Scriptures, you will bring them into submission to your reason, accepting what you wish and rejecting whatever does not please you. The minute you make yourself judge of which parts of Scripture are authoritative and which are not, you slide into a morass of subjectivism from which there is no escape. As soon as you add another standard for belief or behavior, you take away from biblical authority. Here adding is subtracting, and the bottom line is no authority... That is why conservative Christians affirm that the Scriptures are inerrant, the sole rule of faith and practice.[51]

Did you hear that? *"As soon as you add another standard for belief or behavior, you take away from biblical authority."* As Christian counselors we must believe in the inerrancy of Scripture or we have no real hope of ever truly being able to help anyone.

As we continue to pursue our study, constructing Christian cognition in counseling is crucial; in this structuring of thought processes there are primarily four elements that must be addressed in order to construct a process that contains the mind of Christ. Just like the process of constructing a building, once we get the proper materials in place and start putting them all together, when correctly constructed these four elements will give us the ability to succeed. The four elements are: Authority, Beliefs, Presuppositions, and Theology. While these elements are interrelated we will, for ease of understanding and study, look at each one individually, beginning with: Authority.

Authority to Counsel

In order to avoid any confusion it is always crucial for us to be on the same page concerning terminology. Because of this I will always attempt to establish working definitions at the outset of each topic. For *authority* we

---

[51] Jay E. Adams; How To Help People Change (Grand Rapids, Michigan; Zondervan; 1986); Page 20.

will begin with excerpts from Webster's Dictionary:

Authority: *A citation (as from a book) used in defense or support of one's actions, opinions, or beliefs; also:* **the source from which such a citation is drawn...(he quoted extensively from the Bible, his sole authority.)**...

An individual (as a specialist in a given field) who is the source of conclusive statements or testimony: **one who is cited or appealed to as an expert whose opinion deserves acceptance**...

Power to influence the outward behavior of others: *practical personal influence*...

Justifying grounds: basis, warrant, **(on what authority can you act as you do)**...[52]

While there are other secular definitions that I could have cited they were not pertinent to our current study; but notice again that, even in a secular modern-day dictionary there are multiple definitions that correlate with our discussion. For example: as Christian counselors we should often quote from the Bible; we appeal to God and His Word as an expert on humanity; we are or should be involved in influencing thoughts, opinions, and behaviors; and, as ministers of Christ we operate under God's authority.

As we attempt to further our progression with the element of authority as it pertains to constructing Christian cognition in counseling, it is necessary for us to realize that there are three kinds or types of authority we need to consider. For the sake of our study I have opted to call them: *Non-existent Authority; Given Authority;* and *Limited Authority*. Now, I understand that the category of *Non-existent Authority* really isn't any authority; so, if you were swift enough to catch that, great! However, before you shut down, read on for it will become clear as to why I chose that phrase.

Non-Existent Authority

Secular counseling models do not have either *Given* or *Limited*

---

[52] Philip Babcock Gove (Editor in Chief); (Webster's Third New International Dictionary of the English Language: Unabridged; Springfield, Massachusetts; Merriam-Webster Inc., Publishers; 1993); Page 146.

authority because they have no definitive authority to draw from. Some methods will actually let you know they have no authority. The Rogerian method, and those similar to it are prime examples of this style. Rogerians believe in the *Common Knowledge* approach to counseling and starts with the basic assumption that every human being has the resources within them to heal their self; apart from the Creator - God. In fact, *The counselor,* wrote fundamentalist Stanley E. Anderson, *should listen,* **show no authority***, give no advice, not argue, talk only to aid or relieve or praise or guide the client to clarify his problem.*[53]

In opposition with the Rogerians' other techniques or methodologies believe there is some authority within their chosen model. Unfortunately, the distorted perception of authority they maintain is not real. All they have are theories and speculations, which have been put forth under the guise of truth and authority from other sinful men, i.e. broken cisterns (Jeremiah 2:13).

In order to solidify this last statement let me give you this analogy: I have very little working knowledge concerning the mechanics of a vehicle, in fact, it has only been a few years ago that a friend taught me how to change the oil in my vehicles. Don't get me wrong; I could have watched YouTube videos and figured it out on my own (it isn't rocket science) but I, for multiple reasons chose to have a friend teach me. So, here I am without the necessary knowledge or know-how to do any thing when my car breaks down or simply will not start. How smart would I be to go to someone else with the same or similar knowledge of vehicles that I have? Not very smart. Why? Because they neither have the wisdom nor the understanding to fix the problem. Don't misunderstand me I have done this and we have, on occasion, been lucky enough to find and fix whatever was broken. Remember, even a broken clock is right twice a day. However, if I truly expect the problem to be properly dealt with I need to go to the expert: the one who has the proper knowledge and authority to fix what is broken.

It is the same with all secular counseling and psychotherapy models; they are not derived from mankind's Creator and, while they may have a breakthrough from time to time, if you truly want and need legitimate help, go the one that is an "authorized agent", which in this case

---

[53] Jay E. Adams (Competent To Counsel; Grand Rapids, Michigan; Zondervan; 1970); Page 78, emphasis added.

must be a properly trained minister of Christ or a competent Christian counselor.

Continuing to follow our previous analogy, imagine if, after you and your friend couldn't figure out what was wrong; instead of going to the car manufacturers' authorized repair shop for assistance you call all of your friends together in order to find and fix the problem. How many different theory's do you suppose they could put forth both individually, and then, corporately? And yet, if you are still unlucky, all you have created is a huge headache and possibly some arguments. It is the same with counselors and their various models. If all authority is derived from God as Creator, then He is the only One who has the authority or right to bestow that authority; and it would be a violation of His revealed will to place a stamp of approval on any method that widened the great chasm between Him and His fallen creation.

In summation of the *Non-existent Authority* category I will defer to Adams who states:

The modern counselor knows that he has neither authority nor power. All he can do, therefore, is arrogate to himself titles and respect growing (largely) out of the counselee's ignorance and fear. Such power is found in one place only - in God's Word (the Bible) - in the Word that not only brought order and meaning out of chaos on that creative morn, but which alone can give order and meaning to the chaos brought about by modern psychotherapeutic failure... Human substitutes, the counsel of the ungodly, do not have power to enable a human being to live harmoniously with God, with his neighbors, or with his world. They fail to supply what is necessary to give purpose to living or to provide motivation and strength to pursue that purpose.[54]

Given Authority

Given Authority means exactly what it sounds like. There are individuals on this earth whom God has chosen to bestow His authority upon. This divine authority is an absolute must if we have any expectation of truly helping others: it's like taking your vehicle to the authorized mechanic for repairs; not only can they make a proper diagnosis of the problem, they can also repair any thing that is broken. Fortunately, unlike auto makers, God never makes a mistake and He will never have a

---

[54] Jay E. Adams (A Theology of Christian Counseling; Grand Rapids, Michigan; Zondervan; 1979); Pages 34-35, emphasis added.

hard time diagnosing the problem. He knows what every person needs better than they themselves know.

Remember one of our definitions involved the question: *On what authority can you act as you do?* In order to properly answer this query we might say, "I am here as a duly authorized agent of God, and as such, He has bestowed upon me the authority to help you deal with whatever you are going through!" Now that's authority - the kind of authority needed by ministers and Christian counselors; an authority that can come from no other source.

There is need for divine authority in counseling. Only biblical counseling possesses such authority. The counselor, as an ordained man of God, exercises the full authority for counseling that Christ gave to the organized church (1 Thessalonians 5:12-13).[55]

As a duly authorized agent of God, operating with His *Given Authority* to counsel, we must maintain strict adherence to the integrity of the Scriptures. Failure to do so could result in even a Christian counselor with a biblically based method to, knowingly or unknowingly, operate within the previous category of authority; that is, *Non-existent Authority.*

The Word of God is the authoritative standard for all Christian counseling; the counselor never implies or assumes that the authority is of his own accord. It is God's *Given Authority* and He (God) must always be accorded the appropriate praise for its bestowal. For this reason we are always directing counselees toward both God's unmerited favor and His ability to empower them to change, which I commonly refer to as the two sides of God's grace.

We are not helping anyone if we don't teach them how to depend on God in their time of need. Does this mean that we are to abandon them at some point in the process? No, this simply means they need to learn how to depend on God and operate under His authority on their own; this is all a part of "making disciples" as referred to in Matthew 28:19.

Once again, contrary to all secular models, the minister and Christian counselor operate under *Given Authority*. This kind of authority is actively involved in both authoritative and directive instruction, which is in

---

[55] Jay E. Adams (The Christian Counselor's Manual; Grand Rapids, Michigan; Zondervan; 1973) Page 15.

contrast to most secular models. *But you must continue in the things which you have learned and been assured of, knowing from whom you have learned them, and that from childhood you have known the Holy Scriptures, which are able to make you wise for salvation through faith which is in Christ Jesus.* **All Scripture is given by inspiration of God, and is profitable for doctrine, for reproof, for correction, for instruction in righteousness, that the man of God may be complete,** *thoroughly equipped for every good work.* (2 Timothy 3:14-17 NKJV, emphasis added)

If, as God says here, we are to be involved in teaching doctrine, reproof, correction, and instruction in righteousness then, we must be prepared to do just that: teach, rebuke, correct, and instruct. All four involve authority as well as dispensing adequate amounts of direction. True Christian counselors will strive to reverse any harmful thought patterns or sinful actions in their self and others. This will be especially true if they have been granted authority to speak into and help an individual via the counseling process: it is the Christ-like thing to do.

God refused to accept Adam's finger pointing and excuse making in the Garden of Eden and neither can a minister or Christian counselor; it does no one any good. *When (Adam) disobeyed God, his conscience was awakened, and out of fear, sinful man fled, covered himself and tried to hide from God. When confronted by God, finding that he could not successfully avoid Him, he (Adam) resorted to blame-shifting and excuses. In antithesis to running and hiding, Nouthetic Counseling stresses turning to God in repentance. Instead of excuse-making or blame-shifting, Nouthetic Counseling advocates the assumption of responsibility and blame, the admission of guilt, the confession of sin, and the seeking of forgiveness in Christ. In His dealings with Adam and Eve God literally did not allow them to get away with what they had done. Adam tried to make a getaway... But God confronted him noutheticaly...*[56] If God didn't allow Adam and Eve to get away with wrong thinking and actions, how can a minster or Christain counselor, acting under God's *Given Authority*, allow others to get away with it? We can't. But, like God, we must confront in a loving manner.

The question of godly love in biblically based methods is always at the heart of whatever issue needs to be handled: attitudes or actions are not at the forefront of the minister or Christian counselor's thought processes;

---

[56] Jay E. Adams (Competent To Counsel; Grand Rapids, Michigan; Zondervan; 1970); Page 55.

first and foremost all teaching, reproof, corrections and instruction must involve God's unconditional love. In his first letter to Timothy the Apostle Paul said, *the goal of our instruction is love from a pure heart, a good conscience, and a sincere faith.* (1 Timothy 1:5, paraphrased) It is crucial that we never loose sight of these godly requirements. Our conclusion here is that, while biblically based models actively involve both authoritative and directive instruction, it is imperative that all counsel be dispensed in a loving manner.

Then, as love is properly expressed within the confines of a truly biblically based method, *Given Authority* is both imparted and understood because the God of the Bible is the final authority over all His creation: and as such, any minister or Christian counselor using properly interpreted Scripture in their counseling model actually becomes a duly authorized agent of God.

The purpose of preaching and counseling is to foster the (counselee's) *love toward God and love toward one's neighbor which God commands. Jesus summed up the keeping of the whole law as love. Any notion of authority as antithetical to love is inconsistent with Scripture. Love* (or the lack of it) *is precisely man's problem...*(and) *God's authoritative instruction through the ministry of His Word, spoken publicly (from the pulpit) or privately (in counseling), is the Holy Spirit's means of producing love in the believer.*[57]

As we are all aware there have been incredulous abuses and misuses of authority in every walk of life. Regrettably, the ministry and every form of psychotherapy or counseling have not found immunity from this heinous activity. Because this is an unfortunate reality every facet of life has also been negatively affected and, at times, certain areas have even been annihilated. Fortunately, for those seeking relief, the vast majority of ministers and Christian counselors are deeply concerned about every aspect of life. This is why we must understand the differences between *Given Authority* and *Limited Authority.*

Limited Authority

All of you must yield to the government rulers. No one rules unless God has given him the power to rule, and no one rules now without that power from God. So those

---

[57] Jay E. Adams (A Theology of Christian Counseling; Grand Rapids, Michigan; Zondervan; 1979); Page 54.

who are against the government are really against what God has commanded. And they will bring punishment on themselves. Those who do right do not have to fear the rulers; only those who do wrong fear them. Do you want to be unafraid of the rulers? Then do what is right, and they will praise you. The ruler is God's servant to help you. But if you do wrong, then be afraid. He has the power to punish; he is God's servant to punish those who do wrong. So you must yield to the government, not only because you might be punished, but because you know it is right... Show respect and honor to them all. (Romans 13:1-5, 7b)

As previously stated, the God of the Bible is the final authority over all He has created and, since this is true, He also has the authority to place certain limitations on that authority. Let's return for a moment to our broken-down vehicle analogy. You have finally given up on all the conjecture; had enough of the arguments; and have finally taken it back to the manufacturer for the needed repairs. However, your car is an older vehicle with a couple hundred thousand miles on it, so you tell the repairman, "Find out what's wrong with it but don't fix it until you contact me with an estimate." In essence, you have given him *Limited Authority*. Limited in the fact that there are some things he can do and some he cannot. God says the same thing.

In the above Scripture reference God sets forth the limits of His authority. Parents, rulers, and church elders (including ministers and Christian counselors), while being duly authorized agents of God, all have had limits placed on the authority God has given them. Just like you placed limits on your vehicle repairman. God tells all believers everywhere that governments have certain rights of protection, control and civility over those they govern. And yet, when that same government pursues or insists upon a rule of law in contradiction to God's law, the believer has every right to obey God over the government as referred to in Acts chapter 5.

God has given parents authority over their own children, but He limited that authority when He had the Apostle Paul instruct the Ephesian children to *obey your parents - **in the Lord**.* (Ephesians 6:1, emphasis added)

Ministers and Christian counselors have also had their authority limited by God. For example: The minister or Christain *counselor must neither add to nor subtract from God's Word, but offer those needing help "the whole counsel of*

God," which Paul declares "beneficial" to the church (Acts 20:20, 27).[58]

What this means is that, as authorized agents of God, we must comply with and confirm what God says on any given subject in the Bible. We do not operate under our own authority. Apart from Him we have no authority - none, which means that anytime we employ authority, it must be in accord with His instructions and commands. Adams' comment concerning this topic is clear and concise in that it is expected of us to pay meticulous attention to Scripture. He says:

Although they (counselors) must use the authority vested in them by God, they must not exceed the biblical limits of that authority. Nor by their (perceived) authority may they conflict with the valid God-given authority or the state or the home. Counselors who advise illegal acts or who teach children to dishonor parents violate God's authority rather than act according to it.[59]

This is, yet another reason, why a Christian counselor must use a model or methodology wherein the foundation has been established solely on upon the Bible. If our foundation is wrong then it will be very easy to give direction or instruction which is contrary to Scriptures; ultimately, finding ourselves at odds with God Himself. This, we must never do intentionally and make every attempt to drastically reduce the chances of doing so inadvertently.

You may be asking, "But what happens if, even with multiple reduction techniques in place, I still dole out some bad counsel?" First of all, set your mind at ease: as broken wells and cracked cisterns (Jeremiah 2:13) ourselves, we will, at some point, give the wrong direction or counsel. When this happens we must be quick to repent, ask forgiveness from both God and the counselee, restore both relationships, and move forward.

I am reminded of another time when, after following my pastor's earlier referenced advise, I had developed a fairly secure theological foundation. In fact, by this time I had earned my Associates degree in Theology, was a licensed minister, and had been placed in a position of leadership and responsibility within our local assembly. My pastor had

---

[58] Jay E. Adams (How To Help People Change; Grand Rapids, Michigan; Zondervan; 1986); Page 46.
[59] Jay E. Adams (The Christian Counselor's Manual; Grand Rapids, Michigan; Zondervan; 1973); Page 16.

decided to have a fund raiser that would involve, basically the entire congregation. However, one of the things he had opted for was a raffle. We had someone willing to donate a nice used vehicle for this purpose and it was going to be raffled off in conjunction with a silent auction. While I was in complete support of the auction, my conscience would not allow me to be involved in any thing where "casting lots" were involved. Since the Holy Spirit convicted me of the "casting lots" issue I have personally refused to gamble in any way, even the lotto. Many Christians believe it is okay; that it is between them and God. But as for me, the Holy Spirit has counseled me to stay away from all its various forms and I intend to obey Him.

So, with my understanding of both the Word of God and my submission to those authorities over me I prayerfully made an appointment and met with my pastor. During the meeting I lovingly expressed my concern with the raffle and that I would support him and his endeavors one hundred percent in every area of the fundraiser except that one area. He said he understood my position and that I had legitimate Scriptural support for my beliefs. My pastor also told me that he had not even considered this raffle from that viewpoint before and now he needed to pray some more about holding the raffle. I told him that I understood, we prayed, and I left.

God is so awesome. The following Sunday morning my pastor stood before the entire congregation and informed them that God had dealt with him concerning the raffle and, while we were still going to hold the fundraiser and silent auction, the raffle would not happen.

The reasons I have taken so much time dealing with this one incident is to show you that, not only that you will make mistakes, but also how to deal with them from both a counselor's and a counselee's perspective.

From a counselor's perspective we must be willing to listen to the concerns of those we counsel. We must not only be willing to listen about their concerns pertaining to the actual issue; we must also be willing to listen to their concerns about our advise and directions. If the counselee does not have much confidence in our instructions, the chances for change will, in all likelihood, be greatly hindered. As minsters and Christian counselors, if we take the time to truly listen to the counselee we will be able to either calm their concerns, or, if we have made an honest mistake, we will be able to correct it before any real damage occurs.

The second reason, as I have already stated, for passing on the aforementioned "raffle" story to you was to reveal, from a counselor's perspective, how to deal with legitimate differences in beliefs and/or theologies. Whether the counselor is right or wrong, it is always improper to approach anyone in authority with disrespect: unfortunately, this truth has been lost in much of our post-modern world. Now, I know that some say, "respect is earned, not given". While that may be the case in specific individual, worldly, situations, circumstances, and relationships; if we are referring to the God-given authority of government, parents, and church leaders (Romans 13:1-7; Ephesians 6:1); respect is commanded: *render therefore...tribute to whom tribute is due...honor to whom honor* (is due). (Romans 13:7)

For this reason when a counselee approaches the counselor questioning their tactics or counsel it should always be done with respect. Even if their approach is wrong, however, it does not give us the right to let fly a verbal tirade demanding respect: that is one of the quickest ways to forever lose whatever respect they had for us. When we are approached wrong, we walk in love; remember one of our earlier questions: "Am I willing to walk in love with the unlovable?"

One last word of caution, which by no means is the least of importance; as counselors we must never confuse biblical commands and instructions with principles: for example, it is perfectly within our authority to instruct a counselee that he cannot rob a bank, but we have no authority to command him to bring all of his money to the church elders so they can distribute it appropriately. If the latter should happen we have stepped out of our God-given *Limited Authority* boundaries and into becoming an authoritarian (dictatorial) leader, which is wrong according to Scripture. And all God-given authority (whether *Given* or *Limited*) will ultimately be minimized or completely forfeited.

At each and every stage of the Christian counseling process our authority is granted by the Bible itself. And if our Scriptural references used in dispensing direction and guidance are not abundantly clear to the counselee it is our responsibility to expound upon them until the counselee can understand our counsel well enough to apply them to his situation. Should understanding occur before the end of each session? It is wise to try, but there are times when full comprehension will simply have to wait; it may take several sessions before a more comprehensive understanding can be realized.

In closing this section on authority let me simply add the following: *No other system of counseling has authority (even though Ellis and Skinner, et al. pretend to it) because no other system has an authoritative base. I cannot help but agree with most criticisms of the use of authority in counseling since they grow out of a recognition of the utter arrogance of* (another) *fallible man who attempts to speak authoritatively. No counselee should entrust his life to the hands of another unaided fallible sinner. Unless the counselor has been converted, and is able to demonstrate that there is biblical authority for the direction he gives, a counselee ought to back off.*[60]

Beliefs and Presuppositions

As we transition to beliefs and presuppositions, our previously stated second and third elements involved in constructing Christian cognition in counseling, we will, once again begin with some basic definitions; which, once finished, will answer any questions concerning the teaming up of these separate, yet intricately connected elements of the Christian counseling process.

In Webster's Third New International Dictionary we read: *Belief... a state or habit of mind in which trust, confidence, or reliance is placed in some person or thing: faith... something believed... trust in religion: persuasion of the validity of religious ideas... a statement of religious doctrines believed... A statement or* **state of affairs** *on the basis of* **which one is willing to act... A deliberate habitual readiness to act in a certain manner** *under appropriate conditions... immediate assurance or feeling of the reality of something...*[61]

In short, what this implies is to have such a strong conviction in someone (in our case, God) or something (in our case, the totality of God's Word) that it causes us to simply not act in certain ways in specific situations; that we deliberately and habitually act in certain ways (in our case, ways the please God) in other situations.

From Vines Expository Dictionary of Old and New Testament

---

[60] Jay E. Adams (A Theology of Christian Counseling; Grand Rapids, Michigan; Zondervan; 1979); Page 20.
[61] Philip Babcock Gove (Editor in Chief); (Webster's Third New International Dictionary of the English Language: Unabridged; Springfield, Massachusetts; Merriam-Webster Inc., Publishers; 1993); Page 200, emphasis added.

Words we have the verb *pisteuo*, which is defined as: *to believe, also to be be persuaded of, and hence, to place confidence in, to trust, signifies, in this sense of the word, reliance upon, not mere credence*... Now we turn to the noun form: *pistis*, which means: *Faith, and is translated "belief" in Romans 10:17; 2 Thessalonians 2:13. Its chief significance is* a *conviction respecting God and His Word and the believer's relationship to Him*.[62]

So, not only do we, as ministers and Christian counselors, understand that "belief" actually involves a strong conviction and deliberate, habitual actions that are pleasing to God; we must also be persuaded deep-down inside that our ability to properly guide and direct another individual's life requires our utter reliance upon God and His grace: mere mental assent, will not suffice.

Closely related to beliefs we find presuppose, which is defined by Webster's as: *To suppose beforehand:* **form an opinion or judgment of in advance***... it indicates a taking for granted of something as true or existent, ranging from hazy, casual, uncritical* **acceptance** *or belief to certainty through the requirements of logical causation...*[63]

I hope that you are already beginning to see why I have chosen to discuss these two separate and distinct elements of Christian counseling cognition at the same time. Both involve: the formation of an opinion by means of judging whether a person or a thing, ending in a certain level of confidence in the person or thing under consideration; in both cases the resulting conclusion may be either right or wrong, or somewhere in between.

For us to end up 100% of the time, being 100% correct we would have to be hearing from the Holy Spirit 100% of the time, with 100% efficiency and accuracy. How often are we able to accomplish this? While this is actually meant to be a rhetorical question it does not require much forethought to realize we spend nearly all of our time somewhere in between. In order to reduce our wrongs, moving us closer to the rights we are compelled to learn and actually live by a few simple things, which were

---

[62] W.E. Vine (Vine's Expository Dictionary of Old and New Testament Words; Nashville, Tennessee; Thomas Nelson Publishers; 1997); Pages 108-109, emphasis added.

[63] Philip Babcock Gove (Editor in Chief); (Webster's Third New International Dictionary of the English Language: Unabridged; Springfield, Massachusetts; Merriam-Webster Inc., Publishers; 1993); Page 1796, emphasis added.

included in our definition of presuppose. We need to stop forming opinions and making judgments with little or no information; we need to be extremely careful to not take things for granted; and, for our purposes of laying a foundation to constructing Christian cognition in counseling, we must utterly end the uncritical acceptance of anything coming down the psycho-babble road.

Uncritical acceptance of secular models and techniques have done grave damage not only to individuals; it has proven to be a huge detriment to the propagation of the Gospel of Christ. For example: The secular "professionals" have shanghaied one of the primary functions of the ministry, namely, the act of deferring or referring. Even though, in the past few years there has been a resurgence of this crucial element of ministry there is still a strong belief that ministers are not properly equipped to offer counsel: I even had one, well-intentioned, brother in Christ tell me that a pastor had "no right" to tell a couple during pre-marital counseling that they should not get married. When I asked him why he simply said, "Because they're not qualified". This is exactly what is meant by defer/refer: to not make any attempt to help a brother or sister in their time of need. Secular teachings say that ministers should always refer to a "professional" counselor.

The uncritical acceptance of these beliefs have so permeated the Church that, when a pastor, operating within his God-given authority and responsibilities, acts in a way that pleases God he often ends up at odds with church elders and the congregation. Unfortunately for the body of Christ, this is exactly what secular institutions, psychologists, and psychiatrists want us to believe. In reference to this very topic Adams writes: *Christian workers who have been called by God to help His people out of their distress, will be encouraged to resume their privileges and responsibilities. Shall they defer and refer? Only as an exception, never as a rule, and then only to other more competent Christian workers. Their task is to* **confer...**(to) **qualified Christian counselors** (who are) **properly trained in the Scriptures** (and) **are competent to counsel...**[64]

One perfect example of an improper belief or presupposition involves the use of transference and countertransference techniques

---

[64] Jay E. Adams (Competent To Counsel; Grand Rapids, Michigan; Zondervan; 1970); Page 18, emphasis added.

employed in many "Expert Knowledge" psychotherapies. (We will discuss this more in chapter 10.) Other areas that are more common, and in some cases, more damaging to the individual is where Christians have, came to the wrong conclusion include: Autonomy (The belief that man is autonomous: i.e. separate from and without accountability to God.); Sin (The doctrine of Hamartiology, which is covered in chapter 7.); Personal responsibility, confession, and moral judgment, which we will spend some more time with now, in the next section.

I have recently heard where the historically, most commonly quoted verse in Scripture, John 3:16 (*For God so loved the world that He gave His only begotten Son, that whoever believes in Him should not perish but have everlasting life.*) has been replaced by Matthew 7:1 (*Don't judge others, or you will be judged*).

Once again, we have a belief based upon an uncritical presumption that has permeated not only the postmodern society in which we live, but it has now taken hold of believers across the nation. Society says, "no one has the right to judge another." Judging another is not allowed: even if our concerns are biblically true and we are attempting to express concerns of morality. When one speaks out about their concerns they are not accorded with the same freedoms and are likely to hear: "Who are you to tell me what's right?" Or; "Now, you're the moral police!" Or maybe, "You can't tell me what to do!" We have all heard these types of comments either directed at us personally or at someone else; hopefully, as ministers and Christian counselors, we have not been caught up in this improper thinking. If you have, stop it! It is not in the Bible. Read it for yourself: *Don't judge others, or you will be judged. You will be judged in the same way that you judge others, and the amount you give to others will be given to you. "Why do you notice the little piece of dust in your friend's eye, but you don't notice the big piece of wood in your own eye? How can you say to your friend, 'Let me take that little piece of dust out of your eye'? Look at yourself! You still have that big piece of wood in your own eye. You hypocrite! First, take the wood out of your own eye. Then you will see clearly to take the dust out of your friend's eye.* (Matthew 7:1-5 NCV)

Not only are there situations of all sorts in which judging is essential, but the Scriptures specifically command believers to make judgments (cf. John 7:24). The passage only condemns illegitimate judging. Christ assumed that Christians would find it necessary to judge others and in Matthew 7 was therefore specifically directing them how to do so. The passage in question condemns judging in a hasty manner, without evidence. Judging others before straightening up one's own life is also forbidden. Judging intended to denounce another in order to raise one's own ego is condemned. But judgments or moral value in counseling are precisely what the Scriptures everywhere commend.[65]

Jesus' intended usages of these verses have been violated for so long that even some ministers and Christian counselors have bought into the deception: maybe there is some truth behind the statement, *even a lie will be considered as true, if it is repeated enough.* To help combat this error in beliefs and presuppositions as well as some others the *American Association of Christian Counselors* have developed the following list of *control beliefs.*

All counselors operate from presuppositions that serve as a priori control beliefs. We have developed ten root values and baseline ministerial ethics that direct Christian counseling:

1. ***Christ, our Lord of life and our model for counseling, is the embodiment of love and truth...*** *Everything about Christ - His behavior, questions, attitudes, parables, wisdom, emotions, prayer life, humility, teaching, death, and resurrection - is fit for study and for application as Christian counselors...*

2. ***The Bible is the sourcebook of revelation and relationship - the guidebook for treatment and renewal.*** *Christian counseling asserts dedication to Christ, the God incarnate, who was foretold in the Old Testament and revealed in the New Testament. The Bible is not only our source good, the ground of truth from which our helping proceeds, but it is also the guidebook from which we derive the principles for understanding, assessing, and treating others. Either by precept and direct instruction or by inference from...the Scriptures.*

3. ***The church is the center of counseling and care activity.*** *Christian counseling must be Christ-centered and church-related since Christ lives in and dwells in His Church (Colossians 1:18)...*

4. ***Science is synthesized within a larger construct of supernatural theism.*** *Christian counseling... judiciously respects the findings of the clinical sciences and calls upon all Christian counselors to submit*

---

[65] Jay E. Adams (Competent To Counsel; Grand Rapids, Michigan; Zondervan; 1970); Page 85.

all our success claims to tests of empirical validity... God's truth and His ways in helping ministry are never contradictory...

5.   **Maturity in Christ is our ultimate goal; spiritual formation is our primary means...** *While the goals of many clients are shaped around better health, happiness, restored relationships, and greater well-being - goals that we can assist them in achieving - our ultimate goal is intimacy with our Heavenly Father and maturity in Christ (Ephesians 4:20; Philippians 2:1).*

6.   **Christian counseling spans the bio-psycho-social-spiritual spectrum...** *Christian counseling... respects the common factors of change and uses assessments and methods that best help the client across the entire biological, psychological, social-environmental, and spiritual-theological spectrum... The Holy Spirit, the Paraklete of God, is the third person present at all times in counseling. We consciously invite the Holy Spirit to join a process of spiritual formation...*

7.   **Orthopraxy is as important as orthodoxy.** *As committed evangelicals, we regard biblical orthodoxy and the credal history of the church to be of great importance. However, right belief without living it out is a seductive fallacy and is all too prevalent in the modern church. As James put it, faith without works is dead (James 1:19-27; 2:14-26)...*

8.   **Counseling is a two-phased, sequential process: Brief therapy is mandatory for everyone, and long-term therapy is discretionary, chosen by some.** *Solution-based brief therapy* (has shown) *promising results and is being well received in the Christian counseling community... Brief therapy is not, however, a panacea for all problems... There remains a necessary role for long-term therapy, which may be chosen by clients at the conclusion of brief interventions.*

9.   **Clients are valued over comfort, commodity, and compensation...** *The people we serve must be first with us because they are first with God. This ethic supports the challenge of fitting our counseling models to people, rather than fitting people to counseling models... It also means that we give some service to those who are unable to pay...*

10.   **Christian unity, counseling excellence, and ethical integrity take precedence over every personal theory, discipline, and preference...** *Christian counselors can avoid the*

fractious, divisive squabbles that tear at the unity of so many other helping disciplines. To do this, we must give heed to the call to remain united in Christ (Ephesians 4). This unity requires that our first allegiance always be to Christ; and it challenges us to pursue excellence in all our work and to maintain integrity in all our relationships, as befits anyone who would follow Jesus...

Christian counseling must be dedicated to life in the body of Christ...let us deliberately and passionately lift up Christ in Christian counseling.[66]

As we live our lives from day-to-day we often say that we have certain beliefs and yet, our actions do not align with what we confess. One of the major truths of all humanity is that of *automatic thoughts.*[67] Thoughts that, while they are frequently unconscious, are still very real and seriously shape both our emotions and actions.

Automatic thoughts have neither caught God off-guard, nor escaped His counsel to all believers everywhere; as is testified by His instructions for us to "renew our minds" (Romans 12:2).

For us to be able to effectively construct Christian cognition in counseling we must completely rely on biblically based beliefs and presuppositions as well as submitting every thing we do to a critical analysis of the Scriptures. For this to successfully come about we need to be proficient at *rightly dividing the Word of truth* (2 Timothy 2:15) and closing with a legitimate theological conclusion. This leads us to the final element in our attempt to construct proper Christian cognition in counseling.

Theology and Counseling

In the opening statements of this chapter I stated that *lines have even been drawn within the church concerning whether or not the Bible is accurate and error free. Unfortunately, there are segments of the Christian community teaching that parts of the Bible can be trusted and believed, while other parts cannot. Consequently, each person is left to their own sinful, distorted opinions as to which verses are accurate and which ones are wrong.* In this final section we will take a brief look at this all-important element and how it pertains to Christian cognition in counseling.

---

[66] Dr. Timothy Clinton and Dr. George Ohlschlager (Competent Christian Counseling Volume One; Colorado Springs, Colorado; Waterbrook Press; 2002); Pages 54-57, emphasis added.
[67] Dr. Timothy Clinton and Dr. George Ohlschlager (Competent Christian Counseling Volume One; Colorado Springs, Colorado; Waterbrook Press; 2002); Page 36

In an earnest attempt at dispelling any confusion, just as we did with the prior three elements, we will begin with some basic definitions of theology as it pertains specifically to the counseling process. We will, once again, start out with Webster's dictionary which states: *Theology... rational interpretation of religious faith, practice, application, and presentation of the traditional doctrines of a religion or religious group...* **B: The study of God and His relation to man and the world... C: The analytical and historical study of religious beliefs in relations to contemporary thought and life...**[68]

Theology, in its most basic sense is the study of God. However, we must also realize that any "study" of God we orchestrate involves the inference of being from a human perspective. Please don't get me wrong; I understand that we have the inerrant, inspired Word of God, but that very same Word tells us that right now - at this stage in the game - we only know in part (1 Corinthians 13:12). Even though this is true, it should never dissuade us from striving in prayer and study of the Word so that we might obtain the ability to rightly divide the Word of truth (2 Timothy 2:15).

While discussing our fourth element in constructing Christian cognition as it pertains to the counseling process, it would greatly enhance our ability to help others if we extend our study of theology far beyond what I have discussed here. Let me reiterate the importance of our ability to *rightly divide the Word of truth* again; if we are not able to successfully bring Scripture to bear on a counselee's concerns we have already began the process of failure.

God expects ministers and His authorized appointed helpers to have the ability to Scripturally teach, either by principle or precept, what He has to say concerning virtually any subject. *This means that, in order to do biblical counseling, the human counselor must know the good counsel of the Scriptures, and develop those skills by which he may confront others directly in deep concern.*[69] This is also included in our Webster's dictionary definition: *the study of God and His relation to man and the world.*

Because it is so critical for the minister and Christian counselor to

---

[68] Philip Babcock Gove (Editor in Chief); (Webster's Third New International Dictionary of the English Language: Unabridged; Springfield, Massachusetts; Merriam-Webster Inc., Publishers; 1993); Page 2371, emphasis added.
[69] Jay E. Adams (The Christian Counselor's Manual; Grand Rapids, Michigan; Zondervan; 1973); Page 17.

have a hands on, practical understanding of Scripture and the ability to explain what the Bible has to say on any given subject. I believe it is proper, upon the initial contact by an individual wishing to set an appointment, to ask what their primary issues and concerns are so that I may have some time to "brush-up" on the actual scripture references as well as praying for wisdom and specific guidance from the Holy Spirit. Even though some may disagree with this belief, I am convinced it is a legitimate function of the initial contact.

If we are unsuccessful in providing scriptural references to support our instructions, guidance, and direction we may short-circuit the necessary authority to affect change. Our ability to use the actual references will accomplish primarily two things, which will enhance the counseling process:

1.   It helps to set the counselee's mind at ease concerning whether or not we know what we are talking about; and

2.   It adds to the weightiness of God's authority to the needed change, i.e. it is one thing for me to confront or direct another and something totally different for God to do so.

In the counseling process, Adams writes, *not only is it necessary to have a theological...orientation toward Scriptures to avoid misleading counselees and to correct errors in the thought and practice of counselees, but it is vital also to have this orientation in order to communicate truth authoritatively. The counselor who himself is theologically unsure will communicate his biblical insecurity in the way that he speaks... Authoritative proclamation of the Word in preaching and counseling (not authoritarian) grows only from a sound knowledge of theology.*[70]

As it pertains to counseling, theology is simply having the ability to create a bridge that allows the counselee to cross-over from fear to faith; from addiction to freedom; from being bound by the world's system to accepting freedom in Christ. All counseling will be somewhat directive in nature because we are explaining and guiding others in the way they should be living their life before God and others.

While we could continue with the subject of theology in perpetuity

---

[70] Jay E. Adams (A Theology of Christian Counseling; Grand Rapids, Michigan; Zondervan; 1979); Page 13.

our purpose here is not a lengthy diatribe on this topic and its virtually limitless issues. While we are not concerned with creating an exhaustive treatise there are eight areas that are common to nearly every Christian counseling session. If, as a minister or Christian counselor, we have not grounded ourselves in the following areas we need to stop and solidify our foundation upon them. They are:

1.   *Connectedness in the body of Christ is the key to transformed living; connectedness invites and releases the Spirit of Christ to do His life-changing work...*

2.   *The divine inspiration of the Bible, which allows us to confidently tell the truth - that we cling to by faith - to those who need to hear it*

3.   *The existence of an infinite, personal God, who calls us to an allegiance that demands we forsake the 'gods' we create for ourselves.*

4.   *The uniqueness of Jesus Christ, the only God-man of all history, the promised Messiah and Savior of humankind.*

5.   *Salvation by grace alone, which enables us to see and communicate God's gracious life continually offered to us, a life that is impossible to realize by our own efforts.*

6.   *The substitutionary atonement of Christ - we are sinners who deserve death, but Christ chose to die in our place so that we might live in Him.*

7.   *Personal spiritual regeneration, being born again in newness of life by the Holy Spirit.*

8.   *Personal spiritual sanctification, the lifelong process of progressive maturity that is the fruit of God's forming in us the very life of Christ.*[71]

As it pertains to the counseling process, theology is as critical to a proper godly solution as water is to fish: no water and the fish cannot survive; no theology and Christian counseling cannot survive: using the wrong water with the wrong fish, the fish will get sick and, if not corrected, die; improper use of Scripture will not help the counselee get well and could make matters worse; feed a fish bad food and they flounder; feed a counselee bad theology and they will become confused, discouraged, and

[71] Dr. Timothy Clinton and Dr. George Ohlschlager (Competent Christian Counseling Volume One; Colorado Springs, Colorado; Waterbrook Press; 2002); Page 61.

flounder. Get the picture? The relationship between theology and Christian counseling leads to life or death: true Christian counseling cannot be accomplished apart from theology and yet, the un-theological use of the Bible will result in death of the Christian based counseling method.

We have discussed the four primary elements necessary for constructing Christian cognition in counseling, i.e. authority, beliefs, presuppositions, and theology. Next we will turn our attention to breaking out the hammer and nails; the tape measure and saws; and the levels and squares in order to actually take these four elements and construct a process that greatly enhances our ability to succeed.

The Ability To Succeed

As we proceed with our discussion on constructing Christian cognition in counseling there are a few other issues that we need to discuss. Along with our comprehensive understanding of authority, beliefs, presuppositions, and theology there are certain issues common to every counseling session that the minister and Christian counselor needs to understand. The following list does not contain every possible issue involved in helping others but these specific areas must be addressed if we truly have a desire to succeed; they are: relationship; communication and listening; minimization; feelings versus behavior; moral neutrality; and the possibility of failure.

Relationship

Some have said that the relationship between the minister or Christian counselor and the counselee is the most important aspect of success. We can have an in-depth comprehension of the four foundational elements concerning Christian counseling however, if we have not established the proper relationship there can be no real trust. For example: Adam walked and talked with God in the cool of the day. And yet, when he violated God's trust by partaking of the fruit from the tree of the knowledge of good and evil their relationship was broken. In fact, if you recall, it was so broken that Adam attempted to hide himself from God.

A good relationship is so crucial to a successful counseling relationship that, if it becomes broken, it must be repaired quickly: trust must be re-established. This may be accomplished by following the "R³" principle. "R" to the third power is an easy way to remember a truth that can easily be deduced from 1 John 1:9, which reads: *If we confess our sins, he is faithful and just and will forgive us our sins and purify us from all unrighteousness.* Within the confines of this single verse we find three things that we must do when trust has been lost in a relationship; they are:

1. **Repent**: Repent of the act that brought about the violation of trust within the relationship.

2. **Restoration**: Restoration could involve anything from the simple act of giving or receiving forgiveness to financial compensation. Restoration may involve any number of factors or conditions, but forgiveness is always a necessity.

3. **Re-establishment**: The relationship must be re-established or all is lost.

One final note concerning the "R³" principle: for the relationship to be properly repaired the elements of repentance, restoration, and re-establishment must be followed in consecutive order, any other order violates Scriptural principals.

Communication and Listening

Communication and listening are at the heart of nearly every thing we do in life. As some wise person once said, "listening is twice as important as talking, that's why God gave us two ears and one mouth." This quaint saying, while not scripturally based, is especially true from the counselor's perspective because we have no way of providing authentic help until we know what the concerns of the counselee are. Jesus, in multiple passages of Scripture, said, *he who has ears to hear, let him hear* (Matthew 11:15; Mark 4:9; Luke 14:35; et al).

We must be willing to sit and listen to the concerns being presented in full before we even begin to form an opinion. This is a very common mistake in every walk of life - someone starts to say something and before they are half-way finished, we already have a response ready: there are even times when we get so engrossed in our own thoughts that we rudely interrupt while they are still speaking. Patience is not only a virtue, it is also one of the fruits of the Spirit and we must practice it often in our daily life - the counseling process is no different.

Another area that is important in this area is misunderstanding brought about by different cultural backgrounds; language barriers; and any number of other areas, but one of the most common problems is having multiple definitions or uses for the same word, i.e. "love" may be equated to "lust," "friendship," "closeness," or "agape". This area also includes the differences between generational understanding of words as well. For example: "gay" being equal to "happy" or "gay" meaning "homosexual"; or "hooking up" meaning simply getting together for a visit verses "hooking up" equaling meeting with another for casual sex, no strings attached. With an ever changing, ever-evolving language such as ours, we must remember to be cognizant of such issues.

Because effective communication and listening methods and materials are in an abundance and available to anyone desiring to go deeper in this subject we will touch lightly on one final factor. This final element is so rampant in our life that some of us; yes, even ministers and Christian counselors, actively participate - some knowingly, others out habit: it involves being less than honest. There is so much deception in politics; in business; in marriages; in advertising; and even in the church that we have a hard time listening to the truth if its something we don't want to hear. Here are two examples that prove this point. In the first example: the telephone rings and your daughter answers. After a brief silence she says, "Dad, it's for you!" You are completely exhausted from a hard days work, how are you going to respond? What are you going to say? The second example: Your wife asks, "Honey, how does this dress look on me?" If the dress does not fit properly or is not appealing, how are you going to respond? And, if you are honest in your response, does she have the wherewithal to properly handle the truth?

It is important to understand that misery, sorrow, disappointment, heartache, and bitterness, come from one's own stupidity. ***Others do not make us bitter or miserable, regardless of what they do to us. It is our problem. By wrongly responding, we hurt ourselves...***[72]

Minimization

Sin cannot be minimized or glossed over. God took sin so serious that He sent His Son to die for sinners. *God's great involvement*

---

[72] Jay E. Adams (Competent To Counsel; Grand Rapids, Michigan; Zondervan; 1970); Page 67, emphasis added.

with His people is evident in Christ's death. Matters such as law and love, irresponsibility, relationship and alienation, guilt and forgiveness, hell and heaven make up the content of counseling. Counselors must be careful not to represent Christ as the member of a first-aid squad who offers bandaids to clients.[73]

Confronting sin in our own life or that of our counselee must be done in love and should never be minimized. We cannot handle either sinful thoughts or deeds lightly because they are deadly: that is how the enemy gets a foothold in our life. First, he will shoot the arrow into our thoughts and, if we do not annihilate it immediately, he will cause us to start dwelling upon it in our imaginations. Then, if not dealt with, step by step we will be led to a point where we yield to our thoughts, giving birth to sinful activity.

When someone comes to us ministers or Christian counselors we cannot stand by and simply watch as they are led away to destruction. Sin is sin. All sin is a violation of God's commands and, as duly authorized agents of God, we cannot minimize another's sin, whether it be a sin of omission or commission.

Additionally, *each individual must bear personal responsibility for...his conduct. No one can blame another for his bad behavior, even when he has been taught that behavior from childhood. What we learned may be unlearned. Since we may reshape ourselves, we are responsible for the shape we are in. Even under the most severe pressures Christ taught us that it is one's personal responsibility to respond properly to wrongs and the one who inflicted them upon us.*[74]

Feelings and Behavior

Fundamentally this is a crucial element in the "R³" principal for us to have a clear understanding before being able to competently counsel another human being. The Bible is so clear when it declares, *we live by faith, not by sight* (2 Corinthians 5:7) and also that we live *by every word that proceeds out of the mouth of God* (Matthew 4:4). Nowhere does the Bible instruct us to live by our feelings. God instructs us to live our life according to the commands, principles, and precepts found within His Holy Word. All human feelings are fickle and subject to external circumstances. In other

---

[73] Jay E. Adams (Competent To Counsel; Grand Rapids, Michigan; Zondervan; 1970); Page 213fn, emphasis added.
[74] Jay E. Adams (Competent To Counsel; Grand Rapids, Michigan; Zondervan; 1970); Page 214fn.

words, the person who "feels" this way or that will change with the winds of political correctness; circumstances; and situations as easily as a flag attached to its pole changes with the breeze.

Something else concerning feelings and behavior that we need to know is when an individual feels depressed, elated, angry, or worried their feelings are real. However, they are not the problem - feelings are simply symptoms of a deeper issue: an issue that, if not organic in nature, is related to behavior. Feelings (i.e. joy, sorrow, anger, worry, etc.) are a direct result of actions.

In relation to this topic Adams says: *Peter often pointed out that good living produces good feelings. (1 Peter 3:10)... So to have good days, one must do good deeds. This is not to say, of course, that good deeds save anyone, or that supposed "good deeds" apart from the energizing power of the Holy Spirit are good in God's eyes, but good deeds (in the full biblical sense of the term) lead to good days... A good conscience, according to Peter* (1 Peter 3:16) *depends upon good behavior. Good lives come from good deeds; good consciences come from good behavior. Conscience, which is man's ability to evaluate his own actions, activates unpleasant visceral and other bodily warning devices when he sins. "When he feels it." These responses serve to alert him to the need for correction of the wrong behavior which the conscience would not tolerate. Bad feelings are the red light on the dashboard flashing out at us... Visceral discomfort is a God-structured means of telling human beings that they have violated their standards... (And) the only satisfactory way to deal with conscience is to set it to rest by lifting the hood on the faulty behavior that activated the warning device. Conscience is a "good conscience" when it gives approval to one's behavior. When conscience has been set to rest with respect to past problems... one's coping level rises... Hopefully now this movement will gain momentum and snowball in the direction of good feelings.*[75]

What is important for us to draw from this rather lengthy dissertation is that feelings are a result of behavior and, contrary to normal thinking, behavior is **not**, at the outset, a consequence of feelings.

Moral Neutrality

Contrary to our "judge not" culture, we cannot become accomplices in moral neutrality. Jesus clearly called right, right and wrong, wrong; and, as His gift to the Church, so should we. There is no place

---

[75] Jay E. Adams (Competent To Counsel; Grand Rapids, Michigan; Zondervan; 1970); Pages 93-96.

either in the pulpit ministry or the the Christian counseling process for standing in a morally neutral place.

When it comes to adultery, homosexuality, lying, stealing, gossiping, or any other sinful behavior we must present biblically based solutions and then be ready to encourage and assist the counselee in pursuing God's guiding principles.

We should also be ready to show biblical proof for our moral judgments and then, unfortunately, stand strong in the face of controversy; or even an out-and-out assault on our stance because the counselee either refuses to accept the truth or is unwilling to listen to God's Word on the subject. This is, yet, another reason why we must be willing to walk in love with the unlovable. Even when they are wrong, if the counselee chooses to remain under our ministry, we can remain hopeful that the Holy Spirit will soften their heart and ultimately open their eyes to the reality of their sinful action and/or lifestyle.

The Possibility of Failure

Including "the possibility of failure" in a list of specific areas we need to address, if we honestly want to succeed, seems somewhat anti-constructive. However, failure is a very real possibility in any endeavor we pursue: even though it is not something we want to experience especially in the area of helping others. Occasionally, however, we will come face-to-face with failure, how we handle it is what determines our response.

Because failure is often so complex and difficult to analyze most of us would like to look for some glimmer of light amongst the ashes to pin our hopes of success on. While this is true, we are obliged to honestly evaluate our skills, experiences, and methods or we will never become adept in our ability to genuinely help others with their struggles in life.

When failures take place, counselors must first ask, "Who failed?" Counseling was a failure, that is evident, but who failed - the counselor, or the counselee?... Counselors must recognize that failure may not be their fault. Sometimes counselees will interpret failures as successes. Sometimes, for instance, they want to settle for something less that a total reorientation of their lives. They often settle for solutions to the immediate problem... rather than digging down and rooting out the preconditioning problem, of which the performance problem was but one instance. Such premature terminations of counseling must be considered failures, even if counselees do not think so. And so the question of failure becomes a difficult matter. Failure has to be looked at from various viewpoints. Counselors expect to fail because they are sinners and because the persons they are working with also are sinners. Failure is a recognized part of counseling and every counselor who works with others will fail.[76]

As we come to a close concerning the construction of Christian cognition in counseling we have learned that biblical authority; beliefs; presuppositions; and theology are all crucial elements necessary to be Christ-like in our thinking. We have also briefly discussed the six issues commonly involved in every session. There is, however, one irreplaceable aspect of all ministry and Christian counseling methods that can never be overlooked or ignored. I have intentionally left this single element out of this discussion because the entire following chapter is dedicated to this issue. This indispensable, irreplaceable, and invaluable element is the guidance and counsel of the Holy Spirit, Who works from beginning to end in all things pertaining to God and His plans.

---

[76] Jay E. Adams (Competent To Counsel; Grand Rapids, Michigan; Zondervan; 1970); Pages 56-57.

Chapter 4 : Counseling and the Holy Spirit

Much of what has been taught and, consequently, believed concerning the Holy Spirit and His work within the Body of Christ has been in error; while some of it has been 180 degrees from right the vast majority of it is only slightly askew. Unfortunately, being slightly askew can be just enough to inhibit a counselees healing. Since the work of the Holy Spirit, or lack thereof, can have such a drastic impact on the counseling process we should spend time clearing up some of the murkiness in our understanding of His function. To begin with let's simply describe a few characteristics of the personhood of the Holy Spirit and His work.

Characteristics of the Holy Spirit's Work

Since we will delve deeper into this later, let's simply say right now that Jesus and the Holy Spirit are one. Being aware of the triune nature of God (i.e. three in one, yet separate) is very important at this stage of our understanding but it goes much deeper: not only are the Father, Son, and Holy Spirit unified in purpose and conviction, they are also alike in manifestation and character. For example: If Jesus came to give life and to give it more abundantly (John 10:10), which He did; then, the Holy Spirit has been sent by Jesus to accomplish the very same thing.

So, what are some manifestations that are common to the Christian counseling process, which might be a strong indication of the Holy Spirit's presence:

1. There will be a genuine expression of Christlike love, patience, and trust in a loving Heavenly Father evident within the counseling session.

2. There will be a spirit of meekness and humility while maintaining bold courage toward the destruction of sin, sickness, disease, poverty, fear, failure, and every other thing that could cause defeat in the believer's life.

3.   There will be a clarity of needed actions in order to complete biblical instructions that pertain to the counselee's Christian duties and personal responsibilities.

4.   There will be significant freedom from fault-finding, disparagement, character assassination, and all other works of the flesh.

5.   There will be a sincerity and unmistakable sobriety toward destruction of all sinful habits and activities.

6.   There will be a genuine lack of desire, especially on the Christian counselor's behalf, to hurt or harm anyone by either thoughts, words, or actions.

7.   There will be a recognized dedication and determination to avoid any conversation and/or action that does damage or disgraces the name of Jesus.

In order to summarize these seven common characteristics of the Holy Spirit's work in the counseling process we might say that He; the Holy Spirit and, by extension, the Spirit-led counselor, will be primarily focused on liberating the counselee *from sin, for the deliverance of the body from pain, sickness, and want, or for some other good thing that someone needs to have done for* (them).[77]

We are compelled to learn the importance of not believing any thing that cannot be supported by properly interpreted Scripture. Throughout history far too many well-meaning believers have been led astray by others. The Apostle Paul asked the Galatians, *"who has bewitched you..."* (Galatians 3:1) No individual should be willing to blindly follow any minister or Christian counselor; and we should not expect them to mindlessly follow us either. Many leaders, both past and present, have been led astray and we must be honest enough to admit that we too, could also find ourselves in error.

This is why we strenuously encourage every Christian counselor, especially in the beginning of their practice, to opt for a strictly Bible-based counseling method. The beginning stages of our practice is a time for

---

[77] Jay E. Adams (Competent To Counsel; Grand Rapids, Michigan; Zondervan; 1970); Page 97.

learning to distinguish truth from error. Unfortunately, if we choose to be all-encompassing at the start of our ministry we greatly increase the possibility of incorporating unbiblical ideas and methods into our counseling model, which will need to be unlearned later. Then, after we get to know the truth, accept it, and conform to it, we can, with a rich understanding of the things of God, begin to incorporate other tactics presented by the secular counseling community, as long a they do not violate God's Word or inhibit the Holy Spirit's work in any given situation.

As we proceed in our study of the Christian counselor and the Holy Spirit let's explore some of the biblical truths concerning Who He is.

The Truth About the Holy Spirit

The Holy Spirit is spoke about over 130 times in Scripture by at least 21 different titles. Some of which truly lend themselves to a deeper understanding of His role in the Christian counseling process. Names such as the Spirit of *Holiness* (Romans 1:4); the Spirit of *Truth* (John 16:13); and the Spirit of *Wisdom, Understanding, Knowledge, Counsel,* and *Might* (Isaiah 11:1-2) as well as *Comforter* are all of specific interest for our current purposes.

The Holy Spirit has the same divine attributes as the Father and the Son, (i.e. omnipresence; omnipotence; omniscience; etc...). He has divine works that are attributed to Him, such as:

Convicting of sin. (John 16:7-11)

Distribution of gifts. (1 Corinthians 12:4-11)

Changing lives. (John 3:3-5)

Frees from sin. (Romans 8:2)

Brings to our remembrance, teaches, and guides us into all truth. (John 14:16-17, 26; 15:26; 16:17-25)

Imparts love, joy, peace, long suffering, goodness, meekness, faith, and self-control to believers. (Galatians 5:22-23)

Then, as if all these things were not enough, the Bible reveals that the Holy Spirit fills numerous offices within the divine plan. For example: He is the General Overseer of the Churches (Acts 20:28); He is the Comforter, Helper, and Guide to all the saints (John 14:16-17; Romans 8:26); He is the Power of God in the Earth (Acts 1:8; 10:38); He is the Great Teacher of men (Isaiah 11:1-2; 1 Corinthians 2:10-12); He is the Preserver of all things (Psalms 104:29-30); and, among many others functions, He is the Healer of the Saints (Romans 8:11).

With all of this and much, much more about the Holy Spirit in Scripture, how can we dismiss or ignore His active role in the Christian counselor's process? *We must learn that the Holy Spirit is not a mere power that we need to get hold of and use, but we must learn that **He is a person** who is infinitely wise, holy, just, and gracious, and who seeks to get hold of us and use us. What makes a difference is one's attitude and inner motivation: does he do what he does in reliance upon his own efforts, in dependence upon methods and techniques, or does he acknowledge his own infallibility and ask the Spirit to use His gifts and methods? Gifts, methodology and technique...may be abused; they may be set over against the Spirit and may be used to replace His work. But they also may be used in complete subjection to Him to the glory of God and the benefit of His children. (W.T.) Davison has well stated this point when he rightly warns against the attempt to secure a spiritual end by the adoption of habits, the multiplication of rules, and the observance of external standards; excellent in themselves, but useful only as means subordinate to the Spirit.*[78]

The Parakletos (The Comforter)

While the above lists are only a partial listing of the Holy Spirit's characteristics, attributes, names, titles, and offices they give us a fairly good view of God's all-encompassing work in us - touching our heart, our character, and our conduct - is accomplished by the Holy Spirit. Armed with this information let's look a little deeper into Jesus' words in John 14:15-17: *If you love me, keep my commandments. And I will pray the Father, and He shall give you another Comforter, that He may abide with you for ever; even the Spirit of truth; whom the world cannot receive, because it sees Him not, neither knows Him: but you know Him; for He dwells with you, and shall be in you.*

In the first part of John chapter 14 we are informed primarily on

---

[78] Jay E. Adams (Competent To Counsel; Grand Rapids, Michigan; Zondervan; 1970); Pages 24-25.

man's habitation of God. However, in verse 16 Jesus changes streams of thought and begins to speak of God inhabiting humanity.

In John 16:7 Jesus declared, *I tell you the truth; It is important for you that I go away: for if I go not away, the Comforter will not come unto you; but if I depart, I will send Him* (the Comforter) *to you.* This *Comforter* was and is the Spirit of God, who indwells the believer and desires to accomplish all of the things we have already mentioned. Prior to getting overly involved in this discussion lets deal with some fundamental definitions in order to, hopefully enhance our effectiveness as we continue.

The word used by Jesus, which has been translated as "Comforter" is the Greek word *Parakletos.* In Strong's Exhaustive Concordance of the Bible it says (He, the Comforter) is defined as *an intercession, counselor: - advocate, comforter.*[79] However, Vine's Expository Dictionary of Old and New Testament Words reveals a fuller, deeper, and more useful definition for our purposes. It says, *Parakletos (3875), lit., "called to one's side," i.e. to one's aid, is primarily a verbal adjective, and suggests the capability or adaptability for giving aid. It was used in a court of justice to denote a legal assistant, counsel for the defense, an advocate; then, generally, one who pleads another's cause, an intercessor, advocate, as in 1 John 2:1, of the Lord Jesus. In the widest sense, it signifies a "succorer, comforter". Christ was this to His disciples, by the implication of His word "another (allos, "another of the same sort," not heteros, "different") comforter," when speaking of the Holy Spirit, John 14:16.*[80]

While the word is rather difficult to fully pin down in English, the Parakletos of the Bible fundamentally expresses the office of one who comes to the aid of a person in need. Titles such as *Comforter, Helper,* and *Counselor* fit into the context of our scripture references, however, the Holy Spirit is much, much more than this. He is also our Advocate, our Teacher, and our Exhorter. I once heard someone describe the work of the Holy Spirit like this: He comes along side of us in order to encourage, help, strengthen, and give support similar to the stake that a farmer places next to his tomato vine. The tomato stake supports and strengthens the vine and in

---

[79] James Strong;)Strong's Exhaustive Concordance of the Bible; Nashville, Tennessee; Thomas Nelson Publishers; 1990); Page 55.
[80] W.E. Vine (Vine's Expository Dictionary of Old and New Testament Words; Nashville, Tennessee; Thomas Nelson Publishers; 1997); Page 200.

so doing encourages and helps the plant to produce beautiful fruit that is so appealing to both the eye and the palate.

Another Comforter

Since we have already made reference to Jesus' words *"another Comforter"* twice let's turn our attentions to this for a few minutes.

Jesus called the Holy Spirit *"another Comforter; another Helper; and another Advocate"* etc. What is crucial for us to realize and accept as truth is His choice of words when He opted for *"another"*. As we have already mentioned in our definitions Jesus opted to use the Greek word *allos* as opposed to *heteros*, which literally means *another of the same sort*. In other words, the Holy Spirit fulfilled Jesus' promise to send His disciples a *Helper* that is loving, compassionate, and completely sufficient in meeting all their needs; exactly as He had during the time He was physically with them.

While we are digesting the deep significance of what Jesus was actually telling us in John 14:16, let's look at one more aspect: none of us would consciously question Jesus' ability to get to the heart of any situation. (I'm reminded here of His conversation with the Samaritan woman at the well when He said, *You have well said, "I have no husband"* - John 4:17. Now, that is getting to the root of the situation!) As our example, Jesus' abilities in successful counseling are unparalleled. Through advice, leadership, and counsel He was able to totally transform the apostles and, consequently, they radically changed the world: but, they were not alone. They had *"another of the same kind"* - the Holy Spirit had came to live inside of each one: to empower, to strengthen, and to encourage them.

Spirit of Holiness

Through the Holy Spirit, Jesus now dwells in His Church, which is the New Testament fulfillment prophesied by Ezekiel when he, under the guidance and direction of the Holy Spirit, wrote, *I will put my Spirit in you, and you will come to life...* (Ezekiel 37:14). When this occurs the Holy Spirit causes a regeneration in the soul of an individual and that person then *becomes a new creature in Christ; old things have passed away and all things have become new* (2 Corinthians 5:17). At that point the Holy Spirit takes up residence in that life and begins His work of sanctification.

In Romans chapter 1, verse 4 the Apostle Paul called Him the *Spirit of Holiness* because *He is the Source of all holiness... The holiness of God's people that results from their sanctification by the Holy Spirit must be attributed entirely to Him as He works through His Word. The "fruit" of the Spirit is just that: it is the result of His work. If the counseling is in essence one aspect of the work of sanctification... Then the Holy Spirit, whose principal work in the regenerated man is to sanctify him (cf also Ezekiel 36:25-27), must be considered the most important Person in the counseling context... Ignoring the Holy Spirit or avoiding the use of Scriptures in counseling is tantamount to an act of autonomous rebellion. Christians may not counsel apart from the Holy Spirit and His Word without grievously sinning against Him and the counselee.*[81]

For counseling to be called "Christian" it must be completed in unity and harmony with the sanctifying work of the Holy Spirit; the primary means He uses to effect sanctification in the believer, is the Word of God. Jesus prayed, *Sanctify them through thy truth: thy word is truth* (John 17:17) and, as His representatives and gifts given to the Church for their mutual growth and maturation, we should ordinarily perform our work via the same sanctifying word. Adams writes:

The point that needs to be made is that since the Holy Spirit employs His Word as the principal means by which Christians may grow in sanctification, counseling cannot be effective (in any biblical sense of that term) apart from the use of the Scriptures. The fact of the Holy Spirit in counseling, therefore, implies the presence of the Holy Scriptures as well. This fundamental relationship in itself should be decisive for any Christian who carefully thinks through the counseling situation. Counseling without the Scriptures can only be expected to be counseling without the Holy Spirit.[82]

The Spirit's Indwelling Presence

One of the greatest things we can ever learn is that God has not given the Holy Spirit to a select few. No, God has allowed the Holy Spirit to dwell within every true believer and not only for the work of sanctification. God has given the Holy Spirit as an *earnest* (Ephesians 1:14). Strong's tells us that this is *a pledge, i.e. part of the purchase-money or property given*

---

[81] Jay E. Adams (The Christian Counselor's Manual; Grand Rapids, Michigan; Zondervan; 1973); Pages 6-7.
[82] Jay E. Adams (Competent To Counsel; Grand Rapids, Michigan; Zondervan; 1970); Pages 23-24.

in advance as security for the rest.[83] In other words, He is a kind of down payment; an identifying seal that sets us apart: we are different; He made it so and we must come to the place where we realize and accept it. All spiritual blessings in heaven have been given by the Father; made available to us through His Son, Jesus; and Jesus entrusts the Holy Spirit to convey them to us.

The Holy Spirit, who knows and searches all things - even the deep things of God (1 Corinthians 2:10-11) - has work to do and He often looks for a willing child of God to help Him. *At the core of all true Christian helping...is the influence of the Holy Spirit. His presence and influence make Christian counseling truly unique... He is the comforter or helper who teaches "all things," reminds us of Christ's sayings, convicts people of sin, and guides into all truth... This should be the goal of every believer...to be used by the Holy Spirit to touch lives, to change them, and to bring others toward both spiritual and psychological maturity.*[84]

As ministers and Christian counselors we have been given a scared trust and it is absolutely imperative for us to learn how to be on the same page with the Holy Spirit and His work - failure to do so can have devastating results: this is one reason why we should never fear change. Even though all change is messy and hard, God will provide the grace needed to accomplish what He is asking of us. Unfortunately, far too many believers prematurely give up because they have disconnected, for whatever reason, from the Holy Spirit, Who empowers them. This is one of the greatest reasons why we all need encouragement - life is not easy and genuine change is even harder, but victory can be attained.

The role of the Holy Spirit and all Christian counseling is about change - changes in thinking, changes in attitudes, changes in activities, and changes in relationships. Being actively involved in counseling is not so much focused on closure as it is about change. As we decide to step out to help someone, we must be assured that both (the counselee and counselor) are not alone in our endeavors. It is God who does the work through us (Philippians 2:13) by the same power of the Holy Spirit who replaces the

---

[83] James Strong (Strong's Exhaustive Concordance of the Bible; Nashville, Tennessee; Thomas Nelson Publishers; 1990); #728; page 16.

[84] Dr. Timothy Clinton and Dr. George Ohlschlager (Competent Christian Counseling Volume One; Colorado Springs, Colorado; Waterbrook Press; 2002); Page 43.

old sinful thoughts, actions, and attitudes with new, godly ones.

All *Christian counseling…involves three persons at the very least: the client* (the counselee), *the counselor, and God, who wants to be invited to participate in every session. The true power to change comes from the Holy Spirit's active involvement in the process as He encourages, consoles, challenges, convicts, and transforms the client* (counselee) *into the likeness of Christ… When we are working with members of the covenant community, He is the One who, from His positions as indweller, empowers people for radical change. Humbled in a partnership with the divine, we must seek always to be in step with the Spirit - to not lag behind or rush ahead of Him. When we work in harmony with the Sprit, we frequently witness the miracle of regeneration and subsequent transformation.*[85]

In closing this chapter, it is extremely important for us, as ministers and Christian counselors to wholeheartedly believe what the Bible says concerning any subject, including the works of the Holy Spirit. If we cannot believe all of the Word, let us be honest and say that we truly do not know what part of it to believe and what part not to believe. And, if this is the case, let us throw the Bible away and simply do the best we can to make it through this life on a purely natural, worldly level in hopes that, in the end, we will not find ourselves standing before a just Creator trying to answer His questions involving why and why not. As for me, I choose to believe that His Word is true from beginning to end; and also that, from Genesis to Revelation it is without error. This is the God I serve; the Son I trust; and the Holy Spirit that I depend upon both personally and professionally.

---

[85] Dr. Timothy Clinton and Dr. George Ohlschlager (Competent Christian Counseling Volume One; Colorado Springs, Colorado; Waterbrook Press; 2002); Pages 65 and 111.

Chapter 5 : Belief That Change Is Possible: A Prerequisite to Counseling

Embarking upon any journey concerning the topic of beliefs within the counseling process as a prerequisite requires us to first declare that true, honest, and effective believing can only be present when there is a combination of faith and hope involved. Because of this, our pilgrimage will be focused on biblical faith and hope; and how these uniquely intertwined elements, which affects everyone's life, has either an advantageous or destructive effect on the counseling process.

That being said, along with the fact that this work is intended to be an introduction to the counseling process, we will take some time to layout a few basic definitions. While this may appear to be academically trite, it is indispensable in helping to prevent confusion, distortions, and misunderstandings: as previously discussed, one of the most common mistakes in communication occurs when words are being used that have multiple meanings. Hopefully, we will be able to avoid many of these pitfalls.

Defining Faith and Hope

As in previous chapters we will begin with the common, modern-day definitions and then see how well they fit in with our biblical definitions. In Webster's dictionary we find a rather lengthy explanation on the various meanings of the word *faith*; it includes the following:

*[1]Faith...1a: The act or state of **wholeheartedly and steadfastly believing in the existence, power, and benevolence of a supreme being, of having confidence in his providential care, and of being loyal to his will as revealed or believed in: belief and trust in and loyalty to God...** b(1): An act or attitude of intellectual assent to the traditional doctrines of one's religion... (2): A decision of an individual entrusting his life to God's transforming care in response to an experience of God's mercy... a supernatural virtue by which one believes on the authority of God himself, all that God has revealed or proposes through the Church for belief. 2a(1): Firm or unquestioning belief in something for which there is no proof... (2): Uncritical grounds for belief - used chiefly in the phrase "on*

faith"... b: confidence; esp: firm or unquestioning trust or confidence in the value, power, or efficacy of something... 3a: An assurance, promise, or pledge of fidelity, loyalty or performance... often used in the phrases "to keep faith" or "to break faith"... 4: Authority, credit, credibility. 5: something that is believed or adhered to exp. with strong conviction: as a (1): A system of religious beliefs... b: The cherished values, ideals, or beliefs of an individual or people... c: The fundamental tenets, views, or beliefs of an individual or group on a particular subject or in a particular field... 6: The true religion from the point of view of the speaker...[86]

Most of these individual definitions will be dealt with as we proceed through our study in one manner or another - but, it is nice to have it laid out for us in a single location. Now, we will dig slightly deeper into our definition for the purpose of adding another level to our understanding of what true biblical belief involves. That word is, *hope*. Turning, once again to Webster's dictionary we find the modern-day definition of *hope*:

Hope... 1: To cherish a desire with expectation... 2: To place confidence or trust - usually used with "in"... 1a: To desire with expectation or with belief in the possibility of obtaining... b: Desire, trust... 2: Wish...

Hope... 1: Trust, reliance... 2a: Desire accompanied with expectation of obtaining what is desired or belief that it is obtainable... b: One on whom hopes are centered... c: A source of hopeful expectation... d: Something that is hoped for: an object of hope...[87]

A simple review of these two definitions makes it easy to see why faith and hope are so intricately intertwined: *the act or state of wholeheartedly and steadfastly believing in the existence, power, and benevolence of a supreme being...* While maintaining an *expectation of obtaining what is desired or belief that it is obtainable...*

What an awesome conclusion for us to have reached; and all of this, before we even get into the Word of God. For our purposes, this *"supreme being"* referred to in Webster's dictionary is God; the Creator of the heavens and the earth; the One who has revealed Himself to us through His written Word. He is the One in whom all ministers of the Gospel and

---

[86] Philip Babcock Gove (Editor in Chief); (Webster's Third New International Dictionary of the English Language: Unabridged; Springfield, Massachusetts; Merriam-Webster Inc., Publishers; 1993); Page 816, emphasis added.
[87] Philip Babcock Gove (Editor in Chief); (Webster's Third New International Dictionary of the English Language: Unabridged; Springfield, Massachusetts; Merriam-Webster Inc., Publishers; 1993); Pages 1089-1090.

Christian counselors must wholeheartedly and steadfastly place their trust in. Then, as we press on, we must ask, *What would any biblical study on faith and hope be without taking a brief look in the book of Hebrews?*

Faith means being sure of the things we hope for and knowing that something is real even if we do not see it. Faith is the reason we remember great people who lived in the past. It is by faith we understand that the whole world was made by God's command so what we see was made by something that cannot be seen. It was by faith that Abel offered God a better sacrifice than Cain did. God said he was pleased with the gifts Abel offered and called Abel a good man because of his faith. Abel died, but through his faith he is still speaking. It was by faith that Enoch was taken to heaven so he would not die. He could not be found, because God had taken him away. Before he was taken, the Scripture says that he was a man who truly pleased God. Without faith no one can please God. Anyone who comes to God must believe that he is real and that he rewards those who truly want to find him. (Hebrews 11:1-6 NCV)

Here in verse one the author chooses to use the word *"Faith"* and yet, as we have already deduced, faith has several possible meanings: so, which one is he trying to get us to understand? For a more pinpointed comprehension of his intentions let's turn to two extremely valuable study tools that any minister or Christian counselor should have access to; the Vine's dictionary and a Strong's concordance.

Vine's dictionary reveals that the Greek word used here is *pistis* and informs us of the following: *pistis (4102), primarily, "firm persuasion," a conviction based upon hearing... is used in the New Testament always of "faith in God or Christ or things spiritual"... The main elements in "faith" in its relation to the invisible God, as distinct from "faith" in man, are especially brought out in the use of this noun and the corresponding verb, "pisteuo"; they are (1) A firm conviction, producing a full acknowledgement of God's revelation or truth, e.g. 2 Thess. 2:11-12; (2) A personal surrender to Him, John 1:12; (3) A conduct inspired by such surrender, 2 Cor. 5:7;* **All this stands in contrast to belief in its purely natural exercise, which consists of an opinion held in good "faith" without necessary reference to its proof.**[88]

Pistis (faith) includes a fervor born of an inward confidence and conviction that God exists and, that He is the Creator of all things. That He

---

[88] W.E. Vine (Vine's Expository Dictionary of Old and New Testament Words; Nashville, Tennessee; Thomas Nelson Publishers; 1997); Page 401, emphasis added.

is the Provider and Bestower of our assurance of eternal salvation through Christ Jesus. Faith is also a strong reliance on God; that He is, not only capable, but willing to fulfill all He has said.

For our purposes, faith and hope, when combined contain an explosive propensity for change, which is ultimately, the impetus for all counseling. Both faith and hope are, in every respect, a crucial prerequisite to any successful counseling method. In fact, biblical faith also involves an element of active obedience to the will of God. It is more than a simple believing in God's existence, His desire and His ability to provide for all our needs. It also requires that we do what He tells us to do. James said, s*o also faith, if it does not have works (deeds and actions of obedience to back it up), by itself is destitute of power (inoperative, dead).* (James 2:17 AMPC) Some of those works simply involve *actions of obedience* to Gods Word with a confident expectation that He will be true to His Word.

Faith is simple. It is believing God without a waver, without doubting, and without questioning what He says. It is taking God at His Word and believing that what He has promised He is able to perform… It is believing not only that He is able, but that He will do it. It is the quality of counting those things that be not as though they were (Rom. 4:17). Faith is also the absolute conviction that what God has promised and what we have asked according to His Word is done already. It is the substance of things hoped for and the first payment on things that we desire from God (Heb. 11:1-3).[89]

Now faith is the substance of things hoped for, the evidence of things not seen (Hebrews 11:1 KJV). Many of us have been taught that this verse is where we find the biblical definition of faith; some of us have even taught this to others. While it is, at least in part true, we cannot stop there. If we did we would simply be scratching the surface of what faith truly is. As we have already alluded, from the Vine's definition, *Faith in its relation to the invisible God* (is) *distinct from faith in man* in that, we can have a certain kind of faith in natural, visible things; things that we can experience by simply engaging our natural senses, i.e. taste, smell, touch, etc… However, the faith that pertains to having a firm persuasion and assurance of an invisible Creator is a work of grace, which in and of itself is a gift of God; after-all doesn't God allot *to each a measure of faith?* (Romans 12:3)

---

[89] Finis Jennings Dake (God's Plan For Man; Lawrenceville, Georgia; Dake Publishing; 1977); Page 33.

Upon accepting the wooing or drawing of the Holy Spirit, God supernaturally graces and empowers us with the *measure of faith* necessary for us to believe in the invisible, immutable Creator of all things. Then, immediately afterward, God puts the proverbial ball into our hands and tells us of certain things we can and should do to grow this free gift of God. We should "add" to our faith by repeatedly hearing the Word of God and we should be "growing" our faith by virtue of exercising it.

Before leaving this point on defining faith and hope we need to understand that, while many believe Hebrews chapter eleven verse one includes the biblical definition for faith, not all agree. Since we are attempting to reduce any confusion surrounding this vital topic it would be wise for us to include another perspective, which does not necessarily disagree with our previous understanding: it simply takes us a little deeper.

In the King James Version Bible Commentary [*computer file*] we find the following concerning Hebrews chapter eleven, verses one through three:

Verse 1 **is not so much a definition** *of what faith is as it is a description of what faith does. Two truths concerning its activity are stated here. First, faith provides* **substance** *(Gr hypostasis). Precisely what this word means here is difficult to determine... The first connotation is that of* **substance** *as an essence of something... The second connotation is that of* **substance** *as the foundation of something... The third connotation is that of* **assurance**... *The fourth connotation, that of a* **guarantee**... *Thus faith might be looked upon as the "title deed" of things hoped for... Within all the connotations "there is the central idea of something that underlies visible conditions and guarantees a future possession..." Assurance may be the best translation...*

Second, faith provides **evidence** *(Gr elegchos). It is evidence in the sense of proof which results in conviction. Now, the difference between substance or assurance of the first part of the verse and the evidence or conviction of the last part may seem minimal; but the contrast within the verse focuses upon the qualifying phrases:* **of things hoped for** *and* **of things not seen.** *The first involves future hopes; the second involves present realities, which are unseen... Hope is faith relating to the future; conviction is faith relating to the present. Because of faith, objective reality is not required. Faith is the affirmative response to God's will and Word. Man possesses faith when he takes God at His Word. One does not need to see something to believe it. Faith is the acceptance of* *something merely because God has said it...⁹⁰*

As we previously stated, faith "is a work of grace" - God's grace, which enables us to *believe* in and accept something *merely because God has said it*. Faith is not a new invention as some would have us to believe; and it is not man's own creation either. God established faith and expects all of His children, especially ministers and Christian counselors, to abundantly add to and strengthen it by following His instructions and plans.

The great evangelist Oral Roberts succinctly sums up what faith is when he writes: *So the first part of understanding faith is to know that what we hope for is not just a pipe dream or something we imagine. It has reality and substance. Then he* (the author of Hebrews) *says faith is not presumption. It is something we just think is going to be. We have to have evidence. Therefore, faith is strong when it has evidence and not presumption.⁹¹*

Someone has said that *faith is not a force upon the understanding, but a friend and a help to it.* In concluding this particular section we will conduct a short study in contrast. By pinpointing a few simple things that faith is not, we will help to alleviate even more areas of potential misunderstanding where faith and hope are concerned. Faith and hope are not:

- Sense-Knowledge: biblical faith and hope are not affected, either positively or negatively by the physical senses (i.e. sight, sound, touch, etc...).

- Works: while the grace gift of faith is not a "work", true biblical faith will result in activity or, as it were, "works". Simple activity does not generate faith; however, biblical faith will generate works.

- Something Borrowed: Bible faith is not something that can be borrowed from another person, it must be a "personal assurance" based upon personal conviction.

- Merely Talked About: having one conversation after another about the need for faith is not sufficient, true biblical faith

⁹⁰ Logos Library System; http://www.logos.com; King James Bible Commentary; January 13, 2012.
⁹¹ Oral Roberts (The New Testament Comes Alive Volume Three; Nashville, Tennessee; Parthenon Press; 1984); Page 22.

must be received and then, grown by regularly hearing the Word (Romans 10:17) and then following the instructions therein.

- Mental Assent: simply acknowledging God's truth is not faith; true faith must be alive and active within one's heart.

We could spend hour upon hour delving into what faith is not but most of it would become a mere repetition of the principles we have already discussed. However, the final point we made concerning "what faith is not" deserves a bit more clarity. Because there some extremely legalistic teachings "out there" we need to spend more time with "Mental Assent".

Mental Assent

To begin with let's re-examine a specific definition that we previously found in Webster's dictionary: *¹Faith... 1b(1): An act or attitude of intellectual assent to the traditional doctrines of one's religion...⁹²*

Some neoorthodox theologians...in their zeal to stress the transcendent...have denied that saving faith is a human psychic act at all. Faith "crosses over into the absolutely trans-subjective, is a negation of human activity (and as such) *falls outside the field of psychology...put(ing) both feet on the other side of human experience..." Faith "is not a neutral organ that accepts divine revelation; it 'belongs itself to revelation'. It is not a function of 'this side' which takes to itself 'the other side'; 'it is itself something from the other side;* **it is a miracle'**... **Everything human in faith is 'unworthy of belief'**... *Faith is 'not an act of man, but the original, divine believing'... There is only divine subjectivity; God does the believing* (and simply provides us with the measure of faith - Romans 12:3).⁹³*

In short, what this says is that man has absolutely nothing to do with faith. It is simply Divine in nature and "everything human in faith is unworthy of belief". But where does that leave us with the Scriptures that tell us *with the heart man believes unto righteousness* (Romans 10:10)? Or, as the Amplified Version of the Bible explains that the word *believes* means "adheres to, trusts in, and relies on Christ" all three describe the human side of faith and activity, which assists us in working out our own salvation with

---

⁹² Philip Babcock Gove (Editor in Chief);)Webster's Third New International Dictionary of the English Language: Unabridged; Springfield, Massachusetts; Merriam-Webster Inc., Publishers; 1993); Page 816.
⁹³ Dr. Robert L. Reymond (A New Systematic Theology of the Christian Faith; Nashville, Tennessee; Thomas Nelson Publishers; 1998); Pages 729-730, emphasis added.

fear and trembling (Philippians 2:12). The Word also declares that Abraham, *staggered not at the promise of God through unbelief; but was strong in faith, giving glory to God; **And being fully persuaded** (and assured) that, what He (God) had promised, He was able also to perform. And therefore it was imputed to him for righteousness.* (Romans 4:20-22 KJV, emphasis added)

In one respect and since it is not natural for man, in his fallen condition, to positively respond to the presentation of the Good News, the aforementioned theologians are correct. However, once God sows the seed (i.e. the measure of faith) in an individual's heart, it becomes that person's responsibility, not God's. It is up to the free will of each individual, once the seed has been sown, to employ faith. Each person opts to express a belief that God not only exists, but that He is also a rewarded of them that diligently seek Him (Hebrews 11:6).

Other theologians have referred to this active expression of believing in an invisible, omnipresent Creator as *the voluntary element.* As a matter of fact two such individuals, in dealing with the Doctrine of Salvation have stated that; *The voluntary element. After knowing what God has promised, and after assenting to the truth of that promise, then faith reaches out and appropriates what is provided. Knowledge (or intellectual/mental accent) itself is not enough. A man may have the knowledge that Christ is Divine and yet reject Him as Savior. Knowledge affirms the reality of these things, but it neither accepts or rejects. Nor is assent enough. This is an assent of the mind which does not convey a surrender of the heart... Real faith is in the realm of the will. It appropriates. It takes. Faith always has the idea of action in it. "Faith has legs". It is the soul leaping up to embrace the promise.*[94]

So, what does all this have to do with counseling? Good question. James tells us that even *demons believe* in God and that they *tremble* (James 2:19) because of their faith in God's existence as well as His ability to perform what He has said in His Word. This reveals that demons possess and express true faith. Unfortunately, many men and women in the counseling setting may "say" they "believe" in God: when, in reality, there is no firm conviction of heart, nor surrender to the assurance of God's promises of provision and protection for themselves, personally. They have nothing to pin their hopes on. They are ascribing to an intellectual/mental

---

[94] Guy P. Duffield and Nathaniel M. Van Cleave (Foundations of Pentecostal Theology; Los Angeles, California; L.I.F.E. Bible College; 1987); Page 218.

assent of God's existence and nothing more. When this is the situation on either the counselor's or the counselee's behalf, the effectiveness of any Christian counseling model will be greatly inhibited at best, and at worst, completely ineffective.

Adams writes, *No counseling system that is based on some other foundation can begin to offer what Christian counseling offers... For several reasons, the hope that Christian counselors offer is unlike hope given by others. First, this hope is based on the unfailing promises of God that He has recorded in the Scriptures. That makes all the difference... Secondly, every command in the Scriptures implies hope: God never tells His children to do anything that He fails to supply both the directions and the power to achieve... Thirdly, God Himself is the Counselor Who guides and directs through His Word. The Christian counselor is not alone... He depends not on his own strength... When a Christian counselee sees for himself that his counselor adheres closely to biblical principle, this too brings hope...*[95]

In all fairness to Adams, he does continue and gives us a fourth reason, which he says is *as important as these three may be* (possibly even) - *excels them.* How much better can it be? He continues to explain: *What the Bible means by the word "hope". That word signifies far more than our pale approximation of the meaning in modern Western society. To us hope means "hope so"... But in Scripture, hope never has such uncertainty connected to it.*[96] This fourth element is simply another way of expressing what we have already discussed when we said that intellectual/mental assent leaves nothing for us to pin our hopes to; resulting in a mere "hope so".

Biblical faith is the only guarantee that we can legitimately attach our hopes on, before we can honestly believe that change is possible. As we have already stated, faith in God says that we are willing to trust Him with our very lives and the we are willing to follow His instructions for living. Unfortunately, everyone who comes to us for help will not be at the same level of faith so we need to have the ability to discern where each one stands. The Bible speaks of various types or kinds of faith - one might even say, levels of faith - which means that the minister or Christian counselor should have, at the very least, a cursory comprehension of each level of

[95] Jay E. Adams (A Theology of Christian Counseling; Grand Rapids, Michigan; Zondervan; 1979); Pages 177-179.
[96] Jay E. Adams (A Theology of Christian Counseling; Grand Rapids, Michigan; Zondervan; 1979); Page 179.

faith.

Several kinds of faith (are) *mentioned in the Scripture, of which the following list will be helpful in arriving at the kind of faith one should have:*

1.   *Common Faith (Titus 1:4)*

2.   *Weak Faith (Romans 4:19; 14:1-23; 15:1-4; 1 Corinthians 8:1-13)*

3.   *Strong Faith (Romans 4:20)*

4.   *Little Faith (Matthew 6:30; 8:26; 14:31; Luke 12:28)*

5.   *Great Faith (Matthew 8:10; 15:28)*

6.   *Unfeigned Faith (1 Timothy 1:5; 2 Timothy 1:5)*

7.   *Temporary Faith (Luke 8:13)*

8.   *Historical Faith (1 John 5:10-13)*

9.   *Mental Faith (James 2:14-26)*

10.   *Active Faith (James 2:14-26; Hebrews 10:19-38)*

11.   *Wavering Faith (James 1:5-8)*

12.   *Unwavering Faith (Hebrews 10:23; 11:6)*

13.   *Human Faith (Mark 11:22-24)*

14.   *Divine Faith (Hebrews 11:3; Galatians 2:20; 1 Corinthians 13:14)*[97]

While there is so much more we could discuss concerning the various kinds of faith referenced above; if, as individuals, we will prayerfully read the aforementioned verses associated with each one, the Holy Spirit will lead us into a deeper revelation and understanding than we are able to delve into at this time.

Adding to Faith

Throughout our study we have said that faith and hope are absolutely essential elements if any Christian counseling method has a chance of being effective. Unfortunately, life happens: life has a way of

---

[97] Finis Jennings Dake (God's Plan For Man; Lawrenceville, Georgia; Dake Publishing; 1977); Pages 504-509.

throwing obstacles across our path that will test our faith. Some of these obstacles include: a lack of sympathy or empathy on behalf of others; unbelieving friends; scoffers; divine delays; or any other obstacle that may cause us to question God and His Word, or His ability and desire to fulfill His promises. And yet, the author of Hebrews tells us to be careful that we are not found having *an evil heart of unbelief* (Hebrews 3:12) that would lead us away from our loving Creator.

To help us with this let's refer to a biblical account wherein a man named Jairus, a ruler of the synagogue, approached Jesus, fell at His feet, and pleaded with Him to come to his house and heal his 12 year old daughter who was dying. However, while Jesus was on the way to Jairus' house He became "sidetracked" by a woman with an issue of blood. We pick up on this dissertation where Jesus is telling her that her faith has made her whole and to go in peace. *While* (Jesus) *was still speaking, someone came from the ruler of the synagogue's house, saying to him, "Your daughter is dead. Do not trouble the Teacher." But when Jesus heard it, He answered him, saying, "Do not be afraid; only believe, and she will be made well."* Luke 8:49-50 NKJV

What an opportunity for Jairus' faith to be destroyed! *Your daughter is dead!* How many of us would have agreed with the messenger and simply decided to tell Jesus to forget it, we're too late? But Jesus, upon overhearing the report looked at Jairus and said, *Do not be afraid; only believe, and she will be made well.*

There is power in God's Word. It was by this Word that the world took form (Genesis 1), Jesus Christ Himself is called the Word (John1; 1 John 1), and we must not think of the Scriptures, which are called God's Word...as any less powerful. The Bible is not just another book; it is unique because it is God's Word... When God speaks, it is so; His Word is as sure as the thing itself.[98]

So what can we do when we believe in the power of God's Word and yet life beats us up so bad that we lose faith and hope? Listen, if not guarded against, ministers and Christian counselors will be as susceptible to this as the counselees they are attempting to help. Scriptures have much to say regarding faith; remaining in faith; continuing in the faith; staying rooted, built up and being established in the faith in Christ. Fortunately for

---

[98] Jay E. Adams (A Theology of Christian Counseling; Grand Rapids, Michigan; Zondervan; 1979); Page 34.

everyone involved we are not simply encouraged in these things; we are also given methods for building up and strengthening our faith.

So then **faith comes by** *hearing, and* **hearing** *by* **the word of God.** (Romans 10:17 NKJV, emphasis added)

Have the roots [of your **being]** **firmly and deeply planted** *[in Him, fixed and founded in Him], being continually built up in Him, becoming increasingly more confirmed and established in the faith, just as you were taught, and abounding and overflowing* **in it with thanksgiving.** (Colossians 2:7 AMPC, emphasis added)

Let us draw near with a true heart in full assurance of faith, having our hearts sprinkled from an evil conscience and our bodies washed with pure water. Let us **hold fast the confession of our hope without wavering,** *for He who promised is faithful. And let us consider one another in order to stir up love and good works,* **not forsaking the assembling of ourselves together,** *as is the manner of some, but* **exhorting one another,** *and so much the more as you see the Day approaching... Therefore do not cast away your confidence, which has great reward. For you have need of endurance, so that after you have done the will of God, you may receive the promise: "For yet a little while, And He who is coming will come and will not tarry. Now the just shall live by faith; But if anyone draws back, My soul has no pleasure in him." But we are not of those who draw back to perdition, but of those who believe to the saving of the soul.* (Hebrews 10:22-25, 35-39 NKJV, emphasis added)

Hearing the Word, being and remaining firmly and deeply rooted in Christ with thanksgiving; guarding against negative speaking; assembling together as believers; being exhorted and exhorting others; holding onto Him with fearless confidence and patience; and refusing to be connected with those who draw back to eternal misery and utter destruction. While this is not a complete list of the ways and means of building and strengthening faith it is a great start. As we live by the instructions found in God's Word we will find it much easier to guide counselees through their own faith minefields.

Examine yourselves, whether ye be in the faith; prove your own selves. Know ye not your own selves, how that Jesus Christ is in you, except ye be reprobates? (2 Corinthians 13:5 KJV)

Smith's Bible Dictionary defines *reprobates* as *(Heb. Nimas, worthless,*

101

rejected), (Jer. vi. 30). **Hardened in sin and unbelief** *(Rom. i. 28).* [99]

We must make regular and honest evaluations of our own faith, ensuring that we have not become hardened in sin or unbelief. Then, following these hard but necessary examinations, allow God's Word and the Holy Spirit to change us, we will be in a much better place to assist others. **If we can** change and remain steadfastly adhered to God while enduring all the discouragements of family and friends; and, **if we can** resist all the temptations of the flesh and the devil; we will be better able to show the truth of our faith to others. Resulting in leading the counselee to a place where their hope and faith will develop into a fervent and sincere passion to see the love of God expressed in all areas of their life.

This is one of the primary reasons we should be in a continual state of *adding to* our *faith.* Notice however, the emphasis we have placed on the "if we can" in the above paragraph: the "ifs" are greatly conditioned upon our individual belief that righteousness is possible. The righteousness spoke of here is not the "righteousness in Christ" that is most commonly referred to in Christian discussions and sermons; it is the opposite side of what I call, the righteousness coin: actions and deeds.

Growing Our Faith

Boys (lads), let no one deceive and lead you astray. He who **practices righteousness** *[who is upright, conforming to the divine will in purpose, thought, and action,* living a consistently conscientious life] is righteous, even as He is righteous.* (1 John 3:7 AMPC, emphasis added)

While adding to our faith is an absolute prerequisite for every believer, for the individual minister and Christian counselor, we must also strengthen and grow our faith by virtue of *practicing righteousness* through *conforming to the divine will in purpose, thought and action*; i.e. faith must be exercised. Recall, if you will, the discussion where we described a few simple things of what faith is not; one of them was that faith and hope are not **merely talked about...faith must be received and then, exercised.**

Think of it this way: you may be a personal trainer and have a great desire to help others in training through the use of both aerobic and

---

[99] Dr. William Smith (Smith's Bible Dictionary; Philadelphia, Pennsylvania; A.J. Holman Company; Original copyright 1863, current copy has no date included); Page 260, emphasis added.

anaerobic techniques. So you go to school, acquire all of the knowledge you need that pertains to the human anatomy, the skeletal and muscular systems, dietary necessities, and whatever else you think will make you smarter and better prepared to help others. How many employment opportunities do you think will come your way if you are personally so out of shape that you can't walk up a flight of stairs unwinded; or you cannot lift a five pound dumbbell?

As ministers and Christian counselors it is extremely hard to be effective in helping someone else if their problem is one that we have not yet personally gained victory over. Does this mean that we need to have every thing figured out and have all of the answers before we can ever help another? No; it simply means that we must know our own, personal limitations and be actively involved in strengthening and growing our faith.

But how can believers, who are "new creations" and have new hearts of flesh that replace the hearts of stone (Ezekiel 36:26), yet sin? How can they be freed from the old master, sin, be enlisted in the service of righteousness, and yet not do all that they ought? In short...he can do so because, although he is counted perfect in Christ, he is not yet perfect in himself. (For more on sanctification see chapter 9.) ***The Christian is not a consistently faithful slave of righteousness; he is in the learning process.*** *There is sin yet in his life. But it is precisely because he has a new outlook on life, serves a new Master, and desires to do the will of the Lord, that his failure to please God becomes a matter of sorrow and remorse... But, because he has a new orientation and the Spirit dwells within him, he is concerned and distressed over his shortcomings... Speaking about this same experience we all know,* Paul (in Romans chapter 7) *was describing a body that often acts contrary to one's mind. Failure to recognize that has kept counselor's from helping many people with what is a universal problem.*[100]

The Christian is...in a learning process. We are all in the "same boat" because, just as it did two thousand years ago, the fact still remains that sin *is a universal problem* and, if we ever have any hope of possessing overcoming faith, we must add to our faith via knowledge and understanding as well as through use and exercise.

However, before we can ever choose to exercise our faith we must

---

[100] Jay E. Adams (How To Help People Change; Grand Rapids, Michigan; Zondervan; 1986); Pages 1860187, emphasis added.

first believe that righteousness or right actions are actually possible. To assist us with our comprehension here let's look at what the Bible calls "righteousness."

Strong's #1343: *dikaiosune: just* **the quality of being right. Broadly, the word suggests conformity to the revealed will of God in all respects.** *It is both judicial and gracious. God declares the believer righteous, in the sense of acquitting him, and imparts righteousness to him (2 Corinthians 5:21).*[101]

Vine's dictionary adds, *dikaiosune: right action is frequently in Paul's writings, as in all five of its occurrences in Romans 6; Ephesians 6:14; etc. But for the most part he uses* **it of that gracious gift of God to men whereby all who believe on the Lord Jesus Christ are brought into right relationship with God. This relationship is unattainable by obedience to any law, or by any merit of man's own, or any other condition than that of faith in Christ... Righteousness is not said to be imputed to the believer save in the sense that faith is imputed ('reckoned' is a better word) for righteousness.** *It is clear that in Romans 4:6 'righteousness reckoned' must be understood in the light of the context, 'faith reckoned for righteousness,' vv. 3, 5, 9, 22. 'For' in these places eis, which does not mean 'instead of,' but 'with a view to.' The* **faith thus exercised brings the soul into vital union with God in Christ, and inevitably produces righteousness of life, that is, conformity to the will of God.**[102]

To summarize the two previous paragraphs: God, upon our acceptance of Christ as Lord, reckons righteousness to us as a free gift. Then we are tasked with excising that righteousness by using faith filled words, intermingled with faith filled actions and deeds. This process *inevitably produces righteousness of life* and *conformity to the will of God.*

This clarifies the two of the most commonly asked questions by believers around the globe: Is true righteousness really possible this side of heaven? And, Is it possible for all believers to follow God's plan?

Pertaining to this very subject Adams writes, *you know you are saved, but there seems to be little growth, little victory over sin. And so you wonder, is it really*

[101] Jack W. Hayford (General Editor); (Spirit Filled Life Bible: New King James Version; Nashville, Tennessee; Thomas Nelson Publishers; 1991); Page 1857: Word Wealth, emphasis added.
[102] W.E. Vine (Vine's Expository Dictionary of Old and New Testament Words; Nashville, Tennessee; Thomas Nelson Publishers; 1997); Pages 970-971.

*possible in this life for a Christian to be **different** after all?*[103] "Different" from what? The unsaved world. Why do so many believers walk and talk and live virtually every aspect of their life in similar fashion to unbelievers?

We could spend the rest of our lives attempting to answer the depths of this question, which we will not; it is fairly safe to say that the vast majority of issues pertaining to a lack of righteousness on the believer's behalf are either directly or indirectly related to the individual's free will. God, in one of His greatest acts of love toward all of humanity, made us free moral agents. In a nutshell, this means that every human being has the freedom to choose right from wrong concerning every decision we are required to make in life.

We actually have the option as to which master we will serve - righteousness or sin. Since this is a scriptural reality, our Creator, through His only Begotten Son and the Holy Spirit has empowered us with the ability to enforce righteousness in our own life, if we so choose.

Contrary to some modern teaching, we are no longer dominated by sin. Unable to live righteously, and stuck in a bumbling, miserable existence of no spiritual growth... A Christian's life can be different...[104] because God has provided to us the legitimate ability to choose; unfortunately, far too many believers are either unaware of this biblical truth; they have failed to *add to their faith;* or they have not grown their faith *by virtue of use.*

My friends, do not be surprised at the terrible trouble which now comes to test you. Do not think that something strange is happening to you. (1 Peter 4:12 NCV)

*In this verse Peter says several things: (1) that because of our identification with Christ's substitutionary death in the flesh, the problem of sin in the flesh **(described as human desires)** has been dealt with; (2) that whenever we face the temptation to sin, there will be a battle (he uses a military term, arm, which means to take up one's battle gear); (3) **that we are equipped to resist sinful human desires** by remembering that in Christ we have died to sin; and (4) **that it is therefore possible to live differently for the rest of our lives.***[105]

---

[103] Jay E. Adams (How To Help People Change; Grand Rapids, Michigan; Zondervan; 1986); Page 179, emphasis added.
[104] Jay E. Adams (How To Help People Change; Grand Rapids, Michigan; Zondervan; 1986); Pages 180-181, emphasis added.
[105] Dr. Timothy Clinton and Dr. George Ohlschlager; (Competent Christian Counseling Volume One; Colorado Springs, Colorado; Waterbrook Press; 2002).

Because, in Christ, we are equipped to resist sinful human desires it is possible for us to live differently for the rest of our lives. As ministers and Christian counselors, if we have not added to and grown our faith and hope in this area, how can we ever expect to instill into a counselee that it is possible? And perhaps, even more importantly, how can we legitimately challenge them to live a changed life?

While effective and strong faith may be revealed in as many different ways as there are stars in the sky, there are some very common characteristics displayed in the life of any individual who possesses such faith. These common characteristics include:

• A complete and humble obedience to God's will as well as a readiness to do whatever He calls them to do.

• Strong faith will be more concerned with the existence of faith than it is it's size: a small amount of faith is enough, if it is alive and actively growing.

• Effective faith realizes that a believer has been delivered from their past by Christ's death and also, that, as they learn more of God's plan for their life, including the promise of a bright future: hope will grow.

• Tenacious faith and hope will persevere when confronted with persecution and pressure. In fact, this is often a time when God's presence will be greatly enhanced in the believer's life.

• Compelling faith not only perseveres during times of persecution and pressure; it quite often becomes even stronger by virtue of added use. (Remember our strength training example?)

• Powerful faith is filled with and thrives on hopeful anticipation.

• Robust faith has a calming quality supporting it: it truly believes that God is who He says He is and that He will accomplish or fulfill His promises.

Let's reiterate, faith and hope are more than simply a belief in God's existence: even demons believe in His reality and tremble (James 2:19). This faith is a wholehearted conviction that says we are willing to trust God and follow His biblical instructions for our life even in the midst of ridicule, pessimism, and persecution; because we have a holy fervor and conviction that God really does exist and, as the Ruler of all things, He actually has the power to provide for us all things that pertain to life and godliness (2 Peter 1:3).

Windows and Doors: Modern Day Fleeces

Unfortunately, many in the church and without (by that I refer to those who profess to be Christians, yet fail to be attached in any real sense to a local assembly of believers as instructed in Hebrews chapter 10, verse 25) have unconsciously concluded that "when God shuts a door, He will open a window." Or that "God opens and closes doors or windows based on His plan" for our life. This, both in principle as well as in effect, is the exact same thing that Gideon did with his fleece. Let's read that account in Judges:

Then Gideon said to God, "If you are truly going to use me to rescue Israel as you promised, prove it to me in this way. I will put a wool fleece on the threshing floor tonight. If the fleece is wet with dew in the morning but the ground is dry, then I will know that you are going to help me rescue Israel as you promised." And that is just what happened. When Gideon got up early the next morning, he squeezed the fleece and wrung out a whole bowlful of water. Then Gideon said to God, "Please don't be angry with me, but let me make one more request. Let me use the fleece for one more test. This time let the fleece remain dry while the ground around it is wet with dew." So that night God did as Gideon asked. The fleece was dry in the morning, but the ground was covered with dew. (Judges 6:36-40 NLT)

By affixing natural conditions to God's revealed will for our life we are giving the devil, other people, and even our own peculiar emotions the potential of leading us down the wrong path. Referring specifically to answered prayer Finis Dake writes, *men fail to get all the benefits provided in God's plan because of unbelief and because of the many conditions they manufacture...*[106]

The psalmist tells us to *commit your way unto the Lord; trust also in Him; and He shall bring it to pass.* (Psalms 37:5) What is "it"? Whatever He has told you. However, our trusting and committing does not mean there is nothing for us to do. I recall many years ago when God first started dealing with me

---

[106] Finis Jennings Dake (God's Plan For Man; Lawrenceville, Georgia; Dake Publishing; 1977); Page 208.

concerning His plan for my life. One day when I finally accepted the fact that He wanted me to become a Pastor and itinerant teacher I put my hand to the proverbial plow and started doing what I knew to do. Even though it had been over fifteen years since I graduated from high school, I enrolled in my first Bible school. You want to talk about "open doors"? My wife and I both decided that we would go to this school: six classes a week for two years. Now that may not sound too horrible until you consider:

1.   We both worked full time jobs: my wife worked Monday through Friday in the daytime while I worked Tuesday through Saturday on the midnight shift. Combine this with...

2.   My wife worked twenty-five miles north of where we lived; I worked thirty miles west of where we lived; and the Bible school was 35 miles east of our house. Most nights we ate our dinner "on the way" to school and then we had to leave ten minutes early so I could drive the sixty-five miles to work without being late, dropping my wife off at home on the way there. And, if that were not enough...

3.   We had a very active teenage son, not yet driving. And...

4.   All three of us held positions of leadership and responsibility at our own home church.

Talk about the grace of God! But we knew what He wanted us to do and we refused to sit back and wait for open doors and windows - we kicked in doors and busted out windows, proverbially speaking. We did what was in our power to do and simply trusted God to do the rest. However, for this to happen we had to first believe that God loved us and that He was with us; giving us the strength to overcome every obstacle and hindrance to our successfully fulfilling His will for our life.

Modern day fleeces will always cause us to hesitate; and, more often than not, lead to yet another *"if it is truly you God"* comment, which opens the way for even more error and confusion. Consider Abraham for a moment: God told him to leave his family (mother and father, not his wife) and go to a place where He would later reveal - Abraham went, not knowing where he was going. Later, God told Abraham to take his son Isaac and sacrifice him to God; Abraham did not hesitate. He not only went, but he took everything needed for the sacrifice (i.e. wood, fire, knife, etc.) with him. Once again, Abraham went at God's instructions not really understanding God's plans or intentions even though he was completely committed to trusting Him. How many of us, on either occasion, would have said, "If this is really You God, then You need to..."

The Bible does not tell us to look for open or closed doors as a way of determining God's guidance. True, God often opens and closes doors, but in determining His will beforehand, it is perilous to try to do so on the basis of one's prejudiced (or limited) view of circumstances. Selective interpretation is all too frequently at work. I shall not take time to discuss the futility of trying to determine God's will by means of "feelings," "urges," "deep convictions," "peace" and "leadings". Behind each are unrecognized reasons. Sometimes they are biblical, sometimes they aren't; sometimes they are noble, often they aren't. One must get back to these reasons in counseling to analyze and evaluate them according to biblical principles. Anything less than this results in decision-making that shifts with whims and whatever - or worse than that! And what a tragedy when such decisions are stamped with divine approval and authority as "God's leading!" [107]

So, we must ask, if we are not supposed to use "urges," "feelings," "convictions," "peace," or any plethora of other guidance whims, what are we to employ? God's Word; direction of the Holy Spirit - but only if that direction aligns with the written, unadulterated Word; any counseling that runs contrary to Scriptures does not originate with the Holy Spirit; and faith. Yes, faith.

But the man who has doubts (misgivings, an uneasy conscience) about eating, and then eats [perhaps because of you], stands condemned [before God], because he is not true to his convictions and he does not act from faith. For **whatever does not originate and proceed from faith is sin** *[whatever is done without a conviction of its approval by God is sinful].* (Romans 14:23 AMPC, emphasis added)

The Apostle Paul is very clear when he establishes this principle: *whatever is not done in faith is sin.* We should never do anything until we are confident that what we are about to do is not sin; or possibly even a sin to us personally. Let me tell another personal account that seems to fit-in right here. At one time God had dealt with me about the things I was drinking. He told me very specifically not to drink any thing but water until He told

---

[107] Jay E. Adams (A Theology of Christian Counseling; Grand Rapids, Michigan; Zondervan; 1979); Page 301.

me it was okay to drink something else. I complied and for six months I drank nothing but water; then, one day, without a preconceived thought the Holy Spirit impressed upon me that it was now okay to have something besides water and, I did. You may be asking yourself just how this is relevant to our conversation. Well, during that six month period, if I had consumed any beverage other than water; for me, it would have - without a doubt - been a sin.

Whoever doubts is condemned...whatever is not done in faith is sin. Don't get caught acting in unbelief; wait until you are convinced in your own heart and mind of God's instructions. Jay E. Adams has called this the *Holding Principle*.

The principle, to hold back till certain that you are not sinning, **applies to any and all situations in which a Christian discovers that to come to a particular decision, begin a practice, etc., raises scruples in his mind. Until he is sure that the move forward is proper in God's sight, he may not make it.** *The holding principle calls a halt to acts, decisions, etc., made when in a condition of doubt. Until he is "fully convinced in his own mind"...he must refrain.*[108]

While this principle must never be used to support laziness or simple procrastination it is entirely justifiable until we can prayerfully study God's Word and receive His direction concerning any given situation. The end result of this principle is biblical practicability - it is practical for us as well as our counselees to be able to include a wholehearted confidence and expectation of obtaining from God what He has promised, which is tantamount to faith in action.

Specifically commenting on the *Holding Principle* Adams concludes: *Christian's who regularly put it into practice find that frequently it allows time for new information to be gathered (that brings new clarity to an unclear situation) or new developments to take place (that help clarify the situation). Much of the doubt that arises in counselees grows out of haste. God often wants to slow us down to take a harder look at something before we commit ourselves to it.*[109]

---

[108] Jay E. Adams (A Theology of Christian Counseling; Grand Rapids, Michigan; Zondervan; 1979); Pages 32-33, emphasis added.
[109] David Hansen (The Art of Pastoring; Downers Grove, Illinois; InterVarsity Press; 1994); page 33.

Maintaining Hope During Times of Loss

Unfortunately, even if we do every thing right we will still suffer loss from time to time. The most common experience to mankind is the loss of a loved one. While death is both horrific and grievous it is not the only "loss" individuals will experience. Loss can involve finding ourselves without gainful employment; it can mean a loss of family through divorce; it can involve losing ones health, youthfulness, or any number of other issues in life that can result in grief and sorrow; both of which are simply an honest expression of our own feelings. And yet, even in the midst of these intense feelings we can look forward, confidently trusting in God to take care of all our needs.

As ministers and Christian counselors we must be able to help counselees grab a hold of hope in the midst of seemingly hopeless situations. It is our responsibility, by the grace and aid of the Holy Spirit, to find a way of expressing to others that God supplies hope even when life seems impossible.

Once again we are not discussing the modern condition of a "hope-so" mentality; we are dealing with the kind of hope that is essential to our perseverance; the kind of hope that is found in and arises out of a right relationship with Christ and empowers us to get through the toughest of times and situations. Without this kind of hope we give up; and, if the sorrow and pain turns into despair, real trouble may be on the horizon. How can we tell the difference or see when an individual is sliding from loss into despair? The answer to this question is fairly easy - faith and hope in the midst of loss will still have an eye toward the future. When we find someone in despair this element of anticipation for a future will be missing.

For I know the plans I have for you, says the Lord. They are plans for good and not for disaster, to give you a future and a hope. (Jeremiah 29:11 NLT)

*Brothers and sisters, I know that I have not yet reached that goal, but there is one thing I always do. Forgetting the past and straining toward what is ahead, **I keep trying to reach the goal** and get the prize for which God called me through Christ to the life above.* (Philippians 3:13-14 NCV, emphasis added)

God revealed to the Old Testament prophet Jeremiah that His plans for the prophet were good plans; plans that point toward a hopeful future. Since God does not show favoritism (Romans 2:11; Ephesians 6:9;

111

Colossians 3:25) we can grasp onto one of my favorite sayings, which is: "If God will do it for one, He'll do it for anyone!" What an awesome reality - if we, or anyone else, will reach out to God in faith, trusting in His Word - we can say, with complete and total anticipation of receiving: that, if He did it for one, He will do it for me. God never plans evil or hopelessness for believers. In the grand scheme of things His is a plan to take us to heaven where loss, pain, suffering, sorrow, and grief do not exist. A proper understanding of this future hope should result in hopeful anticipation: that is why the Apostle Paul could say, *...there is one thing I always do. Forgetting the past and straining toward what is ahead...* Keep trying to reach the goal.

Then in Romans 12:12 Paul tells the believers in Rome to *be joyful because you have hope. Be patient when trouble comes, and pray at all times.* It is essential the we make it crystal clear to our counselees at a time of personal loss that they can find solace and hope in Christ because their hope is built on the solid foundation of His faithfulness. Loss and *grieving is affected by hope or the lack of it, and hope is affected by information or the lack of it. Hope does not grow out of misunderstanding and ignorance. Hope is based on information.*[110] And the very best information for us to be able to digest is that man does not control the world; God does. Knowing and accepting this will bring hope now; and a confident expectation and anticipation of a glorious future.

Who Needs Hope

In this section we will simply adapt a list that has been more fully expanded upon in *The Christian Counselor's Manual.*[111] Since our list will neither be quoted, nor given in the same order as in the original, we must be exceedingly aware of the fact that it is an adaptation and yet, we will not change or alter the basic presuppositions and principles found in any of them. Now that this has clearly been established let's begin: as ministers and Christian counselors, who needs hope?

• Anyone who has not accepted Jesus as Savior and subsequently made Him the Lord of their life is in need of hope.

---

[110] Jay E. Adams (Shepherding God's Flock; Grand Rapids, Michigan; Zondervan; 1075); Page 144.
[111] Jay E. Adams (The Christian Counselor's Manual; Grand Rapids, Michigan; Zondervan; 1973); Pages 40-46.

• Anyone who has bought into the ways of the world, accepting the hopeless labels that are attached to specific situations. These individuals need hope because they have come to a wrong conclusion out of ignorance.

• Anyone who has tried and failed. These counselees may be confused, resentful, worried, or even angry at God. They need hope because hope leads to perseverance and perseverance leads to patience in spite of continual delay or difficulty.

• Anyone who has repeatedly had their hopes destroyed. An individual in this group will need hope instilled and then built up in them because, in all likelihood, they have erected a wall around themselves out of a fear of additional pain and disappointment.

• Anyone who has a harassing fear are in need of hope. Fear can traumatize, immobilize, and paralyze so, as ministers and Christian counselors we must find a way to inject hope into what appears to be a hopeless situation.

• Anyone who has long-standing problems will need hope. Often, because of the duration these individuals are just tired and hope can be provided by simply helping them to hold their arms up. (Refer to the biblical account of Moses, Aaron, and Hur in Exodus chapter 17.)

• Anyone who has particularly difficult problems need hope. Although nearly every counselee thinks their problem is the hardest and the worst ever faced by anyone, there are some issues that are particularly more complicated.

• Anyone who has reached an age where they are considered "old" or "elderly" may need hope. The elderly will, at times, believe they are too old to change - it's the *you can't teach and old dog new tricks* mentality. (This also may fall into the second category: buying into the ways of the world.) Then, if the impossibility is not an issue they may feel, because of their age, that they are no longer of any help to others. Both of these issues are very common in elderly counselees and must be countermanded by an injection of hope.

- Anyone who has experienced a life-shattering situation in their own life needs hope. Excessive grief over the loss of a person, possessions, or position tends to lead an individual into despair; but hope is God's antidote to despair.

- Anyone who has been depressed needs hope. We all understand that hope deferred makes the heart sick (Proverbs 13:12). However, when a person is depressed they will routinely stop completing their daily duties and chores. This action will almost always result in a downward cycle sucking the person into an ever-deepening spiral of depression, which must be broken. In these cases the counselee must be made aware of their self-defeating cycle and that the best way to start the healing process is to simply start fulfilling their daily duties and completing their familial/work responsibilities, which will, in turn give birth to hope.

- Anyone who has suicidal ideations needs hope. These individuals are at the pinnacle of hopelessness and must be taken seriously. Most often hope can be infused into the suicidal individual by simply recognizing and acknowledging just how hopeless the counselee appears to be in their current situation.

- Anyone who has ever lived. On the surface this may appear to simply be a "catch all" statement. However, there are times when everyone; believer and unbeliever alike, will find themselves at a junction in life where complicating problems intersect with their path. It is at these times when anyone may need to be encouraged, challenged, or even corrected in order to spur a renewed hope in their future.

As we close this chapter let's reiterate that faith and hope are prerequisites to counseling; this, at least in the beginning of the process, is primarily a belief on the counselors behalf that true change is actually possible. For the minister and Christian counselor to enter into the counseling process without faith or hope is tantamount to nothing more than "going through the motions" which, all too often occurs purely for selfish or monetary purposes and neither are sufficient motivating factors. *The Christian counselor presupposes the possibility of radical change in the personality and life style of the counselee. He believes in conversion and in the sanctifying power of the Spirit. He believes that...change is possible... Hope in counseling belongs, primarily, therefore, to the Christian counselor. He knows that God is in the business of changing lives. Every change that God promises is possible. Every quality that God requires in His children can be attained. Every resource that is needed God has supplied.*[112]

It is also crucial, especially for anyone new to the ministry or counseling process, to learn and get deeply rooted within themselves that we attack the problem, not the person. This may seem to be an elementary statement. Unfortunately, while the minister and Christian counselor has a clear understanding and staunchly adheres to these beliefs, there is a very real possibility of the counselee misinterpreting our actions/intentions. If this occurs it will, in all probability, destroy whatever glimmer of hope they possessed. If this misunderstanding occurs and if the counselee chooses to return for additional sessions, the circumstances surrounding the complicating problems will have to be dealt with prior to being able to explore and investigate the initial presenting problems/concerns.

The Word of God tells us that **there are some things the LORD our God has kept secret**, *but there are some things He has let us know. These things belong to us and our children forever so that we will do everything in these teachings.* (Deuteronomy 29:29 NCV, emphasis added) There will be times that we simply will not have things revealed to us: when this happens it may be the counselee is not being as forthcoming as they should be, or it may simply be a part of God's bigger plan. In either case, if we have done our absolute best and still failed, we cannot allow it to destroy our own faith, hope and beliefs.

The counselor must believe that change is possible not only to communicate hope to doubtful counselees, but also because the process of change can be discouraging to counselors, as well as to counselees. So, the first matter of importance is to believe that people whose lives have been steeped in sin can change. If you do not believe that, you should not counsel.[113] And if, for whatever reasons, we lose faith and hope in the process we must take a break, repent, and restore our own faith and hope; get refreshed, and then, as directed by the Holy Spirit, re-enter the

---

[112] Jay E. Adams (The Christian Counselor's Manual; Grand Rapids, Michigan; Zondervan; 1973); Pages 28-29.
[113] Jay E. Adams (How To Help People Change; Grand Rapids, Michigan; Zondervan; 1986): Page 190.

wonderful world of helping others.

In a letter to the Corinthian church the Apostle Paul, in closing one of the greatest dissertations ever on love, says: *three things will last forever— faith, hope, and love—and the greatest of these is love.* (1 Corinthians 13:13 NLT) In this chapter we have dealt with the faith and hope portions of this verse; in our next chapter we will address love, and how it pertains to the ministry and the process of counseling.

Chapter 6 : The Love of God in the Counseling Setting

In a previous chapter we discussed the prospects of being involved in the counseling process with a counselee that has not accepted the redemption of Christ; i.e. received salvation. For example, some say that effective counseling cannot even begin until evangelism has been effective. Others, such as Jay E. Adams, will not even enter into the counseling process before salvation has occurred. I do not totally subscribe to either of those beliefs because, there are times when we simply need to express the love of God; and, at other times, we merely need to show someone how much we care before they will care how much we know. Showing someone; anyone - especially an unbeliever or potential counselee how much we care is exactly where God's unconditional love enters the Christian counseling process.

Does this expression of God's love require us to agree with whatever they have done or are currently involved in? No. Does it mean that we overlook their actions and simply declare, like non-Christian counseling models, that the past is the past? No. Does expressing the love of God imply that there are no moral judgments to be made on our behalf; no corrective measures are to be expected; or that disciplinary action is never to be taken? Absolutely not.

The very issues that has brought about such distortions concerning the true, unadulterated, unconditional love of God must be dealt with: both within the Church as well as without. The post-modern concept of "judge not" has nearly annihilated the ability of ministers and Christian counselors from actively pursuing effective counseling. For far too long we have been taught or, at the very least, been led to believe in a God that simply cannot be biblically substantiated. Clarifying some of these distortions that surround the love of God are exactly what we intend to address in this chapter.

In Matthew 22:37-40 Jesus teaches us of the two commandments, which, if properly applied in our lives, will fulfill all of the law. He said, *You shall love the LORD your God with all your heart, with all your soul, and with all your mind. And the second is like it: You shall love your neighbor as yourself. On these two commandments hang all the Law and the Prophets.* (Matthew 22:37, 39-40 NKJV)

We are to love God and others. Within these two commandments we find the Church's primary functions. In relation to God, we are to worship Him in Spirit and in truth. In relation to the world, we are to express God's love by declaring the Gospel of Christ Jesus. And, in relation to believers we have an obligation to nurture and build them up in faith. Unfortunately, due to extreme distortions prevalent in our society, many of which have been blindly accepted by large segments of the Church, concerning God's love, we are compelled to start with the basics; our initial concern must begin with uncovering exactly what biblical love is.

What Is Love?

In the New Testament, there are several Greek words for love, but when reference is made to God's love, the word used is always agape. The lexicon defines agape and the verb agapao as follows: "To love, value, esteem, feel or **manifest generous concern for***, be faithful towards, to delight in, to set store upon; whence - love, generosity, kindly concern, devotedness." The noun agape is scarcely found in Classical Greek. It is one of the words given a new Christian meaning in the New Testament.*[114]

The Bible teaches us that true love is a commitment. Because it is a commitment, true love does not depend upon good or bad feelings. Much of what we are inundated with today teaches us that love is a *feeling*. Adams succinctly expresses this reality when he writes:

Hollywood...has taught a pagan philosophy of love. The philosophy that love happens. Love is not something to work at; it just happens... It's the kind of thing that just is or isn't. It isn't something that you develop, it isn't something that grows, it isn't something that you work hard to achieve, it isn't a thinking thing, and it certainly isn't something that you can will. It is something that just happens... Such love at first seems wonderful, but what happens when the happening no longer happens?... In the playboy philosophy, love is getting; it means getting what one can out of another person, using the other person as an object of love. It means grasping and holding and satisfying oneself by using another (...the life of self and desire orientation is based upon the sinful proposition that it is more blessed to receive than to give) and when he (or she) *is through with that*

---

[114] Guy P. Duffield and Nathaniel M. Van Cleave (Foundations of Pentecostal Theology; Los Angeles, California; L.I.F.E. Bible College; 1987); Page 78, emphasis added.

person...that's it. Much advertising is rooted in the philosophy of hedonism. Motivational research people...have been saying that you ought to become out-and-out hedonists...and openly pursue pleasure as the goal of life... The pursuit of pleasure...inundates us in magazines, on billboards, over the television, (the internet), *and in newspapers. Everywhere one turns*[115]

Within this barrage of distortions and downright lies where do we find the biblical definition of love that includes a manifestation of generous concern for the other person?

Godly love involves giving oneself to another. It is not dependent upon feelings, but rather on a consistently courageous decision to extend self for the benefit and well-being of someone else. That dedicated commitment will then result in feeling. As ministers and Christain counselors this reality must be deeply ingrained in our beliefs – we must never become predisposed to the "what's in it for me" attitude; nor can we simply stand by and watch a "wreck" happen in someone else's life because we don't "feel" like helping. Godly love is willing to sacrifice for the good of others.

In his letter to the Ephesian church the Apostle Paul instructed them to act like dear children and "imitate" or "mimic" their Heavenly Father (Ephesians 5:1). The beloved Apostle John informed us that "God is love" (1 John 4:8). And, as we have already referred to, Jesus taught us that the two greatest commandments were to love God and to love our neighbor (Luke 10:27): love should be the utmost concern for us; it must permeate absolutely every aspect of our being.

Love is a commandment of Jesus; as ministers and Christian counselors we must understand as well as believe this is a fact. Godly love is not simply revealed by showing respect for another; it is more deeply expressed through self-sacrifice and servanthood. In fact, godly love may also be defined as "selfless giving," reaching far beyond family and friends; extending all the way to enemies and persecutors. We have also learned that love is a choice and not simply something that "happens" to us, nor is it the unabashed pursuit of "pleasure as the goal in life".

It is especially crucial for ministers and Christian counselors to

---

[115] Jay E. Adams (The Christian Counselor's Manual; Grand Rapids, Michigan; Zondervan; 1973); Pages 150-151.

realize that there will always be a few individuals we will not "like" as well as others. While it is not something we take pleasure in accepting it is, none-the-less, true; and the reasons are not usually of any importance. There will simply be those that we just don't "get" with or have a hard time "warming" up to. This is one of the best reasons for us to learn that love is not a feeling; it is a choice; it is commanded. We can, without any hypocrisy, choose to manifest a generous and genuine concern for someone's well-being and treat them with respect, whether or not we feel an affection toward them. If we choose to love others, God will be gracious to help us express His love toward them - even the so-called unlovable ones.

Since godly love is a command as well as a choice and not a feeling, we must realize that there is one more major factor where love is concerned: the love of God is a verb.

Love Is A Verb

Yes, the love of God is a verb; *it is a word that characteristically is the grammatical center of a...mode of being...and typically has rather* (a) *full descriptive meaning and characterizing quality*[116] *For God so loved the world, that he gave his only begotten Son, that whosoever believes in him should not perish, but have everlasting life.* (John 3:16) By sending His only begotten Son, God expressed His love for all of humanity by His actions.

All Christians believe that love is crucial; unfortunately too many still equate love with feelings and not actions. Quite regularly we will hear comments like, "I just don't feel the love for him that I once had," or "I love God, I just don't feel like _____." (You can fill in the blank with a multitude of different things.) Christians, all believers, not just ministers and Christian counselors, must reveal the genuineness of their love by their actions. God's love always involves action and since we are instructed to imitate Him then, it should go without saying that, our love - if it is godly love - will also involve action.

Jesus is our example of what it means to love; everything He has done and is still doing involves an act of love. And, as ministers and

---

[116] Philip Babcock Gove (Editor in Chief); (Webster's Third New International Dictionary of the English Language: Unabridged; Springfield, Massachusetts; Merriam-Webster Inc., Publishers; 1993); Page 2542.

Christian counselors we must never become accomplices in changing or watering down His love. God is love and while it may sound proper to say that God is loving, in reality, it is not appropriate. Love is the very essence of what God is; then, because He **is** love, He expresses love via His actions. For example, we can love Him because He first put His love into our heart (Romans 5:5). Love is not one of God's attributes; everything He does is imbued with love. When He corrects or teaches He does so with love: just like He corrects and teaches because of love. This concept of correction or even more seriously, discipline, as being a legitimate act of love seems to be a vanishing thing in our society. Why? Because, as a society, we have lost sight of what genuine love is really like; what is truly involved in imitating the love of God.

It is crucial for us as ministers and Christian counselors to begin expressing a pure representation of biblical love: failure on our part to do so will result in even more individuals believing in an unsubstantiated view of love. We must take the reins and start leading people out of these murky waters that have inundated and distorted God's love. Far too many have been hurt; multitudes have become offended; and untold numbers have given up and walked away from God and the church because of a failure to see God's pure love in action at a personal level. All of us can remember a time when we were in need of receiving God's pure love in action, the kind that is seen when a mother kisses her child's boo-boo and says "it'll be okay". We can also recall a time when we failed to act in a loving manner toward others. If we will do our part to reduce these times in our own life on a personal level, God will give us a deeper understanding of the importance of love in the counseling setting.

Importance Of Love In Counseling

I once heard an instructor of mine say that if, as a minister or Christian counselor, you cannot see beyond the sinful actions of your counselee, no matter how heinous their act, and express the pure, unconditional love of God you have no business being involved with that particular case.

On the surface this sounds precisely accurate and in the vast majority of instances I agree. However, there will be a few cases wherein we will know by the Holy Spirit that we must help. Normally in these cases the process will be extremely taxing on our sensibilities and understanding of very specific issues which we thought that were already settled in our own life and beliefs. I prefer to call these cases: God opportunities. A God opportunity is a time where God, through supernatural guidance, causes us to enlarge our tents - to increase our knowledge, understanding, and ability to express His love to everyone, everywhere, all the time. In short, it becomes a time for personal growth.

God Himself, while we were still His enemy, sent His only begotten Son in order for us to be reconciled to Him (John 3:16; Romans 5:10). The Creator of the heavens and the earth; the Creator of all things above the earth, on the earth, and under the earth expressed the true depth of His love for all humanity in that, while we were still enemies He allowed Jesus to die a horrific death so we could experience first hand, the relationship that Adam and Eve had with Him prior to their fall from grace: the uncompromising love of God. Only a loving Creator and Father could bring about such a gracious and merciful blessing. With these thoughts fresh in our mind and heart we must ask ourselves, "who are we to short-circuit that kind of love because of our own prejudices or immaturity?"

The love of God in the counseling process always *looks for opportunities to give; it asks: "What can I do for another?" ...Love "thinks no evil"...Love labors... Love leads to greater love - fulfilling one's obligation brings joy and peace and satisfaction and greater love and devotion...*[117]

The Bible declares that perfect love casts out all fear (1 John 4:18) and when we actively pursue the expression of "perfect" or pure love we are actively opening the lines of communication, which are vital to any effective counseling process. *Communication provides the setting that fosters brotherly love, and (cyclically) it is brotherly love that fosters good communication. Thus communication is the precondition for the spread and maintenance of Christian love, even as love is also the precondition for speaking the truth. Truth without love becomes a wicked weapon. Love, uncommunicated, is a blunted blessing.*[118] So pure love; God's unconditional love must exist and be established before any substantial progress can be made in the Christian counseling process. Additionally, by

---

[117] Jay E. Adams (The Christian Counselor's Manual; Grand Rapids, Michigan; Zondervan; 1973); Page 413.
[118] Jay E. Adams (Shepherding God's Flock; Grand Rapids, Michigan; Zondervan; 1075); Page 386.

opening the lines of communication, when we allow the pure love of God to be exhibited through us, we are fulfilling the command of Jesus to walk in love.

Love of Others Exhibited

When asked about the greatest of Moses' laws Jesus said, the greatest was to love the Lord your God with all our heart, all of our soul, and with all of our mind. However, He did not stop with simply commanding us to love God; He continued by saying, this is the first and greatest and yet there is a second, which is just like it - to love your neighbor as yourself (Matthew 22:36-39).

The Apostle John said, *"If someone says, "I love God," but hates a fellow believer, that person is a liar; for if we don't love people we can see, how can we love God, whom we cannot see?"* (1 John 4:20 NLT). Jesus tells us to love our enemy; to bless them that curse us; to do good to them that hate us; and to pray for them that despitefully use and persecute us (Matthew 5:44). The only possible way for us to observe these commands is to walk in a righteous relationship with our Creator, who is love. And then, release the love that He has poured into us toward others. As ministers and Christian counselors we must remember the old cliche, which says, *You may be the only expression of God they may ever see.* Without the transforming love of God, it will be impossible, not improbable; but absolutely impossible for us to adequately obey and display His commandment to love others.

There are multitudes of reasons why it is impossible to express pure love apart from God. However, we will address what is probably the most vital element involved; one that can only be experienced following the act of regeneration where the love of God is poured into our heart (Romans 5:5). This element is commonly referred to as a fruit of the Spirit.

Now the fruit of the Spirit is love (Galatians 5:22). If there has been a true regeneration of the spirit the fruit of the Holy Spirit will begin to appear in the person's life, those who are only pretending will not have the love of God and others evidenced in their lives. We cannot over-emphasize the eminently noticeable virtue of pure love in the ministers' and Christian counselor's life. *But genuine love for God and His people, heartfelt obedience to His commands, and the Christlike character traits that Paul calls the fruit of the Spirit, demonstrated consistently over a period of time in a person's life, simply cannot be produced by Satan or by the natural man or woman working in his or her own strength. These can only come about by the Spirit of God working within and giving us new life.*[119]

Pure love simply cannot be produced by human effort, such love is the by-product of having a legitimate relationship with our loving Creator. *It comes from abiding in Christ and experiencing His love flowing through the soul. Love is the cement which binds all the other virtues of the fruit of the Spirit together into a united whole (i.e. love-joy; love-peace; love-longsuffering; love-gentleness; love-goodness; love-faith; love-meekness; and love-temperance: against such there is no law [Galatians 5:22-23]). Love is the common denominator of all Christian character. One cannot love and fail to have any of the other virtues. To be filled with the Spirit is to be filled with love.*[120]

D.L. Moody has characterized love and its relationship to the other virtues of the Spirit in the following way:

- *Joy is love exulting.*

- *Peace is love reposing.*

- *Longsuffering is love untiring.*

- *Gentleness is love enduring.*

- *Goodness is love in action.*

- *Faith is love on the battlefield.*

- *Meekness is love under discipline.*

- *Temperance is love in training.*[121]

If we truly love God we will keep His commandments, even the ones that speak of loving the unlovable. We will do what pleases Him; we will love Him and others and we will do all of this because He first loved us (1 John 4:19). However, before we can honestly be expected to truly express the pure love of God we need to have a biblical comprehension of what His love is. While the following characteristics or elements of pure

---

[119] Wayne Grudem (Bible Doctrine: Essential Teachings of the Christian Faith; Grand Rapids, Michigan; 1999); Page 305.
[120] Guy P. Duffield and Nathaniel M. Van Cleave (Foundations of Pentecostal Theology; Los Angeles, California; L.I.F.E. Bible College; 1987); Page 299.
[121] Guy P. Duffield and Nathaniel M. Van Cleave (Foundations of Pentecostal Theology; Los Angeles, California; L.I.F.E. Bible College; 1987); Pages 297-298.

love will help our comprehension level, they are not intended to be an exhaustive list of every element involved in His love. The areas we will address, however, are crucial to any successful, biblical counseling process.

The first characteristic we will discuss is knowledge and its relation to pure love. According to worldly standards "knowledge is power". Unfortunately, even the world knows that "absolute power corrupts absolutely". So, how do we deal with both of these worldly statements - each of which is true, but only partially? We incorporate the element of perfect love.

Knowledge And Love

In writing to the Corinthian believers the Apostle Paul, dealing specifically with a situation that pertained to food, which had been sacrificed to idols said, *while knowledge may make us feel important, it is love that really builds up the church. Anyone who claims to know all the answers doesn't really know very much. But the person who loves God is the one God knows and cares for* (1 Corinthians 1b-3, para).

The fact that love is more important than knowledge honestly cannot be argued against. However, there has been much harm perpetrated during the counseling process in the name of love. Untold numbers of lives have been horrendously damaged because a minister or Christian counselor started doling out advice before they had a proper understanding of Scripture. I did not say, nor did I imply that these damages were intentional - perfect love never intentionally means to harm.

It is crucial for us to realize and firmly declare to be true what Paul says, love is more important than knowledge. However, his statement was never intended to give us an "out". We are responsible to God and others for our actions and advice; and as such, we must be willing to set under the hand of instruction and learn. This training is, without question, critical for us to undergo (and, at times endure) for a plethora of reasons; two of which are extremely germane to our discussion.

First of all, knowledge can make us look and feel good - even important, but it can also degrade into an arrogant, know-it-all attitude: an attitude that will push others away and ultimately cause God to work against us because arrogance has it roots found in old fashioned pride. Conversely, love without knowledge will, in all likelihood, lead to sentimentalism. Sentimentalism will cause us to work from a position of emotions rather than reason; at times, even at the expense of the truth. This is the emotional - feeling kind of love we addressed at the beginning of this chapter; the kind of love that has been so distorted that the simple act of bringing correction to another is viewed as unloving.

While it is true that Paul was addressing a very specific situation above, the principle can apply to any situation where some believers have freedom of conscience in certain things while others do not. This is why the pure, unadulterated love of God, when mixed with the proper amount of knowledge will lead a believer to willingly support and help a weaker believer as opposed to becoming a source of strife or division; consequently causing them to stumble.

The second reason we must undergo instruction and gain knowledge pertains directly to our ability to properly decipher Scripture. There are specific rules for properly interpreting God's Word, which are crucial for us to have a working knowledge and strong comprehension of God's Word and intentions before we can be assured that what we are teaching others is accurate. Without a proper understanding of the rules of interpretation it is very easy to be led, as well as to lead others, astray.

Over the years I have heard numerous individuals, specifically ministers, declare, "if God has called me, I don't need any formal training or education." I am in no way implying that their intentions were to go out and make a mess of things, but their lack of theological preparation ultimately resulted in them having to learn by "trial and error". Many of the problems they had to endure may have been avoided had they opted for prudence in the matter and receive, at least, some instruction from those that have blazed the trail before them.

All counseling, by its very nature...implies theological commitments by the counselor. He simply cannot become involved in the attempt to change beliefs, values, attitudes, relationships, and behavior without wading neck deep in theological waters. I have shown that these theological commitments may be conscious or unconscious, biblical or heretical, good theology or bad, but-either way-they surely are theological... The relationship between counseling and theology is organic; counseling cannot be done apart from theological commitments. Every act, word (or lack of these) implies theological commitments. On the other hand, theological study leads to counseling implications. The attempt to separate the two must not be made; they cannot be separated without doing violence to both. The separation is as unnatural (and as perilous) as the separation of the spirit from the body.[122]

Paul clearly revealed that knowledge alone is not enough to provide a solution to many issues we will face in the counseling setting. And yet, love without proper knowledge of the unconditional love of God can lead us into an entirely new set of problems. With the proper combination of love and knowledge however, any situation can be overcame: remember, people don't really care how much you know until they know how much you care.

Continuing the journey in our search for a more comprehensive depth of the love of God as it pertains to counseling we need to take some time and address another characteristic in the perfect nature of God's love. If we sincerely desire to experience real progress being manifested in the lives of those we help, we must have had a firsthand encounter with His gracious love. This personal acquaintance will greatly enhance our ability to discern what is true, right, and lasting; in short, it helps produce wisdom from within.

Experiencing God's Love and Understanding

Godly wisdom requires a proper application of knowledge gained. However, before we can properly apply any knowledge we have obtained we need to have an understanding of it. The Bible says that God made known His ways to Moses, His acts to the children of Israel. (Psalms 103:7 NKJV)

This basically means that the children of Israel had knowledge of what God was doing but Moses understood His ways. Unfortunately, this still seems to be true today within the church; most have a knowledge of God and His ways while only a few actually acquire an understanding of them. And yet, this in-depth understanding of God's pure love is what the Apostle Paul asked for in his prayer for the Ephesians and, by extension, all believers everywhere.

Paul's prayer was, *may you have the power to understand, as all God's people should, how wide, how long, how high, and how deep His love really is. May you experience the love of Christ though it is so great you will never fully understand it. Then*

---

[122] Jay E. Adams (A Theology of Christian Counseling; Grand Rapids, Michigan; Zondervan; 1979); Pages 14-15.

you will be filled with the fullness of life and power that comes from God (Ephesians 3:18-19 NLT).

Prefacing these comments Paul expresses his deep-seated desire that Christ would be allowed to take up permanent residence in our life. He knew that when Christ is given priority in our lives changes will occur. He understood that God's love is complete; it reaches into every corner of our life and stretches into every experience and encounter we have. The width of His love reaches out to the whole world; its length continues to the very end of our life and beyond; its height far surpasses any level of rejoicing or jubilation we could ever experience; and its depth will traverse valleys of discouragement and despair wherein we may find ourselves. God's love is the total package.

When Christ is at home in our heart we learn to trust Him; faith beyond all natural comprehension develops, and we are transformed from the inside out. This becomes our basis for understanding the greatness of God's love. This transformation also empowers us to be able to articulate and demonstrate it to others. Additionally, the understanding of God's love will enable us to guide, encourage, strengthen, and even, when called upon, to bring about correction in others. This kind of love cannot be explained rationally, it must be experienced; but once experienced if we will continue in it, there will be a fulness of life and power that develops from our relationship with the Heavenly Father. Then, within the confines of this relationship, God pours His love and power into us, making us complete for this life while preparing us for eternity.

Paul's understanding of God's love was so intense that it compelled him to write, *I am convinced that nothing can ever separate us from God's love. Neither death nor life, neither angels nor demons, neither our fears for today nor our worries about tomorrow—not even the powers of hell can separate us from God's love. No power in the sky above or in the earth below—indeed, nothing in all creation will ever be able to separate us from the love of God that is revealed in Christ Jesus our Lord.* (Romans 8:38-39 NLT) What a powerful statement.

As ministers and Christian counselors, experientially having this kind of understanding of God's love is critical; because believers have always been confronted with hardships in one form or another: persecution, prosecution, and even death. If these were the only issues believers had to deal with it could be considered justification to raise questions.

Unfortunately, every believer everywhere will also have to struggle with questions of loss, grief, unanswered prayers, feigned faith, hope deferred, and any number of other issues or scenarios that can arise on a daily basis; all of which will, at times, cause us to question God's presence. It is good that the author of Hebrews makes it clear that it is impossible to be separated from Christ; for He will never leave us nor forsake us (Hebrews 13:5). Christ has conquered death, hell, and the grave (1 Corinthians 15:12-58) and nothing will ever be able to separate us from His love (Romans 8:38-39).

If we, as ministers and Christian counselors, believe in these overwhelmingly assurances at our core, then we will be able to confidently encourage others when they seek our help. We must be able, through personal experience and conviction, express to a counselee that God will never allow any hardship to come between them and Him. There are no powers in existence - demonic or human - that are more powerful than God; and those powers that do exist can have absolutely no effect on their relationship with Him, unless they allow it to happen. Nothing in all of creation can deter, deplete, or disconnect God's love; nothing in all of creation can foil or frustrate His purposes and plans for their life, except their free will.

God's love is beyond measure; it is inexhaustible; sacrificial; and eternal. No matter where one is, God is there; it does not make any difference what happens, His love is ever-present and undiminishing. In fact, hardship and suffering should be viewed as an opportunity for growth because the Bible declares that we *can do all things through Christ, because he gives* (us) *strength* (Philippians 4:13 NCV) and that *we are assured and know that [God being a partner in* (our) *labor] all things work together and are [fitting into a plan] for good to and for those who love God and are called according to [His] design and purpose.* (Romans 8:28 AMPC)

Adverse situations and circumstances should create an impetus that allows us to experience a deeper understanding of His loving grace. *If the God of the Scriptures exists. The Christian's approach to counseling will be totally different*[1] from all other methods. Perhaps the wisest thing for a minister or Christian counselor to recognize and instill into their counselee is that *God was in the events... We may never know in this life all the reasons behind those events, but knowing that there are reasons itself changes everything. Life is not absurd; it has meaning - God's meaning. Beyond that, knowing that for God's children every happening has a beneficent purpose (Romans 8:28, 29) is, perhaps, even more significant. There is nothing more important to tell a counselee, therefore, than that God is in the problem.*[123]

This does not mean that everything that happens to us is good - there is still evil present in our fallen world. But God is able to turn all things around for those who love Him and have received the redemption Christ made available to them. Such individual, even in the midst of horrible circumstances, can maintain the perspective that God's grace will be sufficient; suffering will still bring pain, loss, and grief with it but under God's control the eventual outcome will be for good.

God's love is so powerful and unwavering that He does not even expect us to simply "hold on" or to "hang in there" until the end; no, He gives us the grace to endure and overcome. This grace that equips us to overcome is the subject of our next segment concerning the various characteristics of God's pure love.

Love And Grace

Our modern-day dictionary still includes references to the grace of God within its standard definition: i.e. *divine love and protection bestowed freely upon mankind; the state of being protected or sanctified by the favor of God; an excellent or power being granted by God.*[124]

Years ago, when I was a new believer, I had read of God's grace and learned from other believer's that grace was simply God's "unmerited favor" upon those who, by faith, had accepted Christ's salvation. However, in short order, I came upon another word: mercy; and because of my newfound insatiable desire for learning everything I could about God and His Word, I wondered what the biblical definition of mercy was.

When I inquired of my friends (other believers) they informed me that the mercy of God was the "unmerited favor" of God upon those who believe. This duplication of definitions caused me to begin a more in-depth study wherein I learned that both mercy and grace are the unmerited favor

---

[123] Jay E. Adams (A Theology of Christian Counseling; Grand Rapids, Michigan; Zondervan; 1979); Page 44.
[124] Philip Babcock Gove (Editor in Chief); (Webster's Third New International Dictionary of the English Language: Unabridged; Springfield, Massachusetts; Merriam-Webster Inc., Publishers; 1993) Page 984.

of God. However, God's grace has an added element, which included an "empowerment" of God to overcome or to succeed in whatever He directs. Consequently, one can conclude that God's grace has two vital aspects: 1) His unmerited favor; and 2) His provisional ability to succeed.

Another definition that has often been presented declares: *the primary meaning of grace in connection with God is: free, eternal, and unmerited love and favor of God toward free moral agents who are the product of His own creation, whether human or spirit beings, and who are capable of God consciousness and moral responsibility. Grace is the spring, source, and the very fountain-head of all the manifold benefits and blessings of God to all of His creation.*[125]

The grace of God is not simply extended to every believer in Christ; it is given to all, in both the Old and New Testaments; to all spirit beings as well as to men. As a result of His love, grace moves God to act on behalf of all creation: both in judgment as well as in acts of mercy. This is where we, as a modern-day, post-modern society have acquired a skewed picture of what God's true love is. Am I actually declaring that God's judgment is a loving act of His grace? Definitely. By virtue of Christ's substitutionary work on the Cross, the required price for the sin of all humanity has been adjudicated; this simply means that because of His loving grace God judged Christ's actions as worthy to be a propitiation for sin. God judiciously determined that Christ's payment was sufficient and that anyone who accepted it by faith would be granted eternal life. This is where love and grace became an explosive combination: one that is still available to us today.

Christ was the first to receive the Spirit "without measure" (John 3:34). John said, "of His fulness have we all received, and grace for grace," proving that there are measures of grace (John 1:16-17). The Weymouth translation reads, "grace upon grace" and the Moffatt translation, "grace after grace" thus plainly showing that all of grace is not necessarily decided at once. This is due to the lack of knowledge and faith. According to our knowledge we have faith, and according to our faith we receive grace or God's favor in every stage of growth. There is no limitation to the grace of God or what we can receive from God through grace. The benefits of grace do not come to all alike or all at once, as is taught by many modern teacher. If all men received the same fullness of grace alike, then all would have the same benefits from God alike. The fact that some receive more benefits

[125] Finis Jennings Dake (God's Plan For Man; Lawrenceville, Georgia; Dake Publishing; 1977); Page 336.

than others proves that they come by faith and according to the faith of each person. **Faith governs the benefits of grace and faith in turn is based upon knowledge.**[126]

    Faith governs the benefits of grace and faith in turn is based upon knowledge; this is where we mix in our understanding of the fact that faith is increased by repetitiously hearing the Word of God (Romans 10:17). As we gain knowledge (remember our previous comment that we must undergo instruction and gain knowledge because it directly impacts our ability to correctly decipher Scripture) and a proper understanding of God's Word our faith is increased and strengthened, which will ultimately result in God's empowering us to accomplish even greater things for His kingdom. This means that a manifestation of grace within a person's life is actually, greatly determined by that person. Wait just a minute, I am not saying that man is more powerful than God in any way. What I am saying is that, as free moral agents, God has given us (each person) the ability to either accept or refuse any of God's many blessings.

    The end result is that God's grace is limited to what He can and will do for any specific person by that individual's will, faith, and yes, even their obedience to God's commands. Until a person freely chooses to accept and follow God's plan for their life He simply cannot override their desires. God will not break His own Word and force His desires upon any human being.

    Now, let's take this information and connect it to the counseling setting. God's love and grace, both His unmerited favor as well as His empowerment to succeed, is truly up to each person as to whether or not they are willing to accept it. *If it were left wholly up to God's will in the matter, then all...would conform to His will, and all would be blessed alike, and all would enjoy the grace and favor of God to the full. As it is now, no one can accuse God of not having love for all men if they want to become recipients of that love. The fact that all are not saved and even all the saved do not partake of God's love to the same extent proves that God's blessings according to His grace are not wholly dependent upon Him. Neither are they wholly dependent upon the free will of man. It takes both the will of God and the will of man in full cooperation to demonstrate the fullness of God's love and grace. One cannot*

---

[126] Finis Jennings Dake (God's Plan For Man; Lawrenceville, Georgia; Dake Publishing; 1977); Page 338, emphasis added.

work for the good of one master when he is serving the other.[127]

The church of Jesus Christ, which began with passionate perfection, full of power, faith and wholehearted love for others soon became careless, indifferent, faithless, selfish, and lukewarm. We have these realities revealed to us in the writings of Paul, Peter, John and others who encouraged and admonished them to contend for their faith. These admonishments have been echoed down through the centuries and, while many have accepted God's commands and challenges, many others will not. For those who refuse we must continue to pray for and encourage them: for those who opt to receive God's loving grace we need to support, encourage, and whenever possible lend a hand. The love of God would expect nothing less than for us to reach out and help someone else succeed.

However, before the grace of God can truly be effective in anyone's life their must be, as we have already alluded, a certain level of obedience to God's commands and instructions. Consequently, obedience to God is the next component of our discussion concerning the love of God in the counseling setting.

Obedience and Love

Anyone who has ever raised children knows that it is extremely difficult and rarely effective to simply demand their obedience in any area of life. For those of us who have adventured an attempt at it we know firsthand that it usually ends in pure rebellion. As ministers and Christian counselors we need to realize that counselees will be no different; and yet, oftentimes obedience to God's commands is the key needed to unlock the desired freedom that precipitated the need for counseling.

From the very beginning of this subsection we need to make sure that we are clear on two vital points.

First, no true believer in Christ has to suffer from bad habits, addictions, or sin of any kind. As has already been discussed, the grace of God is always extended and will empower anyone willing to receive it to overcome these things. When a counselee suffers in any of these areas there is a definite reason, and that reason is not God. The cause can, in nearly

---

[127] Finis Jennings Dake (God's Plan For Man; Lawrenceville, Georgia; Dake Publishing; 1977); Pages 341-342.

every case, be boiled down to either ignorance or disobedience. The former cause: ignorance, can be easily fixed through knowledge and training if the counselee honestly desires to see change. In the majority of cases, however, ignorance is not the issue; disobedience is.

Disobedience will be much harder to deal with and overcome because every man is right in his own eyes (Proverbs 12:15, 21:2 KJV) even if it is wrong according to God's Word. *In order to obey, one must be instructed in biblical truth,* (this) *holds for counseling as well as other ordinary life circumstances... The other, more subtle, yet crucial, point...is that in order to be fully instructed one must obey! Learning depends upon obedience. Some...naively accept that all is needed is to tell people the truth, that they will accept and follow it. Biblical counselors know otherwise... Counseling involves more - much more - than instruction... Counselees are sinners who do not always automatically do whatever God wants them to do upon learning the truth. Often they don't (for various reasons) or won't.*[128] When this happens they will experience needless suffering.

Disobedience is rebellion; rebellion is witchcraft (1 Samuel 15:23) and God cannot bless either one. Such individuals cannot be helped if they choose to continue in disobedience to the truth that actually has the ability make them free (John 8:31-34).

Secondly, any believer can be taught obedience to God by resisting every temptation associated with bad habits, addictions, or any other besetting sin. For example, the Bible clearly tells believers not to forsake the assembling of themselves together (Hebrews 10:25); yet every one of us knows someone (hopefully not ourselves) who, at one point would not miss church. Until one day they failed to appear for a service; then one time turned into random absences, but ways with an excuse; finally there were regular absences without any reason or explanation; and ultimately, as the writer of Hebrews continues, it becomes their custom to miss church. What happened? They failed to fight the temptation and eventually their conscience was seared where church attendance was concerned. As ministers and Christian counselors we could apply this same truth to resisting nearly any sinful thoughts, attitudes, or actions.

The truth of the matter is: there is enough suffering in this life and

---

[128] Jay E. Adams (A Theology of Christian Counseling; Grand Rapids, Michigan; Zondervan; 1979); Page 171.

we don't need to increase it through a lack of obedience to God. If we will honor Him, He will honor us; but it involves more than a simple nodding of the head in agreement; action on our part is required, even the Bible declares that faith without corresponding actions is dead (James 2:17, 20, 26) and Jesus Himself said, *Those who accept my commandments and obey them are the ones who love me. And because they love me, my Father will love them. And I will love them and reveal myself to each of them.* (John 14:21 NLT) All believers; ministers, counselors, and counselees included, show their love for God by obeying Him.

While there are as many areas where we might disobey God as there are stars in the sky, one area stands head and shoulders above all others as the most prominent: this area involves forgiveness, or the lack thereof, in all of its various shades. One might say "I've forgiven" and in the same breath include "but I don't want anything to do with him anymore". Does this statement line up with God's commands? Of course not.

Jesus summed up all the Old Testament laws, including the ten commandments, when He said, the most important commandment is that you love the LORD your God with all your heart, all your soul, all your mind, and all your strength. The second is equally important: Love your neighbor as yourself. No other commandment is greater than these. (Mark 12:29-31 NLT) When we are uncertain about something we need to ask ourselves what course of action would best fulfill these two commandments.

Unfortunately, when we are hurt or offended our emotions will often rule the day and we simply, whether in word or action, declare that forgiveness is not an option; yet, no man is free to ignore God's established standards. Even while hanging on the cross Jesus prayed, *Father forgive them, for they know not what they are doing* (Luke 23:34). If Jesus, with all He endured was not free to ignore God's commands, why do we assume that "God understands" when we have our feelings hurt?

From the beginning...people have acted upon their feelings and in accordance with their desires; that is one large reason why they end up in counseling sessions. Such persons inevitably get into trouble. They live according to impulse rather than according to the commandments of God... There are only two options (why) one may live a desire-oriented life or a commandment-oriented life. The first is motivated by feeling and the second by obedience to God...(most) live according to desire rather than according to the revealed will of God. Christian counselors (and ministers) ...while agreeing that it is difficult to do what God requires...must insist that if the counselee knows Jesus Christ, he can and must do God's will no matter how he feels.[129]

It is one thing to say that we love Jesus and others but the real test comes when we are required to obey His commands, when our personal desires run contrary to His will. Obedience to God's commands is not merely knowing and agreeing with His Word, it involves love in action. And the primary indication that an individual truly loves Jesus is when, contrary to emotions, hurts, offenses, or personal tastes, they choose to obey His commandment to love God and others. Fortunately, God does not expect us to stand on our own. If this were true the absolute best we could do would be to act worldly one day and godly the next. Upon accepting redemption the Holy Spirit takes up residence in our life and begins to effect a change in our moral values and personal character. These changes are enhanced and strengthened as our relationship with Him develops: as we come to know God better, obedience to His will simply becomes a natural outworking of our faith in and love for our Heavenly Father and Creator.

Since personal character and moral values (morality) directly impact our desire to obey God's commands, and obedience is intimately related to the love of God we are compelled to address these two areas that, sooner or later, will be tested in everyone's life.

Personal Character and Moral Values

God has made man perfect, in His own image. He had placed him in a perfect environment, supplying his every need, and had given him a beautiful helpmate in Eve. He was also given free will. But it was necessary that his free will be tested, in order for him to be confirmed in positive righteousness or character. Character is the sum total of human choices. It can be attained only through choices. Thus man was on probation, until it should be shown how he would use his power of freedom of choice. He could have chosen to resist temptation. Unfortunately, he chose the opposite.[130]

"If that's for me, tell them I'm not here." "I had to tell that little

---

[129] Jay E. Adams (The Christian Counselor's Manual; Grand Rapids, Michigan; Zondervan; 1973); Pages 296-297.
[130] Guy P. Duffield and Nathaniel M. Van Cleave (Foundations of Pentecostal Theology; Los Angeles, California; L.I.F.E. Bible College; 1987); Page 153.

white lie, or they would have made fun of me." "I just completed my taxes and I had to fudge the numbers just a little, but it's okay because everyone does." These and a multitude of similar comments reveal just exactly where we stand concerning personal character and moral values.

When a counselee doesn't know Christ or simply refuses to obey His direction, they will inevitably make decisions as though this life is all that truly matters; when, in reality, this life is nothing more than an introduction to eternity. As ministers and Christian counselors one of the most critical responsibilities we have is to get a counselee to comprehend that there is no worse tragedy than to see an individual embrace darkness and secrecy in hopes of covering over sinful actions or lifestyles. In order to accomplish this critical task there is absolutely no room for us to be trapped in what many unbiblical methods or techniques refer to as moral neutrality or character indifference. We must be willing to fight to good fight of faith and expose both character flaws and immorality.

Unfortunately, many of these morally neutral counseling models are being used by ministers and Christian counselors, mostly out of ignorance. Some have been given a thin veneer in an attempt to hide the truth while others blatantly espouse their heresy. In fact, some have so perverted moral values and personal character issues that entire systems have been developed to destroy any concept of what "should" or "should not" be; "ought" and "ought not" thinking. Not only have these methodologies and techniques been developed, they have been considered as serious options by some well-meaning believers.

However, *God has made human beings incurably ethical. Everybody knows that he lives in a moral world that cannot be divorced from shoulda and ought (cf. Romans 2:15)... Counselees cannot for long suppress the sense of right and wrong that God put within them. Man was created in God's image as a moral creature... The use of such systems not only lead to ineffective counseling; more to the point - it is sinful... To know about God's revelation in Scripture and to abandon it (or dilute it) in favor of the wisdom of men is serious rebellion.*[131]

Ministers and Christian counselors who subscribe to these systems will have a strong belief that they must always maintain a neutral, non-

---

[131] Jay E. Adams (A Theology of Christian Counseling; Grand Rapids, Michigan; Zondervan; 1979); Pages 45-46.

137

judgmental posture regardless of what the counselee reveals. Whether morally good or bad they will not express a personal opinion, feeling, or viewpoint concerning the topic being discussed; they staunchly stand on the widely misinterpreted "judge not" Scriptures.

However, it does not take much more than a casual reading of the Bible for one to understand that sin cannot be minimized or glossed over; it cannot be ignored indefinitely; even the new terminology being created today will not suffice (a duck by any other name is still, a duck). Anyone attempting to subvert scriptural mandates concerning moral values or personal character issues will, in all likelihood, have deep-seated attitudes that prejudice them in one way or another.

Jay E. Adams says that *an attitude is that combination of presuppositions, beliefs, convictions, and opinions* (and values) *that make up one's habitual stance* (character) *at any given time toward a subject, person, or act. It is a mind set that strongly influences behavior. In counseling, attitudes may be attacked and changed more directly than feelings, which, in most instances can be altered only indirectly through change of attitude* (values) *and action (behavior)* (and character). *This is important, since attitudes* (values) *often stand in the way of solving issues.*[132]

In essence, we can come to no other conclusion except, there is no place in counseling for a morally neutral stance. In fact, value free counseling is a myth. Everyone has personal beliefs about what is true and not true; what is good and bad; what is right and wrong. These beliefs or values and personal character traits, biblical or unbiblical, permeate every decision we make in life. Without a value system of any sort, which does not truly exist, all attempts to help others would be hopeless and without direction.

Throughout the Western world the concept of neutrality of system and method has been preached almost as a sacred doctrine. The modern man thinks that he can hold his Christianity in one hand and a pagan system in the other. He sees no need to compare and contrast what he holds in his hands... The "religious" has been conveniently separated from the "secular". A part - the really operative part - of life has been called "secular" (neutral). Churchly, otherworldly things have been called "religious". This bifurcation of the world - intended to "save" the religious realm from the destructive

---

[132] Jay E. Adams (The Christian Counselor's Manual; Grand Rapids, Michigan; Zondervan; 1973); Page 115.

elements of critical attack - instead has had the effect of relegating it to the ash heap of the virtually unimportant. That should be altogether apparent in the way in which system after system simply ignores the question of God, and in the ease with which even evangelical Christians adopt eclectic positions. It brought about a secular week/sacred Sunday mentality. The same mentality fostered the neutrality concept.[133]

When we read Philippians and First Thessalonians it is easy to see where the Apostle Paul had great joy and pleasure in the relative absence of immorality. Then, after a quick perusal of his letters to the Galatians and the Corinthians, we quickly realize that there were all sorts of immoral issues, which caused a great amount of displeasure and distress to the Apostle. He also dispensed discipline upon those individuals operating in immorality. By addressing each community of believers as Paul did, we cannot assume that God has changed His position concerning personal issues of character and morality: God does not change (Malachi 3:6).

As ministers and Christian counselors *we have a universal moral standard of truth that is embodied in the person of Christ and is revealed in the Scriptures. There are no rigid formulas, however, for applying God's truth, no one right-answer equations for counseling. Staying flexible, applying principles of Christian living, and living by God's grace are crucial to the effectiveness of the competent* (minister or) *Christian counselor.[134]*

Jesus told us, "You shall know them by their fruits" (Matthew 7:15-23). In any discussion of personal character and moral values there cannot be a more telling and truer statement. An individual's fruit clearly reveals where one honestly stands, especially where character and morality are concerned. By a person's fruit we will know who is for or against the truth as it is revealed in God's Word; we will be able to know who is a true believer and who is not. As ministers and Christian counselors it is extremely important for us to discern these things. Unfortunately, there have been far too many godly men and women who have been duped into believing someone has been redeemed because they have learned how to walk and talk and dress the part while, in actuality, being rotten to the core.

Fortunately, for us the Bible clearly teaches that a good tree cannot

---

[133] Jay E. Adams (A Theology of Christian Counseling; Grand Rapids, Michigan; Zondervan; 1979); Page 43.
[134] Dr. Timothy Clinton and Dr. George Ohlschlager (Competent Christian Counseling Volume One; Colorado Springs, Colorado; Waterbrook Press; 2002); Page 64.

bring forth corrupt fruit and a corrupt tree cannot produce good fruit (Luke 6:43-45). Every person, like every tree, brings forth of its own kind whether good or bad - it can do nothing else. This is why biblical discernment and, by extension, moral judgments must be made by ministers and Christian counselors; to do anything less fails to express the true uncompromised love of God. When we endeavor to actively participate in properly judging a counselees fruit we are laying the ground work that has every potential to lead that individual to repentance and restoration on both the vertical and horizontal planes.

Judging, Repentance, and Restoration

Quite some time ago I read where the Scripture, "Judge not lest ye be judged" (Matthew 7:1) had replaced "for God so loved the world that He gave His only begotten Son, that whosoever believes in Him should not perish, but have everlasting life" (John 3:16) as, not only the most recognized Scripture verse in society, but also the most commonly quoted. I cannot attest to the validity of their research and honestly do not remember where I read it, however, based on personal observation I must say that it is most likely accurate.

Previously, we discussed that, in our post-modern culture, there is the prevalent belief of: *Who are you to judge me?* Here, in this section, we will delve deeper into this errant belief as well as its ramifications in the counseling process.

It is absolutely true that Jesus said, *Judge not, that ye be not judged.* However, His comment to stop judging was directed at the hypocritical and judgmental attitude wherein one will tear down another in hopes of making themselves look better. Even though the mentality of not judging has so penetrated our society, the tearing down of another in hopes of receiving special treatment or favor from others still runs rampant from the halls of the schoolhouse all the way to the halls of the Whitehouse; every segment of society - the workplace, the home, and even the church - is forced to deal with it. Biblically speaking, judging, which is intended to denounce another in order to build up one's own ego is condemned. As ministers and Christian counselors we need to accept the reality that unbiblical and secular counseling models are ill-equipped to deal with these issues since their rationale of what is right verses what is wrong changes with whatever the majority agrees upon.

When Jesus said *judge not* He was not giving us the freedom to overlook bad or immoral attitudes, corrupt thinking, and reprehensible actions. He was simply informing us that: first, we must stop excusing our own sins while casting a shadow of condemnation on others who are doing the same thing. In other words, judging others before straightening out our own life is forbidden: secondly, that believers are to be critically evaluating others' actions. This simply means that not everything will always be as it appears to be and, because this is true, we should use great discernment.

Adding weight to this conclusion, Jesus, just a few verses later, said we are to expose false prophets (Matthew 7:15-23). If, as many claim, we are not supposed to judge others, why would Jesus tell us to judge and expose the fruits of false prophets? The Apostle Paul clearly teaches us that we are to exercise church discipline (1 Corinthians 5:1-2). However, before church discipline can be exercised there must be a judging of the fruit being produced. Both Jesus and Paul tells us to be actively involved in judging a person's fruit while, at the same time, trusting God to be the final Judge of each individual. Only God knows what is in the heart of each person so, when we judge the fruit being produced, we must do so in love and compassion; leaving all condemnation in the capable hands of a loving omniscient Creator.

As ministers and Christian counselors we should operate in the fulness of God's love; this not only means expressing His love unconditionally, it also requires us to turn our attentions toward assisting the counselee in purifying their heart and the clearing of their conscience: both of which requires us to judge their fruit. Then, after discerning and assessing judgement we assist and encourage them to reverse the sinful patterns in their life: it matters not whether these patterns are revealed in attitudes, thoughts, or actions.

The Word of God wounds, but it also binds up; it cuts out the soul's cancer, and then it heals the soul (see Isaiah 30:26). Conviction is the unpleasant task whereby the (minister or Christian) *counselor brings a biblical case against the counselee for his sin... When you consider that the Bible is concerned not only with exposing wrongs, but also with righting them, you begin to get some idea about the vast ministering enterprise toward which God's Word is oriented. The Bible boldly claims to supply what is necessary to help one change any attitudes or behaviors out of accord with God's will. The Bible not only shows us God's will and convicts us of failure to follow it, but helps us to get out of the messes into which we fall when we don't obey.*[135] While all of this is unequivocally accurate we must be willing to rightly judge, first our own fruit; and then, the fruit of those we are attempting to help.

We must get to the place in our lives - not just as ministers and Christian counselors, but all believers - where we leave behind any false concepts of God, who He is, and what His Word declares. We should be progressing to the point where we believe the truth as it is revealed in the Bible at all times, concerning any given subject. Jesus declared that *you shall know the truth, and the truth will make you free* (John 8:31-36). God's truth is what makes us free and we can always tell how much of it we truly believe by the fruit we are producing. If we find the wrong kind of fruit in our life we need to correct the cause of the bad fruit: there is no other way.

Recognizing bad fruit requires us to make biblical judgments of our own (or another's) life. However, simply recognizing that there are "issues" is not enough to bring about the desired changes. There was once a very wise man who declared that doing the same thing over and over while expecting different results is the definition of insanity. And yet, that is exactly what we do. The next step involves correction and personal correction invariably requires the element of repentance.

Like judgement, *repentance is a word rarely heard in counseling, even in supposed Christian counseling circles. Yet the vital role of repentance as a biblical prerequisite to correcting a counselee's sin cannot be denied (cf. Revelation 2:5). The counselee who has sinned needs plainly to repent. The English word repent...means "to rethink". Repentance is a rethinking of one's behavior, attitudes, and beliefs. It is coming to a different opinion or viewpoint, one so different that it calls for different thought patterns and a different lifestyle. There is nothing in the [Greek] word metanoia about sorrow; indeed it does not speak of emotions at all. That is not to say that true repentance will not lead to sorrow, but the word itself carries no such connotations.*[136]

Another basic, and possibly more common, definition of repentance is to change one's mind about something, which is then followed by changing one's direction. Changing our mind about anything is the easy part; the real rub comes when we attempt to "change direction",

---

[135] Jay E. Adams (How To Help People Change; Grand Rapids, Michigan; Zondervan; 1986); Pages 139-140.
[136] Jay E. Adams (How To Help People Change; Grand Rapids, Michigan; Zondervan; 1986); Page 142.

i.e. to stop bad attitudes; to control negative thoughts; and breaking bad habits. However, through the act of repenting we have made a decision to stop something or to start something based on choice. Regrettably, there will be times when we fail to live up to our decision. When this happens, and it will, we need to be quick to judge the fruit of our poor decision; then, without casting dispersions on anyone else, accept personal responsibility for our actions and repent.

God never gives up on us. We should always work toward and strive for victory, but even if we happen to give up on ourselves; even if all others have given up on us, God never will. This reality should be cause for great encouragement, for it is our loving Creator who ultimately empowers us to gain the victory; He is also the only One from Whom we truly need to hear *well done* (Luke 19:17).

As ministers and Christian counselors it is pivotal for us to learn that true repentance is more than regret. Throughout history many great men and women have experienced regret for their actions. Normally, however, the regret they have experienced and expressed was nothing more than a simple, "I'm sorry that I got caught". This reality becomes evident when there is not a change in lifestyle or fruit produced; something that always accompanies true biblical repentance. This is one of the many reasons it is vital for us to realize there is always a possibility of the counselee pretending; they may even temporarily suspend the sinful actions while making insincere declarations of faith or change simply to gain our favor (this is especially common when dealing with disputes). *But that seldom lasts long. Since God alone knows the hearts of men...* (we) *must look on the "outward appearance" alone.* (As ministers and Christian counselors we) *have been called to make a functional, righteous judgement, based on fruit that should accompany repentance.*[137]

The Word of God consistently bans gossip, criticizing others, and making rash judgements while at the same time requiring us to circumspectly deal with any sin that can cause damage to self or others, both inside and out of the Church. Even when righteous judgements have been made we must be absolutely sure and make it extremely clear that our judgements are in no way an act of revenge, if our own decisions and

---

[137] Jay E. Adams (How To Help People Change; Grand Rapids, Michigan; Zondervan; 1986); Page 143.

actions cannot endure this scrutiny we should excuse ourselves and defer to another minister or Christian counselor.

Once proper biblical judgements have been made and true repentance has produced good fruit concerning the situation(s) under advisement the final responsibility of every minister and Christian counselor is restoration. This is not restoration on the vertical plane (man-to-God), this is restoration, if necessary, on the horizontal plane (man-to-man). If a situation has became a matter of public knowledge, which is often the case, there must be a setting right of the wrongs.

In the church there are all sorts of people who maintain a de facto second class status because they have never been formerly reconciled or restored to the rest of the body. Having fallen into sin, they either cut themselves off or were cut off from full fellowship, but without formal disciplinary action. (Sometimes people are cut off even though they are not guilty, e.g. the innocent party of a divorce, in whose congregation any or all divorce is seen as illegitimate.) then later, after repentance or perhaps confession and forgiveness, they are more or less restored, though again informally and without public recognition in the church. Others, not privy to the facts of their quasi-renewed status, either are ambivalent about how to relate to them or continue to treat them as deserving of discipline. **Because of the muddled handling of the case restoration is never clearly made, and the people in question find themselves relegated to the back of the Sunday school bus.**[138] Ministers especially must remain cognizant of these situations and deal directly with them. We are not only under a mandate from God to express His love in the corrective process; we are also under command to care for, tend, encourage, and protect any of His sheep that are under our oversight. A failure to properly handle our tasks is a failure to completely fulfill our calling. From judging, to repentance, to restoration we must do things God's way and if we will love Him with all our heart, with all our soul, with all our mind, and with all our strength as well as love our neighbor as we love ourself we will be able to, with the aid of the Holy Spirit, successfully accomplish all He has for us to do.

As we previously discussed, people often associate love with emotions: if they feel the right way they can express the love of God. But godly love does not work that way. The love of God does not ride the roller coaster of emotions: His love is Rock solid. It is important for us to

---

[138] Jay E. Adams (How To Help People Change; Grand Rapids, Michigan; Zondervan; 1986); Page 161, emphasis added.

understand a few things about the emotional, roller coaster kind of love:

- It is not usually discovered until adversity strikes.

- It is intimately connected to natural abilities.

- It is expressed when we choose and withheld when we choose.

Understanding these three elements of the emotional roller coaster kind of love is important for us to know and be on guard against because looking after hurting people is stressful work; and yet, we are called to be involved. As ministers and Christian counselors we must refuse to allow the world to corrupt us. In order to achieve this we need to be committed to God's moral values and character expectations, not the world's system. We cannot allow our values or character to fail because true love - God's love means nothing if we permit it to become contaminated. As we make ourselves available to serve Christ in the counseling setting we are obliged to keep ourselves under His divine protection and filled to overflowing with His unconditional love.

Chapter 7 : The Doctrine of Hamartiology (Sin)

From the very beginning we need to lay a solid foundation to build upon. For this let's look specifically at the word *hamartiology*. *Hamartia*, the Greek word for sin means; *literally, missing the mark, failure, offense, taking the wrong course, wrongdoing, sin, guilt.*[139] The word *ology* means knowledge or the "study of" whatever it is connected with: *Hamartiology* then, is simply the study of missing the mark or the doctrine of sin, which is exactly what we are undertaking in this chapter.

Within the confines of any biblical counseling model there must be ample discussion concerning mankind's origins, pre-fallen state, and the commensurate consequences associated with that fall. In this chapter we will consider these topics and their connection to Christain counseling. Unfortunately, there have been far too many so-called "Christian" counseling methods inducted into the modern church wherein proper exegesis of Scripture has been violated; this has resulted in a non-theological understanding of both the Creator and His creation. As a result of this improper use of eclecticism we need to clearly establish: first, the physical origins of humanity (commonly referred to as: anthropology) and secondly, that all of humanity, because of their fallen nature, is in need of being restored to the Creator.

First, because of the multiple theories and assumptions concerning the origins of humankind we are compelled to declare from the start that we *adopt as an unshakable biblical presupposition, stemming from both exegetical and theological considerations, that human life did not evolve from lower forms, but it was created...by God.* (We) *believe in the existence of a literal Adam, from whom... Eve also was formed by a direct act of God.*[140]

In considering the nature of all ministry and Christian counseling it is both moot and, at the same time, remarkable that any individual could consciously begin with any other supposition. Yet there are a plethora of

---

[139] Jack W. Hayford (General Editor); (Spirit Filled Life Bible: New King James Version; Nashville, Tennessee; Thomas Nelson Publishers; 1991); Word Wealth, page 1575.
[140] Jay E. Adams (A Theology of Christian Counseling; Grand Rapids, Michigan; Zondervan; 1979); Page 98.

manuals, methods, and models available which do not ascribe to the biblical truths commonly referred to as Creationism.

The second issue that must be stated at this juncture is: this entire chapter presumes that salvation through Jesus Christ has already occurred (whether by you, the minister or Christian counselor or by the counselee's personal confession) and that, by the indwelling presence of the Holy Spirit, the following discussion will enhance your ability to assist in their transformation. If salvation has not yet been experienced, there are specific issues which will not be clearly understood until a study of soteriology (chapter 8) is completed.

It should also be said that any study of this doctrine may be viewed as rather sad because, as we will conclude, man was created in perfection and the fall never had to happen. Mankind was created by a beneficent God; a loving Creator who simply desired and expected all of humanity to depend on His direction, counsel, guidance, and provision. This "Garden of Eden" experience occurred for an unknown length of time and all was well. Unfortunately, sin was allowed to enter into the picture and all of humanity, for a season lost the loving Creator's counsel.

During the Garden of Eden experience and prior to the fall, Adam and Eve had never refused to listen to and obey God's counsel so there was no need for any corrective component to His counseling. After the fall however, the basics of counseling had to change. Fundamentally and out of necessity there had to be added the new dimensions of correction, rebuke, and discipline; none of which are easy or desired, but are, at times, necessary. There is also a very common misnomer that declares all counseling (especially Christian counseling) to consistently be nothing more than sharp criticisms and censorship. These beliefs have so permeated our society that many modern models (including some Christian models) have tilted to the other extreme wherein no criticism or rebuke is allowed.

Regrettably, the all-or-nothing stance are both, while being polar opposites, just as wrong. There is a legitimate place in counseling for rebuke, correction, and criticism; there is also a proper time for encouragement, understanding, and simply allowing for love to cover a multitude of sins.

With all of these considerations in mind let's delve into the crux of our current discussion by laying some further groundwork; by defining some crucial things pertaining to this doctrine; specifically we will consider the phrase "free moral agency" and the oft misunderstood word "sin."

Defining Free Moral Agency

Free moral agency *consists of intellectual, sensibility, and free will, and these form the foundation of moral obligation to moral government. The intellect includes reason and self-determination. The sensibility includes self-consciousness, all sensation, desire, emotion, passion, and all feeling. Free will is the power of choice concerning moral law. It is man's faculty of choosing good or evil without compulsion or necessity. It was originally created in man, and he will have it in all eternity.*[141] As our study unfolds many of the various aspects of free moral agency mentioned here will be unveiled. The next word we will attempt to clearly define, however, will not be so easy to pin down.

Defining Sin

Before proceeding any further we need to realize that there are two common categories of sin we will discuss. This can be slightly confusing, if not clarified. The first deals with sins of choice and the second examines inherited sin. In this section our focus will primarily be to address the first category even though, at times, the categories tend to overlap. As previously referenced, many have misunderstood sin to be nothing more that simply "missing the mark." While this is one of the biblical definitions of sin, and probably the most accurate lowest common denominator way of defining it. For the minister and Christian counselor to truly be effective we need to understand that, biblically speaking, sin is so much more.

In reality, defining sin is such a massive undertaking that the multitude of volumes written throughout history have amounted to nothing more than a drop of water in the ocean. However, we all must begin somewhere so let's start with a few common conclusions about sin.

Sin is and always will be an ugly topic; it will be a subject that makes us uncomfortable to one degree or another because sin implies that there has been a violation of God's established standards of moral and ethical behavior. For the minister and Christian counselor to effectively address sin there has to have already occurred some level of judgement on

---

[141] Finis Jennings Dake (God's Plan For Man; Lawrenceville, Georgia; Dake Publishing; 1977); Page 407.

their behalf. This form of judging is something that has nearly been abolished in our post-modern culture. True biblical judging - even judging between good and evil - is no longer acceptable in our society and yet, before any positive changes can be made in the counselee's life there must be an honest evaluation or legitimate judgements made concerning their beliefs and behavior.

God sent His only begotten Son in order for us to live an abundant life (cf. John 3:16; John 10:10) so His concerns about sin are not because He wants to limit our freedom as some tend to think. God understands better than we do about the destructive forces that sin brings into our life and He simply desires to, like any loving father would, warn us of the possible ramifications of our choices.

Sin committed is as much sin one time as it is another. It is as much sin to the saved as to the unsaved. It is the sin itself that is sin, and the time it is committed does not make it unrighteousness at one time and righteous at another, or sin to one and not sin to another. Any transgression of the law is sin, whether before or after one is saved, and the penalty for the broken law must be enforced without exception, as well after salvation as before.[142] Because this is true all sin causes us to fall short of God's holy standards (Romans 3:23); sin in our lives is a violation of God's moral and ethical law (Romans 2:14-15); sin is a power that seeks to influence, enslave, and destroy anyone who will give in to it's control (Romans 6:12-13); in short, sin is obedience to Satan (Ephesians 2:1-4).

We may, as some have, define sin as *any failure to conform to the moral law of God in act, attitude, or nature.*[143] Or we may conclude that sin is *any want of conformity unto, or transgression of, the character or law of God given as a rule to the reasonable creature.*[144] Both definitions are correct as far as they go; unfortunately, *any failure* or *any want of conformity* while being true, may not be sufficient for the minister or Christian counselor to be able to effectively address specific issues in a way that brings enough clarity to cause the counselee to desire a change in their life.

None of us would want to hear our medical doctor say, "You're

---

[142] Finis Jennings Dake (God's Plan For Man; Lawrenceville, Georgia; Dake Publishing; 1977); Page 425.

[143] Wayne Grudem (Bible Doctrine: Essential Teachings of the Christain Faith; Grand Rapids, Michigan; 1999); Page 210.

[144] Guy P. Duffield and Nathaniel M. Van Cleave (Foundations of Pentecostal Theology; Los Angeles, California; L.I.F.E. Bible College; 1987); Page 157.

sick and I'm going to have to operate. I'm just not sure where the problem is so I will keep cutting until I hit the right spot." And none of us should expect a counselee to be satisfied with our lack of understanding of where to surgically remove the sin, which is causing such devastation in their life. For this reason we will investigate the various Old and New Testament words given that are commonly lumped into our single word "sin."

In *God's Plan for Man*, author Finis Dake gives us fifteen definitions of outward sin along with their appropriate Scriptural reference. They are:

1.   *Sin is transgression of the law (1 John 3:4).*

2.   *Where there is no law, there is no transgression (Romans 4:15).*

3.   *By the law is the knowledge of sin (Romans 3:20; 7:7).*

4.   *Sin is not imputed when there is no law (Romans 5:13).*

5.   *Without the law sin was dead or dormant (Romans 7:8).*

6.   *The thought of foolishness is sin (Proverbs 24:9; 2 Corinthians 10:4-5).*

7.   *Every idle word that men speak is sin (Matthew 12:36-37).*

8.   *All unrighteousness is sin (1 John 5:17).*

9.   *Whatsoever is not of faith is sin (Romans 14:23).*

10.   *If ye have respect of persons ye commit sin (James 2:9).*

11.   *He that knoweth to do good, and doeth it not, to him it is sin (James 4:17).*

12.   *All "actions" contrary to the law are sin (1 Samuel 2:3; James 1:13-15).*

13.   *Rebellion is as the sin of witchcraft (1 Samuel 15:23).*

14.   *Any "omission" of the law is sin (Matthew 23:23).*

15.   *All "desires" and "lusts" contrary to the law, inwardly and outwardly manifested, are sin (Mark 7:19-21; Romans 1:29-32; Galatians 5:16-21; Ephesians 2:3; Colossians 3:5-10; James 1:13-15).*[145]

---

[145] Finis Jennings Dake (God's Plan For Man; Lawrenceville, Georgia; Dake Publishing; 1977); Page 408.

These fifteen definitions serve to supplement our previous definitions of sin, however, it would greatly benefit us and our counselees if our understanding was more extensive. For this we will consider a rather lengthy, but genuinely relevant discourse by Jay E. Adams. Many of these definitions will nudge up against our aforementioned area where the two larger categories of sin (outward and inherited) overlap. Adams writes:

> *Sin does have many dimensions; it is many-faceted. We know this because the Scriptures treat sin from a multidimensional standpoint... God has gone out of His way to give us a very clear picture of sin and its effects... Let us consider... 17 words; each says something about the act or the effect of sin that a [minister or] Christian counselor ought to understand.*

> 1.   *Old Testament Words*

> A.   *Avah (lit., "bent"...) This word is similar to our English word* **wrong** *(i.e. wrung out of shape). Picture a bent key that will no longer fit into the lock.... So man, designed to image and honor God, has (by sin) been twisted and warped so that he cannot please Him... Counseling involves straightening bent lives to enable believers to function once again as God intended...*

> B.   *Ra (Lit., "breaking up, ruin") Here is a picture of destruction... Both the act and the tragedy it effects are contemplated in the word. Sin deteriorates... Counseling seeks to reverse these destructive patterns of life. Constructive solutions to problems are encouraged...*

> C.   *Pasha (Lit., "rebellion against a rightful authority;" "revolt") Sin is treason; it is rebellion against God, His law and His government... Here...the core element...is "not thy will be done but mine" ...This wish for autonomy, so prevalent today, must be identified and countered by counselors, or they shall fail. At the bottom, this emphasis is rebellion against God.*

> D.   *Rasha (Lit., "hubbub, confusion, tossing") The picture in this word sees someone running here and there, agitating others, stirring them up, causing confusion... People, agitated, running to and fro, not knowing which way to turn... Biblical counsel guides and directs... Having no standard, man cannot find his way; counseling (when biblical) points to that way.*

E.   *Maal (Lit., "a breach of trust, unfaithfulness, treachery")... The word points to the serious nature of breaking faith, violating a covenantal agreement, with God and neighbor. Sin is spiritual adultery; it is covenant-breaking. When counselors fail to recognize and stress this aspect of sin, they neglect the need for confession and repentance...*

F.   *Aven (Lit., "nothing, vanity, unprofitable behavior") The notion here is effort with no result; the word refers to worthless, pointless, unprofitable, unproductive living. The ultimate result of all sinful living is aven... Counselors are concerned with helping people abandon "their meaningless ways of thinking* (and)... *encourage renewed thinking...that leads to purposeful living.*

G.   *Asham (Lit., "guilt" through negligence or ignorance)... Sometimes the word is connected with the idea of restitution. No sin can be overlooked...even sins of ignorance. Not only is restitution often necessary for counselees, the recognition of guilt for both known sins of ignorance is important.*

H.   *Chatha (Lit., "to wander from, fall short of, miss the mark") Probably, like its N.T. counterpart, hamartia, chatha came to mean sin (in general)... In both the N.T. and O.T. terms, the notion of not measuring up to God's standards of knowledge and holiness; otherwise they would need no counsel...*

I.   *Amal (Lit., "labor, sorrow")... This word stresses the fact that sin has made life a burden. Pain, heartache, the whole "problem of evil" is bound up in this idea. Trouble, travail, weariness are elements of Amal. That is why counselors echo Christ's words, "take My yoke...My burden is light." Sin brings misery and trouble; righteousness simplifies and lightens living.*

J.   *Aval (Lit., "unjust, unfair") This word for iniquity...depicts a departure from what is equal and right... The self-centeredness of sin emerges here. It is the counselors task to help the counselee focus upon God and his neighbor. Where his concern is others, such problems will disappear.*

2.   *New Testament Words*

A.   Hamartia (Lit., "missing the mark") corresponds closely with its Hebrew equivalent chatha... This is the common (general) word used for sin in the N.T. ...It is...a standard...against which human conduct must be measured...

B.   Parabasis (Lit., "crossing the boundary line") The word pictures someone disregarding a "No Trespassing" sign, violating a property line. The word means "trespassing"... Man's sinful nature makes him want to touch to see if the paint really is wet, again, disregarding the sign. This perverted desire to do what is forbidden will be encountered regularly in counseling.

C.   Anomia (Lit., "lawlessness") The lawless are those who live as though God had issued no laws. Every counselee is an outlaw... The clash in counseling occurs when God's requirements do not please the counselee who wants to go on living as a criminal in God's sight. Counselors are lawmen!

D.   Parakoe (Lit., "disobedience to a call")... Counselors echo God's calls for counselees; they remind God's children of their duty to heed God... Counselors help their counselees to want to respond, and show them how to respond to God.

E.   Paraptoma (Lit., "falling" when one should stand upright) Our expression, "falling down on the job" catches most of the nuances in the word. It is failing God by our lack of dependability... Counseling endeavors to develop these qualities in counselees.

F.   Agnoema (Lit., "ignorance" of what one ought to know) "Ignorance of the law is no excuse," puts it exactly. There will be people in hell because of ignorance... Biblical ignorance accounts for many counseling problems.

G.   Hettema (Lit., "defect or shortcoming") When we try to give God a part of our lives, attempt to departmentalize our faith or separate it from other activities, we fail this way. God must be at the center of all we do... Counselors must stress the need for committing all the soul, mind, strength and heart to God in all things... One defect may ruin all.

From this study it seems evident that sin takes many forms. Many of these terms speak of aspects of the act (or state) of sin, others speak of the effects of sin. Some seem to move back and forth over both territories. Either way, it is obvious that sin has many dimensions, all of which bear upon counseling.[146]

As previously stated this was a rather lengthy discourse; however, now that we have addressed these seventeen different Old and New Testament words it should be abundantly clear why our English word (sin) is insufficient to legitimately deal with and handle all issues in the counseling setting.

Mankind's Pre-Fallen State

Throughout the centuries many have attempted to deduce the amount of time that Adam and Eve lived in the Garden of Eden prior to their encounter with the serpent and their subsequent fall. While that may be intriguing we should guard against the improper use of our time. When we realize that the vast majority of these studies are tantamount to speculation; we will see that they serve to be more of a distraction than they are profitable. Additionally, in most instances any speculative musings such as these will only be confirmed when we get to heaven, which, in all likelihood, will not be a priority at that time.

Since our focus is on increasing our ability to be effective ministers and Christian counselors we would be *falling down on the job (Paraptoma)* if we failed to achieve our stated purpose. Therefore, since we have already established and defined some of the foundational terminology pertinent to hamartiology, let's proceed with an exploration of mankind's pre-fallen state or condition. *When we know what human nature was before sin, we shall know something (not all) about God's norm for human life. Man's concepts and his activities grow out of his nature; God fitted him in this world with a disposition* and nature designed to think and act so as to perform certain tasks, and to maintain certain relationships.[147]

Then the Lord God formed the man from the dust of the ground. He breathed the breath of life into the man's nostrils, and the man became a living person. ⁸Then the Lord God planted a garden in Eden in the east, and there he placed the man he had made... ¹⁶But the Lord God warned him, "You may freely eat the fruit of every tree in the garden— ¹⁷except the tree of the knowledge of good and evil. If you eat its fruit, you

---

[146] Jay E. Adams (A Theology of Christian Counseling; Grand Rapids, Michigan; Zondervan; 1979); Pages 147-152.
[147] Jay E. Adams (A Theology of Christian Counseling; Grand Rapids, Michigan; Zondervan; 1979); Page 100.

are sure to die." [18]*Then the Lord God said, "It is not good for the man to be alone. I will make a helper who is just right for him"...* [21]*So the Lord God caused the man to fall into a deep sleep. While the man slept, the Lord God took out one of the man's ribs and closed up the opening.* [22]*Then the Lord God made a woman from the rib, and he brought her to the man.* [23]*"At last!" the man exclaimed. "This one is bone from my bone, and flesh from my flesh! She will be called 'woman,' because she was taken from 'man.'"* [24]*This explains why a man leaves his father and mother and is joined to his wife, and the two are united into one.* [25]*Now the man and his wife were both naked, but they felt no shame.* (Genesis 2:7-8; 16-18; 21-25)

Dealing with the pre-fallen condition of mankind is one specific area where all secular psycho-therapeutic and counseling models fail; as do many of our so-called Christian (or biblically) based models. If we fail to establish an unmovable cornerstone or "plumbline" how can we ever be sure of what is accurate and correct? The two primary assumptions that are commonly encountered are the theory of evolution and, whether actually stated or not, the belief that man (or woman) are broken and have always been so: both of these theories are wrong and in many cases must be dealt with prior to affecting any lasting change.

If, for example, a man comes for advise about how he can get his wife to understand that, because all men do it, ogling a beautiful woman is okay as long as he doesn't touch them: how are we to deal with this? Every minister and Christian counselor should be able to handle this issue scripturally. However, there is something deeper that needs to be addressed: the man's obvious ill conceived belief that, since all men are doing it, it must be okay. In essence he is implying that, "men will always look, always have, and they always will." This confirms that he believes (maybe without even realizing it himself) human nature has always been the way it is now: yet, biblically, this is simply not true.

When this, or any one of a multitude of other similar events, happen we must be prepared to deal with the taproot: that is, the root cause which feeds the sinful thought patterns in the counselee's life. One of the most effective ways of accomplishing this is by establishing what is normal and what is not normal.

One of the many ways we might deal with the issue of sin is to refer to Genesis chapter one, verse twenty-seven where we read that *God created man in His own image, in the image of God created He him; male and female created He them.* When the Creator of the heavens and earth chose and then proceeded to make *man in His image,* He created man as something distinct and unmistakably different from all other forms of life. All of mankind was created first in Adam, then God said, *it is not good for man to be alone,* so He took one of Adam's ribs and created Eve. Because Eve was created from Adam's rib and Adam was created in God's image both were perfect in all aspects (that is without sin in thought or deed) and both possessed free moral agency (a self-determination, which far exceeded any other earthly creature); and both were endowed not only with a pre-eminent place in all of creation, but also with the capacity to be held accountable and responsible for their actions.

In referring back to the aforementioned "ogling" analogy how many, honestly believe that God lustfully leers at women? Of course not! Since Adam, in his pre-fallen state represented exactly the image of God, how can we say that it is normal? Let's consider one more example: Jesus, who walked on this earth in a physical body and experienced every temptation known to mankind; yet we have no historical account, either biblical or secular, that speaks of Him ogling or lusting after the beautiful women He saw. By coming to earth in the form of man, Jesus gave us a perfect example of what the Father expected: in a sense He established normal. Unfortunately, far too many have stopped looking at God's Word and Jesus' life for the plumbline of what should and should not be. Our society has not only become satisfied with establishing "normal" via the most vocal, but also expects everyone else to come into alignment with their distorted views, which can only be biblically described as abnormal and sinful.

The consistent Christian refuses to accept sociology as a norm-setting discipline... The fact that all are sinners (Romans 3:23) does not make sin normal. The norm is righteousness - the sort of life that Christ lived. That all people err does not mean that error is normal...it means only that error is universal... The Scriptures teach that "true righteousness and holiness" is the norm for human living. God sets norms in the Bible; men...have no such right. Alongside true righteousness and holiness God sets "knowledge"...as the last of three qualities that are normal for man, and declares that though they were lost in the fall, He is restoring them to the redeemed.[148]

---

[148] Jay E. Adams (A Theology of Christian Counseling; Grand Rapids, Michigan; Zondervan; 1979); Page 101.

Mankind has declared that "knowledge is power" and yet with all the knowledge around the world mankind continues to lose more and more power over his thoughts and actions. This is because, without God's complete plan, which includes true righteousness, holiness, and knowledge, man is still fighting a losing battle with the god of this world - the very same serpent that was present in the Garden of Eden instigating man's fall.

God gave us the Ten Commandments in order to lay the initial plumbline for normal; in Christ we saw the fulfillment of these commandments being displayed and even summed up into two commandments, which are to *love the LORD your God with all your heart, with all your soul, and with all your mind.' This is the first and great commandment. And the second is like it: 'You shall love your neighbor as yourself.' On these two commandments hang all the Law and the Prophets.* (Matthew 22:37-40)

Christ exhibited a normal life for us to follow. If we sincerely want to know what that life is, then we must look at and listen to the Word, Jesus. While His relationships were antithetical to what the world calls normal, they are nonetheless what God expects of all - both saved and unsaved.

Origins of Sin

We have confidently concluded now that sin in mankind is not normal, so let's move on and deal with the source of, or the origins of sin. The issue of sin has been responsible for such massive amounts of devastation and destruction in this world that, as ministers and Christian counselors, there are some very serious aspects of its origins we must comprehend if we are to have any hope of ever being successful in helping others overcome it in their lives.

Since sin was not an originally inherited quality of the human nature we are obliged to conclude that it was introduced by an outside source. We know also that God is not the author of confusion (1 Corinthians 14:33); He is not the perpetrator of sin and death, so it would be improper for us, in any way, to attribute it to some, yet undiscovered, plan that God has for the future.

God warned sinless man against sin and now condemns sin in every form in the human race. He would be unjust in doing this if He were responsible for sin. Sin entered men from an outside source... When the Bible says of God, "I create evil," it has reference to the reaping of sin which has been sowed. The Hebrew word "Ra" means wretchedness, misery and sorrow which God made **as a result of sin***. It would not be a creation of God.* **God created Satan and all creatures perfect and sinless***... Sin came in by sinless creatures rebelling against God.*[149]

God created Satan and all creatures perfect and sinless means that nothing created was created with sin being a part of its original nature; and yet, sin still exists. Sin is a reality, it can neither be denied, nor ignored. The Bible addresses sin and God Himself has even given us both the instructions and the means of overcoming sin in our lives. Sin is real, but where does it originate? The Word tells us that Lucifer (aka Satan) was created as a glorious, sinless creature who was extremely beautiful. His primary task was to lead one-third of the angels in praising and worshipping God, until one day sin was found in him (Ezekiel 28:12-17) and he declared, in essence, that he would exalt himself to the level of the Creator. (Isaiah 14:12-14)

Because of pride in his heart Lucifer, along with one-third of the angels (those who followed his leading) were cast out of heaven and down to the earth (cf. Luke 10:18) where they roamed around for an indeterminate period. A place where he began to scheme and dream of ways that he might get even with God for what "He did."

However, *God Himself did not sin, and God is not to be blamed for sin. It was man who sinned, and it was angels who sinned, and in both cases they did so by willful, voluntary choice. To blame God for sin would be blasphemy against the character of God.*[150]

Just as Satan attempts to blame someone else for what happened to him, we too must realize that "passing the buck" and "playing the blame game" (i.e. refusing to accept personal responsibility for one's own actions) is still a very common and prevalent character flaw in mankind. As ministers and Christian counselors it is imperative that we recognize this when it occurs in the counseling setting, immediately address it, and not allow the counselee to use it as a crutch or an excuse: since God did not allow Satan or Adam and Eve to shift the blame onto someone else, neither should we allow it by those who come seeking our assistance.

---

[149] Finis Jennings Dake (God's Plan For Man; Lawrenceville, Georgia; Dake Publishing; 1977): Page 414, emphasis added.
[150] Wayne Grudem (Bible Doctrine: Essential Teachings of the Christian Faith; Grand Rapids, Michigan; 1999); Page 211.

Now that we have discovered that sin originated in the heavens with Satan - not God - we need to spend some time reviewing exactly how it was introduced to mankind; for this, let's refer to the only accurate and authentic account we have of this fateful encounter - Genesis chapter 3.

Now the serpent was more cunning than any beast of the field which the Lord God had made. And he said to the woman, "Has God indeed said, 'You shall not eat of every tree of the garden'?" And the woman said to the serpent, "We may eat the fruit of the trees of the garden; but of the fruit of the tree which is in the midst of the garden, God has said, 'You shall not eat it, nor shall you touch it, lest you die.' Then the serpent said to the woman, "You will not surely die. For God knows that in the day you eat of it your eyes will be opened, and you will be like God, knowing good and evil." So when the woman saw that the tree was good for food, that it was pleasant to the eyes, and a tree desirable to make one wise, she took of its fruit and ate. She also gave to her husband with her, and he ate. Then the eyes of both of them were opened, and they knew that they were naked; and they sewed fig leaves together and made themselves coverings. And they heard the sound of the Lord God walking in the garden in the cool of the day, and Adam and his wife hid themselves from the presence of the Lord God among the trees of the garden. Then the Lord God called to Adam and said to him, "Where are you?" So he said, "I heard Your voice in the garden, and I was afraid because I was naked; and I hid myself." And He said, "Who told you that you were naked? Have you eaten from the tree of which I commanded you that you should not eat?" Then the man said, "The woman whom You gave to be with me, she gave me of the tree, and I ate." And the Lord God said to the woman, "What is this you have done?" The woman said, "The serpent deceived me, and I ate." So the Lord God said to the serpent: "Because you have done this, you are cursed more than all cattle, and more than every beast of the field; on your belly you shall go, and you shall eat dust all the days of your life. And I will put enmity between you and the woman, and between your seed and her Seed; he shall bruise your head, and you shall bruise his heel." To the woman He said: "I will greatly multiply your sorrow and your conception; in pain you shall bring forth children; your desire shall be for your husband, and he shall rule over you." Then to Adam He said, "Because you have heeded the voice of your wife, and have eaten from the tree of which I commanded you, saying, 'You shall not eat of it': "Cursed is the ground for your sake; in toil you shall eat of it all the days of your life. Both thorns and thistles it shall bring forth for you, and you shall eat the herb of the field. In the sweat of your face you shall eat bread till you return to the ground, for out of it you were taken; for dust you are, and to dust you shall return." And Adam called his wife's name Eve, because she was the mother of all living. Also for Adam and his wife the Lord God made tunics of skin, and clothed them.

Then the Lord God said, "Behold, the man has become like one of Us, to know good and evil. And now, lest he put out his hand and take also of the tree of life, and eat, and live forever"— therefore the Lord God sent him out of the garden of Eden to till the ground from which he was taken. So He drove out the man; and He placed cherubim at the east of the garden of Eden, and a flaming sword which turned every way, to guard the way to the tree of life." (Genesis 3:1-24)

The third chapter of Genesis describes how sin first entered into human race... The story of the fall of man, as given here, is an absolute contradiction to the theory of evolution which purports to teach that man began at the very bottom of the moral ladder and is now slowly climbing upwards. On the contrary, this chapter declares that man began at the very top, in the image of God, and proceeded to tumble to bottom.[151] This fact is crucial for us to understand in counseling: we are not some amoebae parasite scratching and clawing our way to the proverbial "top of the food chain." Humanity is simply trying to find a way of being restored to their originally created position. Regrettably, multitudes fail (or maybe the proper terminology to use would be, "refuse") to accept God's plan; God's path. What a deceiver Satan is; he will go to any extreme attempting to get even with God.

In verse one of Genesis chapter three we read, *the serpent was more cunning than any beast of the field which the Lord God had made.* In Revelation chapter twelve, verse nine we find the serpent is identified as Satan himself in a tangible, material form. Satan with all his craftiness and shrewdness approached Eve and began his deceptive conversation.

Then, by a simple perusal of verses one through six, we find that Satan's deception worked and in short order both Adam and Eve had ate from the forbidden tree of the knowledge or good and evil. This single act of disobedience to a loving Creator's instructions introduced the initial seed of sin into the previously undefiled, pure, and holy creation which God had so painstakingly created in His own image. It was too late, Satan had already infected all of humanity. When he told our first parents that their eyes would be opened to a new way of life; that they would be like God, he had deceived them into believing something that was not true. He still works in the same way today. He will tempt us to believe something that, on the surface, sounds correct; then, after we, with our natural

---

[151] Jay E. Adams (Competent To Counsel; Grand Rapids, Michigan; Zondervan; 1970); Page 151.

reasoning, come to believe the deception to be truth and take action our eyes are opened to the shame and subsequent pain of that deceitfulness. As a result we, like Adam and Eve, find ourselves standing before a loving Creator stripped of His glory only to be exposed as rebellious children.

Someone once said that to be forewarned is to be forearmed; this is the very reason why we must be acutely aware of Satan's wiles. Our failure to have a substantial comprehension of these basic presuppositions will always lead to unbiblical beliefs, strife, and dysfunction in our personal lives; and ultimately, the unsound dissemination of counsel and direction to our counselees, which will precipitate the further propagation of pain and suffering as opposed to the resolution of sinful lifestyles or destructive patterns of thinking. Paul, the Apostle, sets out a principle for choosing leaders in the church which basically declares that they must be men who are capable of managing their own affairs or they will never be able to handle the affairs of others (cf. 1 Timothy 3:1-13). This must be a prerequisite for all ministers and Christian counselors as well: failure to do so is not only anti-productive, it's downright unbiblical.

There is far more that could be considered at this point; but our study is an introduction and not intended to be exhaustive in nature. This gives us cause to move forward with the following summation concerning the origins of sin. *In Genesis 3...and other passages we have a simple record of the fall of man and what caused him to fall. Without a clear faith in the fall of man there cannot be a clear faith in the redemption of man. Men who...teach that man did not have a fall, that if he did he fell upward* (i.e. evolution), *that man is simply a victim of environment, and that man is incapable of sin...destroy the very foundation of Scripture and of man's eternal life and hope. One must believe in the fall, or he cannot be saved... If man does not believe he is a sinner he cannot be saved.*[152] All of this will be even more relevant as we proceed in our discussion of the Doctrine of Hamartiology; to mankind's conditions after the fall.

The Fallen Condition of Mankind

Through the above discussion we have clarified that initially mankind was created with holy perfection in the image of God; that sin entered in and defiled God's sinless creation; and, as a result, all of

---

[152] Finis Jennings Dake (God's Plan For Man; Lawrenceville, Georgia; Dake Publishing; 1977); Page 155.

humanity fell. Just the same, we have yet to elaborate on exactly what the fall is and the resultant condition of mankind. As with nearly everything we do in life we need to be aware of and guard against the potential of misconceptions and misunderstandings as much as possible. For this reason we will bring some clarity to common phrases that will be used in this section and beyond.

Sometimes the doctrine of inherited sin from Adam is termed the doctrine of "original sin"... If this term is used, it should be remembered that the sin spoken of does not refer to Adam's first sin, but to the guilt and tendency to sin with which we are born. It is "original" in that it comes from Adam, and it is also original in that we have it from the beginning of our existence as persons, but it is still our sin, not Adam's sin, that is meant.[153]

Since the origins of sin do not lie with mankind; that is, it was **first** found in Lucifer when he attempted to exalt himself to be an equal with God and was ultimately cast out of heaven to the earth; we will, for our purposes, refer to "original sin" as that sin which was found in Lucifer. And the sin wherein all of humanity is born with, (since we are all descendants of Adam) as "inherited sin."

The issue of terminology is not new to our time; throughout history men have called *this aspect of sin* (by many names, including) *inherent sin, sin principal, infection of nature, moral disease, contagious corruption, incentive to sin,* **depraved nature**, *sinful propensities, evil tendencies, manifold infirmity, the* **carnal nature, the flesh, the carnal mind**, *the presence and pollution of sin in the heart, the remains of sin, and many other things. These are theological terms and express the same thought of Scripture on this point, that sin is something real in man, separate from man's body, soul, and spirit, as originally created.*[154]

The theological term **depraved nature** as some have opted to use has derived from a word that originally meant "crooked" or "bent out of shape." Recollecting our previous list of various Old and New Testament words for sin we should recall our first one: *Avah*, which when literally translated means "bent."

---

[153] Wayne Grudem (Bible Doctrine: Essential Teachings of the Christian Faith; Grand Rapids, Michigan; 1999); Page 214.
[154] Finis Jennings Dake (God's Plan For Man; Lawrenceville, Georgia; Dake Publishing; 1977): Page 409, emphasis added.

This bending or warping has made mankind - all of mankind because of the inherited sin nature - to no longer reflect the perfect image of God. In fact, this warping of our nature has been so severe that we are corrupted through and through. It is a complete and total annihilation of God's original creation; absolutely every aspect of our fallen nature is bent out of shape - depraved. This is the inherited sin that causes us, apart from the anointed Messiah, to never be able to accomplish anything of any eternal value. For example: in the original creation mankind held within their very being the "keys" to the gates of eternity (eternal life; eternal provision; eternal fellowship with a loving Creator; etc...). These keys worked beautifully until one day the destructive force of sin was introduced and bent up the keys so bad that they no longer worked in the locks.

Because of the devastation brought about by sin, men, as free moral agents, no longer begin life in a perfected, sinless state. Apart from the Messiah we are no longer able to choose to live and practice a life of sinlessness: we are "by nature the children of wrath" (cf. Ephesians 2:3). We are born in sin and iniquity (cf. Psalm 51:5) and, of our own accord, we have no ability to change things.

Sin and death were forever introduced into the world and the results forever changed all of humanity. God's created image bearer's very nature have fallen from holy perfection to total deprivation. This deprived sin nature, which resulted has at least four characteristics that are true of every human-being ever born:

1.   All men are totally and completely void of any original righteousness. (Psalms 51:5)

2.   No one has any innate holy affection toward God. (Romans 1:25; 2 Timothy 3:2-3)

3.   Externally, there is nothing that can defile man; all defilement now proceeds from within a sinful heart. (Mark 7:15, 21-23)

4.   All men possess an unceasing and unbroken prejudice toward evil. (Genesis 6:5)

We have fallen from such heights it would appear that all has been lost; but God was not surprised, He was not caught off guard; He did not even need to call an emergency board meeting of the Holy Trinity in order to come up with an alternative plan. No: God was prepared for this eventuality and He knew that, as a result, man's greatest need would be Divine grace. This Divine grace He has provided via a Redeemer who has already fulfilled the necessary requirements of Divine judgment. He has also provided a means of restoring men to the pre-fallen condition (see Chapter 8).

This is one reason among many reasons why it is essential for any competent minister or Christian counselor to consider not only Adam's pre-fallen status but to look intently into the life of mankind's Redeemer, the last Adam - Jesus. The very One who, in His fleshly body, possessed human nature (i.e. He had free moral agency and could have sinned if He so chose) and yet lived a sin-free life. We can learn vast amounts from a thorough study of both the first and last Adam's lives: and privately we should do so. If we truly desire to become effective at helping others, we need to obliterate the destructive effects of sin in our own lives personally and help others to do the same.

Common Elements of Sin

We have lightly touched on four common characteristics of sin that cannot, from birth, be legitimately denied. Unfortunately, these four characteristics are so wide and far-reaching they barely tell us anything of importance for our everyday use in the counseling setting. For this reason we will dig a little deeper and review some of the more conventional components of sin (autonomy, lust and pride, and temptation), which may not be readily apparent in the earlier stages of the counseling relationship.

By recalling Genesis chapter three it is easy to deduce that the deadly game Satan played with Eve was to make her believe that possessing the knowledge of good and evil would be harmless. He tempted her by making it sound appealing rather than appalling; desirable rather than destructive; and pleasant rather then prideful: he is still employing the same tactics today. *Counseling, therefore, must be understood and conducted as a spiritual battle. The counselor must consider himself a soldier of Christ engaged in spiritual warfare when counseling... The enemy must be defeated in all of his various manifestations. Counselors must be careful not to allow him to take advantage of situations (II Corinthians 2:11) or to give him an opportunity to gain ground (Ephesians 4:27). One way of guarding against such incursions by the evil one is, as Paul noted, to be aware of his tactics' ("we are not ignorant of his schemes" - II Corinthians 2:11).*[155]

As ministers and Christian counselors it is vital for us to understand that a vast majority of our counselees will honestly be convinced of the good in their decisions and choices. For every man believes he is right in his own eyes. (Proverbs 21:2) Some of the hardest areas for the minister and Christian counselor to help a counselee understand are those sins that they do not believe are sinful; areas in their life that does not appear to be sinful according to them. Yet, the Apostle Paul never failed in his writings to all believers, everywhere, and for all of time to address sin, as sin. Refer to the following:

For the wrath of God is revealed from heaven against all ungodliness and unrighteousness of men, who suppress the truth in unrighteousness, *because what may be known of God is manifest in them, for God has shown it to them. For since the creation of the world His invisible attributes are clearly seen, being understood by the things that are made, even His eternal power and Godhead, so that they are without excuse,* **because, although they knew God, they did not glorify Him as God, nor were thankful,** *but became futile in their thoughts, and their foolish hearts were darkened. Professing to be wise, they became fools, and changed the glory of the incorruptible God into an image made like corruptible man—and birds and four-footed animals and creeping things. Therefore God also gave them up to uncleanness, in the lusts of their hearts, to dishonor their bodies among themselves, who exchanged the truth of God for the lie, and worshiped and served the creature rather than the Creator, who is blessed forever. Amen. For this reason God gave them up to vile passions. For even their women exchanged the natural use for what is against nature. Likewise also the men, leaving the natural use of the woman, burned in their lust for one another, men with men committing what is shameful, and receiving in themselves the penalty of their error which was due. And even as they did not like to retain God in their knowledge, God gave them over to a debased mind, to do those things which are not fitting; being filled with all unrighteousness, sexual immorality, wickedness, covetousness, maliciousness; full of envy, murder, strife, deceit, evil-mindedness; they are whisperers, backbiters, haters of God, violent, proud, boasters, inventors of evil things, disobedient to parents, undiscerning, untrustworthy, unloving, unforgiving, unmerciful; who, knowing the righteous judgment of God, that those who practice such things are deserving of death, not only do the same but also approve of those*

---

[155] Jay E. Adams (The Christian Counselor's Manual; Grand Rapids, Michigan; Zondervan; 1973); Page 117.

who practice them. (Romans 1:18-32)

Now the works of the flesh are evident, which are: adultery, fornication, uncleanness, lewdness, idolatry, sorcery, hatred, contentions, jealousies, outbursts of wrath, selfish ambitions, dissensions, heresies, envy, murders, drunkenness, revelries, and the like; *of which I tell you beforehand, just as I also told you in time past, that those who practice such things will not inherit the kingdom of God.* (Galatians 5:19-21)

Therefore be imitators of God as dear children. And walk in love, as Christ also has loved us and given Himself for us, an offering and a sacrifice to God for a sweet-smelling aroma. **But fornication and all uncleanness or covetousness, let it not even be named among you, as is fitting for saints; neither filthiness, nor foolish talking, nor coarse jesting, which are not fitting, but rather giving of thanks. For this you know, that no fornicator, unclean person, nor covetous man, who is an idolater, has any inheritance in the kingdom of Christ and God.** *Let no one deceive you with empty words, for because of these things the wrath of God comes upon the sons of disobedience.* (Ephesians 5:1-6)

Therefore put to death your members which are on the earth: **fornication, uncleanness, passion, evil desire, and covetousness, which is idolatry.** *Because of these things the wrath of God is coming upon the sons of disobedience, in which you yourselves once walked when you lived in them. But now you yourselves are to put off all these: anger, wrath, malice, blasphemy, filthy language out of your mouth. Do not lie to one another, since you have* **put off the old man with his deeds.** (Colossians 3:5-9)

Autonomy

At the core of all sin, whether referenced above by Paul or not, is the desire of man to be autonomous. Autonomous is the equivalent to being independent or self-ruling and yet the Bible says, by failing to submit to God you are obeying the devil - the commander of the powers in the unseen world. That the devil is the spirit at work in the hearts of those who refuse to obey God (Ephesians 2:2). Jesus Himself said that no one can serve two masters, you will hate one and love the other; you will be devoted to one and despise the other (Luke 16:13). The bottom line is that we are never autonomous or "self-ruling."

When Adam and Eve *permitted Satan to challenge God's Word concerning the tree and... remained silent in the face of Satan's lie...*(they) *demonstrated their willingness to reject God's authority over them and their willingness to take God at His word merely on the basis of His sovereign authority... This* (meant) *that the center of authority for man had shifted away from God to himself. Adam and Eve came to believe that they were to be their own authority, that they had the right to determine for themselves by experimentation what is true and what is false... This shows, as Paul says, that men are never truly autonomous, but rather are walking either in obedience to God or according to the prince of the power of the air (Ephesians 2:2). But* **Adam and Eve thought that it was they who were determining the course they would follow, that they were only exercising their autonomous right to determine for themselves the true, the good, and the beautiful**: *they became, in their understanding, their own authority, and their fallen descendants ever since that time have claimed a similar autonomy from God.*[156]

Adam and Eve thought. Just as with most counselees think, and honestly believe what they are doing is fine. Every man, even a fool thinks that what he is doing is right (Proverbs 21:2; 12:15). This reality actually cause problems on two separate fronts.

1.   It causes enormous amounts of confusion and consternation in the counselee when things don't work out the way he/she honestly believed it would.

2.   Since the individual believes he is right, it makes correction very difficult for the minister or Christian counselor to introduce corrective measures in a way that the counselee will accept and allow to affect a change in thoughts or behavior.

Autonomy is an element of hamartiology which is always present in all sin at one level or another.

Lust and Pride

For our next common component of sin we will tackle three at a time; primarily because that is how John, the Apostle of Christ, dealt with them in his first epistle. In First John chapter two, verse sixteen we read: *For all that is in the world—**the lust of the flesh, the lust of the eyes, and the pride of life**—is not of the Father but is of the world.*

---

[156] Dr. Robert L. Reymond (A New Systematic Theology of the Christian Faith; Nashville, Tennessee; Thomas Nelson Publishers; 1998); Page 445, emphasis added.

Since we have already concluded that the belief in an individual's right of self-government and independence (autonomy) is always present when one sins we must also understand the three elements of sin that John refers to here also involves a disregard of God's legitimate authority over an individual's life.

The *lust of the flesh;* the *lust of the eyes,* and the *pride of life* are all intertwined and permeated with the desire for independence: and while they are uniquely inseparable it will be easier for us to comprehend if we will consider each element on its own merits and then fuse them back into their original relationship with autonomy. It is also interesting for us to learn that, barring any organic issues, *all sin stems from at least one of these. It can easily be seen that Eve fell for all three: the lust of the eye - "she saw...it was pleasant to the eyes," the lust of the flesh - "that the tree was good for food," and the pride of life - "a tree to be desired to make one wise." Thus the seed of every sin among men is seen in this, the first sin.*[157]

It is also essential for us as ministers and Christian counselors to remain conscious of the fact that not all worldliness occurs externally, (i.e. how we act; where we go; what we do; and who we spend time with). Much, in fact, nearly all of the foundational elements for all sin are internalized, (i.e. thoughts and desires). In reality all sin begins internally: there is a thought, the thought is meditated upon to the point of visualizing it, and then, it is given birth and acted upon.

Since these are often sins of the heart they are not only subjective, but they are also hard to detect and identify. Especially in the beginning, counselees may appear to be honorable and holy on the outside while defiled and decaying on the inside. All three components reveal selfishness, greed, and a refusal to follow the Creator's rule. Yet, even in our own lives, at the inception, they can be so subtle as to be unrecognized.

This is one reason why Paul commands the believer to *let the Lord Jesus Christ take control of* (our lives) *and don't think of ways to indulge* (our) *evil desires* (Romans 13:14). This means that we are not to spend time trying to figure out different ways of feeding these feelings or lusts; we can, and should, allow Christ Jesus to control us - both in thought and deed.

---

[157] Guy P. Duffield and Nathaniel M. Van Cleave (Foundations of Pentecostal Theology; Los Angeles, California; L.I.F.E. Bible College; 1987); Page 154.

However, the only way for this to be successful is to make a conscious and deliberate decision to make all of our desires subservient to His Lordship and refuse to live a "feelings oriented" life.

The devil appealed to "the lust of the eyes, the lust of the flesh and the pride of life" (cf. 1 John 2:16 with Genesis 3:6)... God's commandment: "you shall not eat." The options given to them are the same options that one faces now. They reflect...two discrete manners of life. The one says: "I shall live according to feelings"; the other: "I shall live as God says"... When Adam sinned he was abandoning the commandment-oriented life of love for the feeling-oriented life of lust. There are only two ways of life: the feeling-motivated life of sin oriented toward self, and the commandment-oriented life of holiness oriented toward God.

The two ways of life are diametrically opposed to one another and force one to choose between them. Throughout the day, one's life consists of many such choices. The two life styles involve patterns of lust or love. They are oriented toward and motivated by the counselees desires for God's commandments. They acknowledge two distinct sources of authority: self or the Bible. They focus on separate goals: temporary pleasure; eternal joy. They acknowledge two masters: Satan or God. They offer two different ways of handling life's problems: the one resorts to running, covering up, lying and blame-shifting, etc., while the other insists upon facing, confessing, speaking truth, and assuming personal responsibility. They bring about their own results: the bondage of chaos in this life and eternal loss, or the freedom of structure and eternal joy.[158]

These two concepts are distinct and must be dealt with either in this life or the next. One critical thing for us, as well as all believers, to learn is that when we become believers the sins of the flesh still exists. While our spirit is reborn we need to remember that the flesh (the physical body) and our minds remain unchanged. Because of His great mercy, God gives us the ability to renew our mind to His ways (Romans 12:2) and then, in so doing we are given the legitimate option of choosing between the feeling oriented and the commandment oriented life. Also, as we renew our minds, there is a commensurate spiritual transformation occurring, which (as we submit to the Holy Spirit's work) supernaturally empowers us to win the battle over the lust of the eyes, the lust of the flesh, and the pride of life.

Furthermore, we must never underestimate the power of the sinful

---

[158] Jay E. Adams (The Christian Counselor's Manual; Grand Rapids, Michigan; Zondervan; 1973); Page 118.

nature, for it is energized by the power of evil and can only be conquered by our obedience to and dependence upon God and His mercy. Then, just as Jesus gained the victory over His wilderness temptations; wherein Scripture tells us that the devil "left Him for a more opportune time" (Luke 4:1-13) we too need to accept that he will return again and again with the same deceitful schemes.

Because the devil never gives up on his quest to cause us to sin we must recognize that victory is based on our present obedience to and relationship with God. In other words, a continual victory over the enemy requires a continual lifestyle of submission and obedience to God's authority. As ministers and Christian counselors we must first settle this issue within ourselves and then encourage our counselees to accept and experience it in their lives.

Temptation

Another area that we must address in this section is temptation. There are far too many victories being thwarted in believers lives because of a lack of understanding. What usually happens are scenarios wherein a counselee (or anyone else) finds themselves being tempted to act in a manner they know is sinful; (this act may or may not be habitual or addictive behavior) so they give in to the temptation believing that, since they were tempted, they might as well go ahead with the sinful act because God knows the desires of the heart and "He will hold me accountable" for these desires anyway, which is another lie of the enemy.

Mercifully, in His wilderness experience Jesus was tempted by all the elements and yet, He never sinned. In other words, a temptation only becomes a sin when we give in to it and act in disobedience to God's commands. This is one reason why Paul instructed us to *cast down every imagination, and every high thing that exalts itself against the knowledge of God, and bring into captivity every thought to the obedience of Christ.* (2 Corinthians 10:5)

Adam and Eve went through the same routine of temptation until actual sin was committed as is true with many men today. James said, "every man is tempted, when he is drawn away of his own lust and enticed. Then when lust hath conceived, it bringeth forth sin: and sins when it is finished bringeth forth death" (James 1:13-16). Sin is not sin until lust hath conceived and the law has been broken. Any temptation short of breaking the law is not sin... for example, it was perfectly sinless and legitimate for

Adam and Eve to eat and to have a desire to be like God, but it was in (the) *eating what was forbidden by the law of God that sin was committed. There is a right and a wrong way and a right and a wrong time to exercise our faculties. When we are tempted to use them in self-gratification and sin the exercise of them is wrong, but when they are exercised lawfully no sin is committed.*[159] This truth should come as a great relief to many for it simply tells us that the fleeting thought (not necessarily lustful imaginations that we enjoy daydreaming about) is not sin.

Prior to closing this section concerning the most common elements of sin let's conduct a short review; all sin falls under one or more of these three elements: 1) the lust of the eyes; 2) the lust of the flesh; and 3) the pride of life. However, there is one element, which we've already discussed, that is involved in sin that permeates each of these three elements: autonomy - the desire to be independent and self-governed. As we come to recognize and understand this reality it will, hopefully make it somewhat easier to begin the process of effectively helping others. Also, as ministers and Christian counselors, there are two more facts that we need to keep in mind: 1) there will never be a loss of someone to help; and 2) we will never have all the answers; so we must continue to study, obey, and grow.

Common Consequences of Sin

Now that we have determined the four most common elements of sin and briefly dealt with the difference between being tempted to sin and the sinful act itself, let's turn our attention to the more common consequential fallout from sinful activity. We will not, however, undertake the issues of sickness, disease, and death. While these issues are very real and the Bible is clear concerning the terminal consequences of sin; we are dealing with the ability to recognize and short-circuit sinful patterns before they lead to eternity.

Excuses

When Adam and Eve partook of the forbidden fruit they, albeit too late, immediately realized a change. Their joy was exchanged for misery, and for the first time they experienced nakedness, the provocation of a loving Creator, and the loss of grace and mercy; their dominion over other

---

[159] Finis Jennings Dake (God's Plan For Man; Lawrenceville, Georgia; Dake Publishing; 1977); Page 157.

creatures was lost; the image of God, innate from creation became distorted and unrecognizable; and finally, they had given birth to the sinful nature, which ultimately permeated all of mankind.

This means that *man cannot help being born in sin, but he can help himself in the matter of continuing in sin. He cannot help his being here but he can help himself as to where he is going.* **Each man is personally and solely responsible for choosing to continue in sin and yieldedness to the devil. He is a free moral agent and can turn to God and get rid of sin at any time he chooses.** *"Choose this day whom ye shall serve" still applies to man, and each one is serving the master of his own choice... God has definitely stated that He is "not willing that any should perish, but that all should come to repentance"; so it is entirely up to man to become reconciled to God or suffer the original penalty for sin.*[160]

Alas, men are still following Adam's lead by choosing to refuse personal responsibility while attempting to blame others (cf. Genesis 3); yet there can be no hope for change until a counselee accepts culpability for their own actions. When any counseling model or system is developed upon Freud's presuppositions, personal accountability will, in all likelihood, never happen because he has made avoidance of responsibility legitimate. Rogerians have been taught to place feelings over responsibility. And Skinnerians, in reality, oppose any concept of personal accountability.

But, the Creator Himself held both Adam and Eve (and countless others in the Bible) responsible for their sinful deeds: as ministers and Christian counselors, who or what gives us the authority to act in any other manner?

Regrettably, when we attempt to "pass the buck," which is what notoriously occurs, there are an plethora of excuses tossed around (e.g. that woman you gave me! etc.). These excuses will nearly always involve an attempt to justify one's personal actions while avoiding personal responsibility. But what the counselee (excuse maker) failed to comprehend is, excuses will never turn away God's required punishment. For example: God can never be considered truly just and holy if He accepts even one persons excuse as being legitimate. For God to do that He would have to, at the very least, hear and judge every individual excuse for every sin of

---

[160] Finis Jennings Dake (God's Plan For Man; Lawrenceville, Georgia; Dake Publishing; 1977); Pages 418-419, emphasis added.

every person that ever lived. I am not saying the God is incapable of doing just this: however, for Him to do so would violate His Word, and that, He is incapable of doing.

God evidently considered His experience with the angels, and decided to make man different, so that if he fell it should be done before he had offspring, in order that all could be classed as fallen. In that case, God could have had mercy upon all (Rom. 3:9; Gal. 3:22). **There would have been innumerable arguments, excuses, and demands upon God by men if they had been permitted to sin in many different ways and times, as each individual came to accountability... As it is now, God can and does deal with each man on the same basis, and all will have to acknowledge in the end that the gospel is fair and just in its demands on all alike. Now God classes all acts of disobedience** (autonomy) **as sin, and all who commit sin as sinners; and He has provided just one way of getting rid of the sin business in the** (human) **race.**[161]

Even though excuses and self justification are a part of daily living, God's plans have never changed; and, He will never make allowances for them. God did not allow Moses to use excuses when he was told to go before Pharaoh (cf. Exodus 3:1-18). God did not accept any excuses concerning the wickedness of individuals, cities, or even His chosen children (the Israelites) of old and, He will not accept our excuses today. As ministers and Christian counselors some of the more common excuses we will hear might include:

- It's not my fault...

- There was nothing I could do about...

- Everyone else is doing it!

- It was a simple mistake; don't take it so serious.

- You don't understand the pressure that I'm under.

- I didn't even realize it was wrong.

God simply will not, indeed cannot, allow for excuses where sin is concerned or He would be unjust.

---

[161] Finis Jennings Dake (God's Plan For Man; Lawrenceville, Georgia; Dake Publishing; 1977); Page 417, emphasis added.

Failure to accept personal responsibility by attempting to shift the blame to someone or something else is not the only pertinent issue when it comes to making excuses. When we either personally or allow a counselee to get away with making excuses we fail to recognize or underestimate the power of sin in one's life. For this cause let's review what Finis Dake says happened when Adam and Eve committed the first act of sin:

He (referring to Adam) *was set upon by the most powerful and subtle of spirit rebels, who caused him to fall and corrupt himself and his posterity* (referring to all of mankind) *and to come under the control of stronger rebels than he himself ever was after the fall. These evil spirit forces are so deep-seated in man's body, soul, and spirit that they seem to be a part of his creative makeup, but they are not. They have control of him as long as he voluntarily remains in sin and rebellion against God. Man in the fall and by subjection to these evil spirit-forces became depraved, polluted, and corrupt in his nature; his understanding was darkened... his conscience defiled... his will made obstinate and rebellious... his affects became carnal and sensual... his thoughts evil continually... his heart full of abominations... and all his posterity with their faculties were constituted sinful by nature and children of the devil by life and practice...[162]*

With these kind of repercussions from a single act of sin, how can we ever logically determine that the power sin exerts either over our own lives or the lives of our counselees be anything but completely diabolical, devastating, and deadly? And yet, when we make allowances for excuses, that is exactly what we are doing. Sadly, society has made excuses far too acceptable and in many cases where severe corrective measures should have been enacted, the perpetrator was allowed to continue on his deadly path without any thought of the possible repercussions.

This culturally induced apathy for personal accountability has effectively led our nation into a situation wherein excuse making (as well as other sinful acts) have became more than a personal issue: it has mushroomed into a national sin. For example: After Jeroboam spent time in Egypt he became king of Israel where he set up golden calves at both Dan and Bethel. This act of personal sin is what ended up causing him to be labeled as the one who caused all of Israel to sin. Jeroboam's personal sin became the impetus for national sin; this same activity still occurs today.

---

[162] Finis Jennings Dake (God's Plan For Man; Lawrenceville, Georgia; Dake Publishing; 1977); Page 158.

Sinful Desires

As ministers and Christian counselors we must begin to do our part in defeating and destroying all excuses as well as the previous four elements of sinful activity in our counselee's lives before they are given the opportunity to progress and proliferate. As sinful activity and excuse making increases we (human beings) actually find ourselves in the cruel condition of struggling with sinful desires and the disastrous effects of sinful activity.

Why should we be concerned with "sinful" desires as opposed to all desires? The answer to this question is a lot easier than it is to actually live by. Desires, in and of themselves, are amoral - without principals; they can be either good or bad; healthy or unhealthy; godly or evil. The primary differentiating factor is the spirit behind the desires. Is it a holy desire or an unholy desire? Is it a desire to please God or self? Is it something that will draw you closer to Christlikeness or away from it?

When we refuse to accept personal responsibility for our own actions by making excuses; unholy, selfish, and evil desires are given all the nutrients they need to promote growth and development within an individual's heart. This explains why Jesus could say, *How can you, **being evil** speak good things? **For out of the abundance of the heart the mouth speaks**.* (Matthew 12:34, emphasis added)

Out of the abundance of the heart clearly refers to an internal condition. Internalized evil and sinful desires are not the same as our previously discussed, "temptations." Temptations are external; an attempt from an outside source that tries to compel us into a sinful act or activity. James brings clarity to this truth when he draws the distinction between a man being *tempted with evil* and when he is being *drawn away of his own lust and enticed.* (cf. James 1:13-14) Then, in verse fifteen, he continues by saying, *when lust* (which is an internal desire) *has conceived, it gives birth to sin.*

One reason why it is easier to define than to experientially live it out is because God has created every human being with desire; it is a part of free moral agency. It is simply something that is a part of who we are; problems arise when we choose not to follow God; when we opt to be autonomous. Anytime we submit to external temptations our internal desires become, in a very real sense, addicted to whatever is feeding them.

If the nutrients are evil and sinful then we will begin to crave sinful things in the heart. If what feeds our desires is holy and blameless we will yearn for more of the same. For example, if a temptation arises we will have no appetite to either partake or participate - it will not even be considered as attractive or enticing.

As ministers and Christian counselors it is easy to see these issues in a counselee and we cannot simply ignore or purposefully minimize them. In doing so we make a way for the seemingly innocuous to permeate their every choice or decision in life, thus, allowing serious issues to become life threatening. Regrettably, failure to recognize these issues or a refusal to accept our conclusions concerning unholy desires and enticements are very common: once again; lack of responsibility and personal accountability will typically lead to further excuses, which ultimately becomes the fodder for even more sinful desires. It is an evil cycle that must be broken before any positive progress can be made in the counseling process.

God has a plan for every life in the world and He has given us the opportunity to have a part in His fulfilling those plans in the lives of our counselees. As such, we need to enter whole-heartedly into God's plan and count it a great honor when He brings someone across our path to assist. When we conform to His plans and His methods we will be greatly blessed by seeing the power of God released as lives are changed, families are restored, and entire communities are affected.

Resisting, Counteracting, and Overcoming Sin

Simply having knowledge of the element and subsequent consequences of sin is not normally enough to witness changes in the lives of our counselees. After we have given them the knowledge or understanding of what has occurred we are obligated to provide them with the tools necessary for resisting, counteracting, and ultimately overcoming sin.

First and foremost, if one truly desires to overcome sin, they must receive a new life, which can only come from faith in Christ Jesus and His atoning work at Calvary. *The first step toward reconciliation with God is to admit that our relationship with Him has been damaged by our sin. Sin hasn't merely bruised our relationship; it has completely severed it. Worse, sin has placed us in an adversarial relationship with God that can cause us to spend a lifetime justifying ourselves instead of allowing Him to repair the relationship. The broken relationship between us and God is not merely a superficial rift. Were it not for God's grace, it would entail a hopeless standoff. But God took the initiative to correct the problem by sending His Son, Jesus, to take our sin upon Himself so that it would no longer be an obstacle between us and God. Grace makes this provision possible, and faith accepts it as a free gift.*[163] (We will deal with this in much more depth in chapter 8.)

Once the severed relationship is restored there are many things or "tools" at our disposal for resisting, counteracting, and overcoming sin. While we will sparingly discuss some of these tools, our purpose is not to be exhaustive; only to provide each minister and Christian counselor with a cursory "starter set." Obviously personal accountability and responsibility, which includes: being open and honest with God; confession and repentance of sin; and receiving as well as granting forgiveness are a necessity. While each of these tools may be considered as simple variations of the same thing they are, in reality, very different. Thankfully, God did not stop with them; we also have at our disposal:

- **"Replacement Parts"**: God has given us the opportunity to replace the old with the new. (i.e. *when the Holy Spirit effects regeneration in a soul, that person becomes "a new creature in Christ; old things have passed away and all things become new." The Holy Spirit takes up His residence in the life, begins to change that life, and **empowers the individual to live according to the promises and commands of Scripture. (Not automatically, nor perfectly, for redeemed men are still sinners who do not yield entirely to the Spirit's will...)** To attempt to effect changes apart from God's power is a colossal mistake.*)[164]

- **Supernatural Ability**: We are given the ability to do all things through Christ Jesus because of His empowerment (Philippians 4:13). This capability includes obedience to God's Word, which is not something that we always feel like doing: irregardless, He still commands our obedience. Submission and conformity to God is how we resist and counteract sinful desires.

[163] Dr. Timothy Clinton and Dr. George Ohlschlager (Competent Christian Counseling Volume One; Colorado Springs, Colorado; Waterbrook Press; 2002); Pages 128-129.
[164] Jay E. Adams (Competent To Counsel; Grand Rapids, Michigan; Zondervan; 1970); Page 68, emphasis added.

Then, when we choose to obey we gain victory over sin and the commensurate feelings will follow. These feelings are the result of fruit being produced by our obedience to God, not the cause of it.

• **"Vice Grips"**: I call them vice grips because they will apply pressure on sin and will not release until their task is completed. This simply means that we have the Word of God and as we continually confess it over any given situation we can rest assured that it will prosper; that it will always produce fruit. God's Word cannot fail; it will do all He wants it to do, it will prosper. (Isaiah 55:11)

• **"Pliers"**: Pliers work in a similar fashion as vice grips with the exception that we are required to consciously maintain continuous pressure. This pressure comes with the realization that we do not have to commit sinful acts. It is similar to our being empowered by Christ, with one vital difference: if the counselee does not comprehend that they have been empowered and commissioned to win the battle over sin, they will never use what has been provided. As we deal with others, getting them to accept the fact that men do not "have to" sin will be much more complicated than getting them to agree with and choose to act upon the, *I can do all things through Christ Jesus* mantra.

• **"Pry Bar"**: This is a multi-use tool because it is one of the strongest and most powerful tools we have at our disposal. If a counselee finds himself being tempted to sin he must know to not hang around and argue; he must not stick around and play with people, things, or even areas and situations where old sins and habits normally exist; he must "pry" himself away from the old haunts and people and get to a safe place. That is, at the very least, until victory is won and lived out for an extended time period.

• **Additional Tools**: These tools should be found in every believer's tool box. They are crucial in resisting and counteracting sin; the more they are used the more adept we will become at engaging and overcoming sin: prayer, faith, submission to godly leaders, fasting, proper interpretation of God's Word, renewing the mind, casting down any thoughts that run contrary to Christ, etc...

All of these tools and many, many others are available to anyone, minister, counselor, and counselee alike. However, before we will ever pick up the tools and put them to use we must come to the conclusion that ignoring, going around, over, or retreating from sin (or any other problem, as far as that goes) is not a fix. When we avoid issues they stay intact and instead of becoming a victorious overcomer we end up adapting to them. The bottom line is this: adaptation does not equal victory.

We must also acquire experiential revelation that, in Christ, God will not allow us to be tested beyond what we are able to handle. *He will not allow the devil to tempt* (any believer) *above that which they are able to withstand... Whatever the test may be at any moment, it is not beyond his ability to withstand in Christ. Given the grace* (help) *of God, given his knowledge of God's Word, given the sanctification that is his to that point, given the resources of the Holy Spirit, no test is beyond his ability to withstand* (and gain the victory over).[165]

As ministers and Christian counselors we have a responsibility to God, our counselees, and ourselves to be aware of evil spirits and their ways. They have no righteousness or moral character so they will take advantage of every weakness, including ignorance, stupidity, and foolishness. Regrettably, hordes of people unknowingly cooperate with the enemy and, because of a lack of understanding, help to propagate his deceit and lies. For example: *Adam and Eve did not need the fruit of* (the) *tree. It was not necessary to either their happiness or well-being...* (and) *it has not added one moment of genuine pleasure to* (their) *life in any way.*[166] Much error can even be attributed to the traditions of man, who have caused the available power of God to be of no effect. (cf. Matthew 7:13) This must be stopped. The unadulterated word of God must be studied comprehensively, believed, and then, released into any and every situation, for God's Word will not fail.

Judgment always follow failure and sin in every dispensation. In this one, God's will had been made known and the penalty for disobedience revealed before man sinned. To be just, it was necessary for God to keep His word and teach the new free moral agents that He was just and righteous in all His dealings and in the exercise of government and that His Word was true and was to be taken literally and obeyed. To be

---

[165] Jay E. Adams (Competent To Counsel; Grand Rapids, Michigan; Zondervan; 1970); Page 132.
[166] Guy P. Duffield and Nathaniel M. Van Cleave (Foundations of Pentecostal Theology; Los Angeles, California; L.I.F.E. Bible College; 1987); Page 152.

lenient would have caused others to rebel and then to expect more and more leniency. If God had started a program like this there would have been no end to rebellion. It never could have been put down with God showing Himself to be a respecter of persons. Sin had to be judged and men taught that it does not pay to rebel against God and do those things that are not for the best good of his being and for the highest good of the universe and the societies therein.[167]

Through Christ Jesus, Satan is already a defeated enemy. And yet he still has great authority over anyone who has not consciously chosen to accept Christ's salvation by faith. For those who have rejected this free gift of God's grace and mercy the devil still has the ability to "take captive at his will" (2 Timothy 2:26); however, he cannot freely exert his will over the believer. As minister's and Christain counselors we must have a comprehensive understanding of Christ's salvation; we must also be ready and willing to lead unredeemed counselees through the process and introduce them to Christ as Lord, via the redemptive process, which is the subject of our next Chapter.

---

[167] Finis Jennings Dake (God's Plan For Man; Lawrenceville, Georgia; Dake Publishing; 1977); Page 158.

Chapter 8 : The Doctrine of Soteriology (Salvation)

This doctrine is one of unimaginable depth; its purposes and effects are so wide ranging that, while it changes where we are destined to spend eternity, it also changes everything from our thoughts to our desires and direction in this life. Because of the extreme depths of this doctrine wherein one might dive into we will intentionally remain very shallow and brief in our discourse. In short, this simply means that this chapter is intended to be a mere introduction to the doctrine of soteriology and should be treated as such.

With such unimaginable depths which one might dig into a study of soteriology (i.e. salvation) the truly ironic thing is that God's plan of salvation is so straightforward and uncomplicated that the most uneducated can comprehend more than enough to experience transformation on an acutely personal level. *The heart of God's plan of salvation centers around the office and function of a Mediator - One who could go between an offended God and a helpless sinful creature, man. Job felt the need for just such a One as he found himself (at least he thought) estranged from God. "He (speaking of God) is not a man like me that I might answer Him, that we might confront each other in court. If only there were someone to arbitrate between us, to lay His hand upon us both" (Job 9:32-33NIV). This is the position which Christ, in His substitutionary sacrifice came to fill.*[168]

In being born into this world, via the natural process of birthing, Jesus became the "Son of Man" (Matthew 18:11) while at the same time being the "only begotten Son" (John 3:16) of God the Father; the Creator of the heavens and the earth; the very same Almighty One that required a penalty for the sin of Adam and Eve that we previously discussed in chapter 7.

This required penalty and the subsequent plan for Jesus to come into this world and pay the price was no afterthought. From *before the*

---

[168] Guy P. Duffield and Nathaniel M. Van Cleave (Foundations of Pentecostal Theology; Los Angeles, California; L.I.F.E. Bible College; 1987); Page 179.

foundations of the world (Ephesians 1:4) He volunteered and was chosen to pay the debt owed by all of humanity. *One must not picture God frustrated over sin, sitting in the heavens wringing His hands, wondering, how He might make the best of a bad situation, suddenly striking upon the idea of sending His Son to die for guilty sinners... All along, God intended to demonstrate His love through sending Christ. Whatever else he sees in salvation, it is important, therefore, for the* (minister and Christain) *counselor to recognize salvation as part of the eternal purpose of God, Who determined that His Son should die. This determination was made not after sin came into the world, but before the world's foundation: before there was a man to sin or a world in which he would sin.*[169]

As ministers and Christian counselors it is paramount that we believe this unconditionally or else every other belief we possess about God and His will is tainted. Therefore, since we believe God had prior knowledge of what would transpire; that He established the process before man was ever created; and also that Jesus agreed up front to be the perfect sacrificial Lamb, we must also conclude that He is an extremely personal God. Additionally, we should also deduce that God still maintains ultimate sovereignty over the world He created and as such, there is a plan behind everything He does. This plan includes providing salvation to all who will receive it by faith.

As defined in our modern dictionary, the word *salvation* includes:

1.   *The saving of man from the power and effects of sin: a) His deliverance from the condition of spiritual isolation and estrangement to a reconciled relationship of community with God and fellowmen: redemption from spiritual lostness to religious fulfillment and restoration to the fulness of God's favor; b) Redemption from ultimate damnation through divine agency; c) The deliverance of the soul from sin or the spiritual consequences of sin: the saving of a person's soul from eternal punishment and its admission into heavenly beatitude.*

2.   *Liberation from ignorance or illusion: deliverance from clinging to the phenomenal world of appearance and final union with ultimate reality...*[170]

---

[169] Jay E. Adams (A Theology of Christian Counseling; Grand Rapids, Michigan; Zondervan; 1979); Pages 174-175.
[170] Philip Babcock Gove (Editor in Chief) (Webster's Third New International Dictionary of the English Language: Unabridged; Springfield, Massachusetts; Merriam-Webster Inc., Publishers; 1993); Page 2006.

In my unabridged dictionary there are four more definitions, however, they have very little relation to the true meaning of what we are studying. For further confirmation, let's review Vine's Expository Dictionary of Old and New Testament Words where we find that salvation (soteria) means or *denotes deliverance, preservation, salvation...of the spiritual and eternal deliverance granted immediately by God to those who accept His conditions of repentance and faith in the Lord Jesus, in whom alone it is to be obtained, Acts 4:12, and upon confession of Him as Lord...*[171]

Crucial Terminology

Salvation is used over one-hundred and fifty times in the Old and New Testaments; it is an all-inclusive term that encompasses all of the redemptive acts and processes involved in the restoration of mankind. In fact, some resources declare that there are at least sixty different words or phrases that express the various phases of the salvation process. Some of these terms we will define and briefly discuss since they are so important to our effectiveness in helping others.

The terminology we will address include: A. Atonement; B. Imputation; C. Reconciliation; D. Redemption; E. Election/Predestination; and F. The Sinlessness of Christ.

A. Atonement

Our first word, atonement, is purely an Old Testament word in that, in it's most basic definition, it simply means "a covering". Unfortunately, among many believers this word is used interchangeably with the New Testament term reconciliation and redemption. This is unfortunate in that Christ did not merely "cover" our sins. For anyone that will receive His free gift of salvation, purely through faith, their sins have already been completely and totally "removed." In the Old Testament the atonement simply hid man's sin from the view of a Holy Creator; in the New Testament our sin has been removed - cast in to the depths of the sea (Micah 7:19).

We no longer have a biblical mandate to have regular sacrifices merely hoping to appease an angry god. Our God has provided both the method and means to fulfill all of the Law's requirements for the righteous

---

[171] W.E. Vine (Vine's Expository Dictionary of Old and New Testament Words; Nashville, Tennessee; Thomas Nelson Publishers; 1997); Page 988.

appeasement of His wrath. Christ became *the propitiation for our sins; and not for ours only, but also for the sins of the whole world* (cf. 1 John 2:2; Romans 3:25; Hebrews 10:10; 1 John 4:10; etc.). This means that, since God's righteous judgement has already been satisfied by the blood of Jesus, all that is required for us to be forgiven is to receive by faith through repentance and confession.

Unlike the temporal sacrifices in the Old Testament, the atonement of Christ is unlimited. In other words it has been made available to anyone, anywhere, at anytime they so choose. It covers every sin, every sickness, and every style or system of corruption known to mankind. *"Behold the Lamb of God, which taketh the away the sin of the world" - the whole world, not just part of it (John 1:29). This proves that atonement was made for the sins of all men, and all who want to accept Christ as their substitute in paying the eternal death penalty, can be saved. On the other hand, those who reject and refuse to believe on His name will be lost; but this does not mean that Christ died in vain. Nor does it mean that every time a saved man becomes a sinner again* (that) *Christ has to die again for him to be restored. The sacrifice of Christ abides for all alike in any generation and men can avail themselves of the opportunity to be saved, and can actually partake of such provision at any time, or they can reject the provision, without destroying it or causing it to be necessary for a new provision to be made each time someone should be restored from sin. One must simply appropriate the salvation provided for him, in Christ; and if he does not, he goes without the benefits provided.*[172]

Somewhere in the annals of eternity past our loving Triune God opted for this plan and in the fulness of time set it in motion; now it is simply up to each individual to accept Christ's payment for the sins of all of humanity as truth; embrace it through faith; and receive it as a free gift from God. One may be inclined to ask how a holy and righteous Creator could seemingly "blink" at sin when He is the One who established the due penalty for sin would be death even before Adam sinned? In response to this query we declare that God is not blinking or winking at sin; He is not simply "turning a blind eye toward it"; and He is not simply ignoring it - He cannot. Because of Christ's death, burial, and resurrection, the penalty of death for sin has been satisfied. In light of this fact, God simply opts not to credit our sins to our account. For example: You and some friends are out

---

[172] Finis Jennings Dake (God's Plan For Man; Lawrenceville, Georgia; Dake Publishing; 1977); Pages 606-607.

for dinner at an exclusive restaurant when the maitre d approaches and tells you that the owner has chosen to cover your bill for the evening (i.e. your debt has been paid). You have the choice to either accept or not. In either case you are no longer held accountable for your expenses.

B. Imputation

The term impute means to assign the cause, source, or origin of a crime or accountability for an act to another. It may also be used when there is a transfer of sinfulness or divine reward conveyed from one to another. This transfer of sinfulness and divine reward from one to another is a very large portion of God's work of justification. Justification is a legal term that shows the sinner standing before God in court ready to receive condemnation for every sin they ever committed. However, instead of being found guilty, God hands down a verdict of not guilty because He has declared the person to be in right-standing - righteous. It has been said that this is an act of God whereby, He declares as righteous the one who confesses their sin to a loving God and who also believes in Christ and His payment for sin - all sin. In essence, to the believer it means that it is "just as if he had never sinned" because God is not imputing; attributing, ascribing, or assigning any of the sinful activity to his account. God chooses to transfer our sins onto Jesus' account wherein He has not only already accepted our death penalty, but has already paid our debt in full - nothing is due, because nothing is owed.

Paul says that there is no longer any condemnation to those who are in Christ (Romans 8:1), which is a reality in this life for those who will receive by faith God's transference of the penalty for sin. While there are no clean cut and definitive statements in the Holy Scriptures that say our sins are "imputed to Christ" there are numerous verses that refer to it. For example: *He became sin and a curse for us and bore our sins in His own body on a tree that we, being dead to sins should live unto righteousness and by whose stripes we are healed. Christ has done this for every man and God has imputed the sins of every man to Christ, but the benefits of this imputation of sins to Christ cannot be received by any person until he repents and accepts Christ as His substitute. Hence, to talk about imputed righteousness for men without being brought to repentance and faith is folly.*[173]

---

[173] Finis Jennings Dake (God's Plan For Man; Lawrenceville, Georgia; Dake Publishing; 1977); Pages 612-613.

So, through repentance and faith in the atonement man's sin can be transferred to Christ; this alone would be great. However, God decided that the removal of sin was not simply enough, so He conveyed the divine reward of Christ's righteousness to all who meet His criteria (i.e. confession of and repentance for sins, and faith in Christ's substitutionary work).

In First Corinthians chapter one, verse thirty the Apostle Paul writes *for those who are in Christ Jesus, God has made Him to be our wisdom, our **righteousness**, our sanctification, and our redemption* (author's translation). This simply tells us that, at the very moment of salvation, God instantly transfers the penalty we deserve to Christ; while delivering the righteousness of Christ to our account.

Simply put, God can justify and declare every true believer justified because He transfers (imputes) Christ's righteousness to us; God reckons it to our account just like He reckoned righteousness to Abraham because he believed God (Genesis 15:6; Romans 4:3). *The sinner must not only be pardoned for his past sin, but also supplied with a positive righteousness before he can have fellowship with God. This need is supplied in the imputation of the righteousness of Christ to the believer.*[174]

For God to have simply removed the death penalty would have been to only complete half of the job: salvation would have only been a partial fix to man's problem. It would have dealt with the sin of man without restoring man's ability to have an undefiled relationship with God. Consequently, due to desperation and an ultimate loss of hope man would have sinned again. But God intensely desires for us to re-establish a relationship with Him on a personal level. Therefore, since there are *none righteous, no not one* (Romans 3:10) and seeing that righteousness is absolutely necessary for this relationship to happen, God, in an expression of great love and compassion, transferred His righteousness to us in order for the fellowship lost in the Garden to be restored.

It is essential to the heart of the gospel to insist that God declares us to be just or righteous not on the basis of our actual condition of righteousness or holiness, but rather on the basis of Christ's perfect righteousness, which God thinks of as belonging to us. This... justification does not change us internally and it is not a declaration based in

---

[174] Guy P. Duffield and Nathaniel M. Van Cleave (Foundations of Pentecostal Theology; Los Angeles, California; L.I.F.E. Bible College; 1987); Page 223.

any way on any goodness that we have in ourselves.[175] Christ simply exchanges our sin for His righteousness. From a human perspective this sounds like Jesus got a really bad deal, however, His love for mankind along with His desire for a relationship through personal fellowship must have made it worthwhile - after all, Christ agreed to it from the very beginning.

As ministers and Christian counselors we not only need to be able to explain imputation to counselees, but we should also freely use it in helping them to find faith in a loving Creator who has and will continue to go to extreme measures to help us.

Moreover, our ability to explain imputation on an elementary level can greatly enhance a counselee's ability to overcome condemnation from many avenues or areas of their life. We have all done things for which we are ashamed we did; things that ended badly; things wherein, if we had three wishes, we would take them back. Mercifully, because of God's grace we don't need to "wish;" we need to confess and repent. If anyone, whether it be a minister, Christian counselor, or counselee, truly confesses and repents of their actions God says that there is no longer any condemnation.

There is no condemnation for those who are in Christ, in part due to God's two-way plan of imputation. The consequences of a genuine confession and repentance of sins instantaneously leads us to God's reconciliation, which is our next area under consideration.

C. Reconciliation

In Vine's Dictionary we read that *reconciliation is what God accomplishes, exercising His grace towards sinful man on the grounds of the death of Christ in propitiatory sacrifice under the judgement due to sin... This stresses the attitude of God's favor toward us... It was we who needed to be reconciled to God, not God to us, and it is propitiation, which His righteousness and mercy have provided, that makes the reconciliation possible to those who receive it...* (It also carried with it connotation) *to change from one condition to another, so as to remove all enmity and leave no impediment to unity and peace... It is the Divine purpose, on the grounds of the work that Christ accomplished on the Cross, to bring the whole universe, except rebellious angels and unbelieving man, into full accord with the mind of God...*[176]

---

[175] Wayne Grudem (Bible Doctrine: Essential Teachings of the Christian Faith; Grand Rapids, Michigan; 1999); Page 319.
[176] W.E. Vine (Vine's Expository Dictionary of Old and New Testament Words; Nashville, Tennessee; Thomas Nelson Publishers; 1997); Pages 932-933.

The biblical definition has changed very little from our modern day meaning, which involves the act of settling or resolving a dispute or divergence of friendship resulting in restoration of consistency and compatibility. When the first Adam sinned, he set into motion a departure from God's established course for all of humanity (for all his posterity). However, the last Adam, (Jesus) through His death, burial, and resurrection resolved and settled forever the conflict between the created and their Creator.

In his letter to the believers at Corinth, and by extension to all believers everywhere, that *if anyone is in Christ, he is a new creation; old things have passed away; behold, all things have become new. Now all things are of God, who has reconciled us to Himself through Jesus Christ, and has given us the ministry of reconciliation, that is, that God was in Christ reconciling the world to Himself, not imputing their trespasses to them, and has committed to us the word of reconciliation. Now then, we are ambassadors for Christ, as though God were pleading through us: we implore you on Christ's behalf, be reconciled to God. For He made Him who knew no sin to be sin for us, that we might become the righteousness of God in Him.* (2 Corinthians 5:17-21)

The need of reconciliation is apparent because of the enmity between God and man brought about by man's sin. Through the sacrifice of Jesus Christ, this condition of enmity can be changed into one of peace and fellowship. This is one of the greatest blessings of personal salvation. Again, this new relationship magnifies the grace of God, for no man can reconcile himself to God. God Himself wrought this reconciliation for us through Christ.[177]

Old things have passed away; behold, all things have become new...that we might become the righteousness of God in Him. Because God was in Christ reconciling the world unto Himself; not imputing their trespasses unto them refers to the restoring of mankind to a place of favor and communion with their Creator, while destroying the hostility and animosity that separated them. Now, all of humanity, as free moral agents, truly have the freedom to choose whom they will serve and befriend with Christ Jesus being the Mediator for both God and man. That is, if man chooses to reestablish the severed relationship.

---

[177] Guy P. Duffield and Nathaniel M. Van Cleave (Foundations of Pentecostal Theology; Los Angeles, California; L.I.F.E. Bible College; 1987); Page 189.

D. Redemption

The word "redemption" signifies a releasing or liberation from captivity, slavery, or death by the payment of a price, called a ransom. Thus the word has a double significance: it means the payment of a price, as well as the deliverance of the captive.[178]

Redemption is a part of reconciliation in that, when sin became a part of the human nature mankind became obligated to the devil. In a sense, when Adam sold out in order to obtain the knowledge of good and evil he made a covenant with God's enemy and now, Satan owns the rights to all of Adam's posterity. Christ, however, has gained the ability for anyone who will receive it by faith to be released from that ungodly contract.

By giving His own life, Christ paid the ransom demanded by the devil to deliver man from his bondage. Through the shedding of His blood, Jesus delivered believers from Satan; the power and guilt of sin; and even death (eternal separation from God).

Counselees must be made aware of the fact that, if they truly accept Christ's redemption, they can be delivered from any bondage; whether it be physical, spiritual, behavioral, or cognitive in nature. The ransom Christ paid for our redemption is wholly complete and, if we will *believe* (cf. Mark 5:26) He will provide us with the power necessary to defeat every work of the devil as well as the works of the flesh in our life. In addition to this ability to become an overcomer, Christ will make available to each believer, the full benefits of God's covenant concerning this life.

E. Election and Predestination (Calling, Foreknowledge, and Foreordained)

This "full benefits" package includes multiple terms which have caused huge chasms between many in the Body of Christ. These differences have resulted in a horrific interruption in the continuity of the Church; they have caused loyalties to be broken; and they have resulted one relationship after another to be destroyed. And yet, God is not the author of confusion, but of peace (1 Corinthians 14:33); He never intended for things to get so blurry and perplexing.

So how can we come together and begin the restorative process

---

[178] Finis Jennings Dake (God's Plan For Man; Lawrenceville, Georgia; Dake Publishing; 1977); Page 608.

within the Body, which has encountered such great devastation? First, *we must clearly distinguish between God's foreknowledge and His foreordaining. It is not right to say that God foreknew all things because He arbitrarily determined to bring them to pass. God in His foreknowledge looks ahead to events much as we look back upon them. Foreknowledge no more changes the nature of future events than after-knowledge can change historical fact.*[179]

This explanation is a great place to start the healing. Regrettably, there are still far too many believers that "know what they know;" too many who are afraid to dig deeper into their beliefs because it might create discomfort or result in a necessary change of beliefs; or it could simply be what someone once said (not about this particular subject, but the mind-set is still the same), "I've had preachers with more experience and more education than you will ever have tell me something else, so you must be wrong." When I hear this comment I simply ask, "Have you studied it out for yourself?" The typical response is something along the lines of, "No, but I believe the person that taught it." At this point, I will usually end the conversation because there is no point in proceeding any further. Sadly, the individual's eternal life or eternal damnation may be hanging in the balance and I don't want to become the one that drives a greater wedge between them and God.

My desire is to end this section with a solid explanation wherein all believers can find some common ground. Without watering down the truth as it pertains to these "doctrines" I will quote Finis Dake rather extensively. He writes:

God predestined that the saved should be holy before God forever, but **who** *and* **which ones** *will be saved and be holy is left entirely up to the choice of each individual to conform to the plan of God. The lost were likewise predestinated to be lost but* **who** *or* **which persons** *will be lost is left entirely up to the choice of the individual who can refuse to the end of life to conform to the plan of God. The plan itself is the thing that is predestinated, not the individual conformity of one single person to that plan...*

Nothing is hard to understand about election, foreknowledge, or predestination when we realize that it is God's plan itself, and not personal conformity to that plan that

---

[179] Guy P. Duffield and Nathaniel M. Van Cleave (Foundations of Pentecostal Theology; Los Angeles, California; L.I.F.E. Bible College; 1987); Page 207.

has been foreknown and predestinated. God decrees that all who do conform will be saved and all who do not will be lost and this is the sum and substance of these doctrines. God's decrees were never made to determine the choices of free moral agents as to whether some will be saved or others will be lost. The decrees of God are those parts of His plan to which all must conform in order to be saved and those who refuse will be lost. **Men have made the great mistake of making the doctrine of decrees,** *to which all must conform to be saved, the same as the free acts of men in conforming to laws. God does not determine our willing and doing but He does decree the basis of the action for free moral agents that will save or damn them accordingly. This does not mean that the initiative of man's salvation is with man. It is with God who chose to make a way of salvation for all men, especially of them that believe and that conform to this plan of their own free choice.*

Election deals with all creatures as sinners and therefore must deal with them on the same basis or the plan is faulty and the Planner is a respecter of persons and unjust in His dealings. The reason God saves only a few is because only a few choose the way of God, and therefore God is free from the final responsibility of the salvation or damnation of anyone.[180]

This simple understanding of these doctrines will be very helpful when - not if, but when - a counselee comes to the conclusion that God only saves some and not others. Once we get a counselee away from this kind of thinking and get them to believe that God has truly made salvation available to anyone who will confess, repent, and believe (i.e. be born from above) we can genuinely proceed with pure, untainted Christian counseling. Until this occurs we can teach principles and precepts to help the counselee live a better life now, even though his innate need for eternal security will never be dealt with until Christ is received as Redeemer and Lord.

Some, indeed most, unbelieving counselees will simply repeat worldly expressions over and over again in a vain attempt to gain the desired relief barring any authentic and legitimate internal changes. One of the most common manifestations or dispositions will involve inquiries as to the difference between Christianity and the multitudes of other religions of the world. In order to sufficiently satisfy their questions we must have a place from which the reasoning process can begin. Since he is an unbeliever, simple repetition of Scripture will be insufficient; we must be

---

[180] Finis Jennings Dake (God's Plan For Man; Lawrenceville, Georgia; Dake Publishing; 1977); Pages 618-619.

able to explain or expound upon the process in a way that helps the un-renewed mind and the unregenerate heart to initiate the process of acceptance. This entire process could be referred to as plowing soil and planting the seed. Thankfully, God has given us a great place to begin plowing and planting when someone says to us, "Why Christianity?" That starting point involves the sinlessness of Christ; the final term we will discuss.

Sinlessness of Christ

From the time he was created until the very moment he chose to rebel against God's instructions, concerning the tree of knowledge of good and evil, Adam lived a sinless life. While there have been some throughout history that have attempted to determine how long Adam and Eve lived in the Garden of Eden prior to their sinful deed, I have not personally came to the conclusion that any of them are accurate.

What we can accurately determine however, is that Adam was created in God's image with a free will and an unblemished, sin free nature: how ever long he lived in that state is purely hypothetical and debatable and has no practical importance for our purposes. The fact remains that he, the first Adam, did choose to sin; he chose to rebel against His Creator's clear instructions; and he chose to make his will of more importance than the heavenly Father's will. Jesus, the last Adam, however, chose not to sin; He decided not to rebel against the Creator's clear mandates; and He opted to make the Father's will more important than His own: Jesus, as the Son of Man had the free moral agency to select His will over and above His Father's and yet, Jesus elected to obey. He was completely free from any kind of sin while He lived in human form on this earth and He still remains sin-free to this day.

Sin, as we have already discussed in chapter seven, has a multitude of names attached to it. For our purposes we can coalesce them all and finally settle with this understanding: sin is anything that fails to conform to God's standards or criteria.

Inasmuch as the Creator established the standards and criteria for sinlessness we must follow His plan or fall short; i.e. fail to conform. When God created all things He commanded that each would reproduce after its own kind, so when sin was found in Adam anyone born through Adam and

Eve's union would be reproduced after the fallen nature. Sin and the inclination to sin are produced from conception and there is absolutely nothing we can do about it from a natural, human perspective.

Jesus is different in that He was the only Child born of God the Father and as such His inherent nature is the sin-free nature of our Heavenly Father, not the sin nature which has been reproduced in all of Adam's posterity. And yet, because Jesus was born through the God ordained natural birthing process He also possessed the free moral agency that all men, everywhere possess. In other words, Jesus, the last Adam, was born sinless but with the fleshly ability to sin; just as the first Adam had been created. This truth is absolutely necessary for us to grasp if we ever hope to explain, why we should choose Christianity over all other religions.

God, as Maker of all things, has the innate authority to establish and enforce every policy and procedure over all of His creation. As such, He has set the rules and guidelines for being acceptable and pleasing to Him; He established these governing standards and made sure that Adam understood them long before he sinned. When Adam chose to violate the Creator's rules he became a lawbreaker and was no longer allowed to enter the sin-free, holy presence of his loving Creator as was specified in the Law. But God, being the merciful Law-giver that He is, opted not to simply stand by and watch as all of mankind followed in the footsteps of His fallen angel, Lucifer.

Since the Law-giver had established the standards, one which demanded a penalty of death for sin, He understood that legally any human could serve the sentence as long as he were sinless and willing: the Law-giver (God, the Creator of all things) had made allowances for a substitution.

With the fullest of love possible God Himself decided to become the substitute for the sins of all humanity. He opted to come into the earth as a man, with free moral agency, and as God, without sin. He did this in order to restore the lost relationship He once had with Adam and Eve by becoming a suitable sacrifice and substitute for their due penalty, which Jesus accomplished upon the cross at Calvary.

If any sin at all had been found in Jesus He would have been required, by the Law of the Creator to pay the penalty for His own sin:

fortunately for all of mankind, there was no sin found in Him. Therefore, because of His sinlessness God, the Creator, resurrected Jesus (the last Adam) from the dead and He now acts as the Intercessor and Mediator between God and all of humanity. Jesus became our Substitute: He took our penalty of death and became our righteousness.

The answer to our initial question of why Christianity over all other religions is fairly simple: Jesus is the only religious leader in the history of mankind that the Creator Himself recognized as a suitable substitute for humanity's sin. This is proved and historically attested to because the grave was empty even though the grave clothes were still there and also by the fact that hundreds of people saw Jesus walking and talking in His resurrected body. The founder or leader of every other religion in the world died and is still in their grave. Obviously because the Law-giver Himself did not accept them as a suitable substitute.

Christianity is unlike all other religions in the place it assigns to the death of its Founder. All other religions base their claim to greatness on the life and teaching of those who founded them, while the Gospel of Jesus Christ centers around the Person of Jesus Christ, including especially His death at Calvary. It has often been said that there is good in every religion. It may be true that there is some ethical value in many other teachings, but only in Christianity do we have redemption from sin, and this accomplished through the substitutionary death of the Son of God Himself.[181]

As one can clearly see, on a very basic plowing and planting level, as ministers and Christian counselor's, we should have the ability to explain deep scriptural truths without spewing verse after verse, which has the potential of becoming more of a hindrance than a help to our counselees.

It is important however to note that *the word substitution is not found in Scripture, but the doctrine is repeatedly found from Genesis to Revelation. Every time an animal was offered in the Old Testament it was typical of Christ our Substitute who took our place and died in our stead so that we might go free and live forever in union with God. Paul says that "Christ our Passover is sacrificed for us" (1 Corinthians 5:7). Christ tasted death for every man (Hebrews 2:9). He was God's Lamb that took away the sin of the world (John 1:29; Revelation 5:6-10; 1 Peter 2:24; Isaiah 53). Men partake of the benefits of the substitutionary work of Christ only as they have faith in*

[181] Guy P. Duffield and Nathaniel M. Van Cleave (Foundations of Pentecostal Theology; Los Angeles, California; L.I.F.E. Bible College; 1987); Page 181.

Him and accept His atonement for themselves (Romans 3:24-25; 4:25; 5:1-11).[182]

Men partake of the benefits of the substitutionary work of Christ only as they have faith in Him and accept His atonement for themselves: this is a personal requirement for each person ever born, if they choose to follow God's plan and desire to receive the benefits of His provision. And yet, this kind of faith only happens as we hear the Word of God (Romans 10:17), which is why, as ministers and Christian counselors, we need to be ready and willing to plow the soil and plant the seed.

The Secret Things of God

Regrettably, no matter how many preparations we make; no matter how much seed we sow the end results may neither be pleasing to us, nor God, which may or may not be due to free moral agency. When this occurs the very best thing we can do is to pray, asking God where we may have erred. We might even review our chosen counseling model in order to see if maybe a different technique could have resulted in a changed outcome. One thing that we must not become involved in is self-defeating, self-destructive condemnation; both of these issues will tear down and render us useless and ineffective to everyone, including anyone else we are trying to help.

There will be times when we simply have to declare that *the secret things belong unto the Lord our God...* (Deuteronomy 29:29a). This verse is not only critical for us as ministers and Christian counselors to grasp and live by; it is also important for us to use during any counseling setting where the counselee is, whether intentional or unintentional, attempting to absolve personal responsibility for their own actions or resolve something that is simply beyond our finite abilities. While we need to be on guard against using this verse as a "catch all" we should also be aware that, by not employing the use of this verse we can end up allowing the entire session to spin off course and out of control, ultimately ending the session without any progress being made.

Every counselor should familiarize himself with this verse to fortify himself against all counselee attempts to spin counseling sessions off into the realms of speculation that are forbidden by 1 Timothy 6:4,5,20,21 and Colossians 2:8... Frequently...this

---

[182] Finis Jennings Dake (God's Plan For Man; Lawrenceville, Georgia; Dake Publishing; 1977); Page 613.

arises from a desire to divert attention from sins in their lives that they would rather avoid. Others are involved in unrestrained sinful curiosity of the sort that led to the first sin in the Garden. Human sinfulness manifests itself in a desire to be like God, knowing all things. It refuses to acknowledge and adopt God's limitations as the standard for human thought and life.[183]

One final word of caution is due concerning this topic: while there are true divine mysteries which God has not yet revealed to mankind and we must honor His will concerning these areas, we should never allow this to become a reason for laziness or procrastination. We need to be willing to seek after, study out, and search for the deep things of God. Then, once found we can rest assured that *...those things which are revealed belong to us and to our children for ever, that we may do all the words of* (God's) *Law* (Deuteronomy 29:29b).

The Use of Scripture in Counseling

I recently had a conversation with one of my past counselees, a believer, that at the time had issues far beyond my abilities so I transferred her counseling sessions to a pastor friend whom I knew would be able to provide her with the proper counsel and direction, but I digress. During this conversation we talked of her outstanding progress (which caused me great joy) and several other things. However, when the subject of using scripture during the counseling sessions arose she said something along these lines, "oh, I've been told that scripture verses cannot be used during counseling - it's illegal."

I immediately said that it was not illegal and that scripture not only could, but should be used in counseling. I informed her that there was one factor that should be dealt with in the pre-counseling interview, which is to tell the potential client that we are in a Christian counseling setting, that we use a Christian counseling model, and that as such we will use the Bible: and, in so doing, we will be teaching Scriptural precepts and commands with an expectation of their (the counselee's) conformity. Finally, after making these things clear from the outset, obtaining a firm commitment from the client that: 1) They understand; and 2) They are willing to proceed. This commitment should be made in the form of a written agreement for

---

[183] Jay E. Adams (A Theology of Christian Counseling; Grand Rapids, Michigan; Zondervan; 1979); Page 54.

the protection of all parties involved. This and other issues pertaining to documentation will be further addressed in chapter ten.

Even though the reasons for using scripture in counseling should be apparent to us a ministers and Christian counselors let's simply touch on a couple to help solidify our rationale.

First, the entire creation was brought into existence by the operation of the Word of God and the Spirit. When God said...the Spirit went into action; and God has told us that His Word will not return void, but it shall accomplish what God pleases, that it will prosper in the thing for which He sent it to do. (cf. Isaiah 55:11) So, if we will use His Word it will not return void: it will be effective; the Word of God will succeed in doing and bringing to pass God's desired results - that is, if we will acknowledge, profess, and believe that it is true.

Secondly, for true Christian counseling models to be properly and effectively employed the counselee must be a believer; and the only legitimate way for this to occur is for the Holy Spirit to bear witness to the Word of God. Man cannot be born from above by any other means. The Bible actually declares that, *of His own will God chose to give birth to us with the Word of* truth. (James 1:18) This "Word of truth" is the seed, which has been planted in prepared soil that the Holy Spirit uses to draw men unto God's loving grace and mercy.

It is the written Word of God, used in everyday life as well as during counseling sessions that *...has the power to bring a person to faith in Christ and* (the) *power to mold him into the sort of person that God wants him to become. That is the power for which the world (and its counselors) is looking, but has not found. Counselors have sought a system with power to transform human lives, but have failed... Such power is found in one place only - in God's Word that not only brought order and meaning out of chaos on that creative morn, but which alone can give order and meaning to the chaos...* (of life).[184]

Satan's goal has consistently been to discredit God and His Word to all of mankind; regrettably, even some ministers and Christian counselors have been bewitched into believing that we should not obey the truth. For those individuals I must echo Paul's words: *How foolish can you be? After*

---

[184] Jay E. Adams (A Theology of Christian Counseling; Grand Rapids, Michigan; Zondervan; 1979); Page 34.

starting your new lives in the Spirit, why are you now trying to become perfect by your own human effort? (Galatians 3:3) We must never allow ourselves to be drawn off course by new models or methods that discount, in any way, the Word of God or its use during the counseling session. Even in this post-modern, litigious society wherein we live and operate, if we will be open and forthright with potential counselees, getting written approval from the beginning, we can and should always involve God's Word and subsequent life changing power in all sessions, without any fear of retribution.

Christian Counseling and the Unsaved

The use of Scripture in the counseling setting invariably leads to the next area under consideration: can true Christian counseling methods be used if the counselee is not a believer; i.e. saved?

While many will disagree with us on this specific topic, if they would be honest, their disagreement would be more in theory than in actual day-to-day operations. We need to reiterate what we have already stated: in a very real way we must be willing to express the unconditional love of Christ to both the saved and the unsaved. Additionally, as we have also stated, "people don't care how much you know until they know how much you care." Because of these two reasons alone we are compelled to answer our query with a resounding: "Yes, Christian Counseling methods can be used even if the counselee is not a believer."

However, the effectiveness of the techniques or methods and the explosive (dunamis) power of God will be gravely limited until the counselee can be properly evangelized and truly receives, by faith (at the heart level and not merely via mental assent) the free gift of salvation.

Evangelism In Counseling

The fact that God's provisional ability to help a counselee change is but one reason why evangelism in the Christian counseling setting is so crucial to success. *Any such counseling that claims to be Christian surely must be evangelistic. Counseling is redemptive. What God has done for sinful man in Christ, conditions what the counselor does. Counseling should follow and reflect God's order in redemption: grace, then faith; gospel, then sanctification. Counseling must be redemptive.*[185]

---

[185] Jay E. Adams (Competent To Counsel; Grand Rapids, Michigan; Zondervan; 1970); Page 67.

Recall, if you will, that redemption involves being released from captivity because the ransom has been paid. Well, if Christ has paid the ransom for all of mankind's sin why are so many still being held in captivity? The answer to this question could take us into a depth of study wherein we could take up a lifetime attempting to answer; only to find that, at the end of our life, we had merely skimmed the surface. However, in a very generalized way, we can say that people are still being held captive out of ignorance, rebellion (to God's Word), or by personal desire: the last two are extremely similar in many ways.

Rebellion and desire implies that the counselee has heard the Gospel and, for any number of reasons, did not receive or respond to God's plan for salvation: this will require a continual sowing of the Word; for one plants, another waters, but it is God who gives the increase (cf. 1 Corinthians 3:6-7). Then we have those who are simply ignorant or untaught about what Christ has already done for them. Regrettably these individuals are rarely "blank slates;" most of them have been taught some things about Christianity, which usually requires a time of clarification or debunking heretical teachings while explaining the Scriptural truths as they exist in God's Holy Word. In either case evangelism is a precursor to the conversion necessary for Christian counseling methods to be effective. *The word converted...means to twist; that is turn around, reverse, turn again, turn one's self about and go in the opposite direction... The true meaning of conversion as applied to men is that of turning from a life of sin to a life of holiness, living a life which is directly opposite to the one lived before conversion (2 Cor. 5:17). Paul expressed conversion thus: "to open their eyes, so they may turn from darkness to light and from the power of Satan to God. Then they will receive forgiveness for their sins and be given a place among God's people, who are set apart by faith in me." (Acts 26:18). It is turning away from sin and all evil to a life of conformity to God and His holiness.*[186]

Another reason evangelism is critical to Christian counseling begins all the way back at the Garden, when Adam and Eve sinned. Immediately upon partaking of the fruit from the tree of knowledge of good and evil they became aware of their sin and ran from God's presence. Both Adam and Eve hid from their loving Creator; the same thing still happens today. Just like God had to coax them out from their hiding spot He (not us) has

---

[186] Finis Jennings Dake (God's Plan For Man; Lawrenceville, Georgia; Dake Publishing; 1977); Page 615.

to persuade unbelievers to come out of their hiding places today; evangelism is the plan He has established as a means of doing this and He expects all believers everywhere to actively be involved in it. As ministers and "Christian" counselors we have no right or freedom to do otherwise.

The Bible says, *two people will not walk together unless they have agreed to do so*. (Amos 3:3) This applies on both the vertical (God-to-man) and the horizontal (man-to-man) planes: anytime a relationship is severed there must be restoration if the two ever hope to walk side-by-side again.

Christian counseling is redemptive in nature so it must be redemptive in operation. For this reason there are no secular models that have the requisite power to restore man-to-God or, for that matter the restoration of man-to-man according to God's original strategy. Not only do they fail to meet the Creator's requirements for restoration, they also fail to supply the necessary motivation and power to pursue true reconciliation. True harmony on both the vertical and horizontal planes can only be found among those who have been converted and made free by the redeeming power of Christ Jesus: commonly referred to as the "new birth."

As explained by Finis Dake, *the new birth is a new creation from above, the direct operation of the Word of God and the Spirit of God upon your life, changing you completely when you truly repent and turn to God. This is brought about in the following manner: first, recognize that you are a sinner and lost, without God and without hope; second, admit that Jesus Christ died on the cross to save you from sin by His own precious blood; third, come to God repenting of your sins and turning away from all sin, pleading the merits of the blood of Christ in the name of Jesus Christ, and you shall be born again; that is, the Holy Spirit will then definitely make you a new creature, cleansing you from all sin by the authority of the Word of God and by the blood of Christ that was shed to atone for your sins; and fourth, you must believe from the heart when you confess with the mouth that God does forgive you of your sins and that He does cleanse you from all unrighteousness.*[187]

Immediately upon completion of these four steps an individual is provided with the power needed for building true relationships, which should be the impetus for hope. Hope for both counselor and counselee; because it is based on God: His unfailing promises; His instructions and the

---

[187] Finis Jennings Dake (God's Plan For Man; Lawrenceville, Georgia; Dake Publishing; 1977); Page 71.

empowerment to achieve them; and His never diminishing desire to see us succeed.

Salvation Is Crucial

Success is why salvation is so essential to the Christian counseling process. *Against all positions that deny either the possibility of significant change (stemming from deterministic views of genetic, social, or environmental influences) or that hold out change as a possibility only after long periods of time, the Christian cheerfully asserts the possibility of thorough, rapid change. This is a very crucial plank in the Christian counselor's platform. As a basic assumption, he presupposes the possibility of radical change in the personality and life style of the counselee. He believes in conversion and in the sanctifying power of the Spirit. He believes that it is possible for one, who, because of his sinful nature, developed sinful living patterns and was taught wrongly by both precept and example from early days, to become a vital Christian possessing the fruit of the Spirit.*[188]

The minister of God and the true Christian counselor has the ability to call upon God and invoke the power of the Holy Spirit via the Word, in the almighty name of Jesus Christ; this along with the fact that we have available to us the supernatural wisdom of God, ought to bring great reassurance to all involved. In fact, Peter informs all believers that God has provided all things that pertain to life and godliness through the knowledge of Him that has called us. (cf. 2 Peter 1:3) The realization of this provision can only be accomplished by and through faith in God, His abilities, and His willingness to do what He said He will do. This kind of faith can never be bought or conjured up by an unbeliever, it is only accessible to a believer as part of God's provision.

Furthermore, as ministers and Christian counselors, we not only need to believe what the Bible reveals when it says that *whatever is not of faith is sin* (Romans 14:23b), we must also help our counselees to accept it. For example, multitudes of studies have proven the affects of attitudes on one's ability to heal. Whether the needed healing is physical, psychological, or spiritual, an attitude of expectation is vital. Faith does this: faith develops an assurance within the believer.

Then, assurance or faith exchanges uncertainty for certainty;

---

[188] Jay E. Adams (The Christian Counselor's Manual; Grand Rapids, Michigan; Zondervan; 1973); Pages 28-29.

instability for stability; failure for victory; doubt for more faith, etc. All of this newfound expectation pleases God and moves Him to action, for it is faith that pleases our loving Creator. (cf. Hebrews 11:6) We are not talking about acting religious or playing make-believe simply to please someone. Our desire must be to see change in the life of the individual we are counseling; change that is possible with God because He says it is so.

Since God has established the means, He also has the right to set the order and techniques, and He has. In like manner as the provision of redemption and restoration are conditional, so are God's blessings. For example, part of God's provision is complete power over Satan. However, *the success of the conflict depends so much upon the ground upon which it is fought. If the devil can cause the Christian to forsake the "high tower" of the name of Jesus and to do battle in his own strength, that arch-enemy of righteousness is sure to win a victory; for if he can even cause a doubt in the midst of the fray, he knows he has the upper hand. But let the same Christian insist that his life is "hid away with Christ in God," and steadfastly refuse to meet the tempter apart from his relationship to the Mighty Conqueror, and the devil will be a defeated foe. There is a conflict of faith, wherein the Christian must boldly claim his position in Christ* and refuse to take a backward step when the enemy assails.[189]

It does not matter what problem has surfaced - **in Christ** we have the victory, apart from Christ the very best we can do is to put a bandaid over it in hopes to calm things down, even if it is only a temporary patch. In Christ we can and should expect radical change, apart from Christ we have no assurances, no guarantees, and no way of instilling the crucial element that is an absolute must for all true victories in life - hope.

In a letter to the Corinthian believers Paul says that, *if Christ has not been raised... your faith is worth nothing* (1 Corinthians 15:14); but Christ did arise; He was raised to life and now sits at the right hand of our Heavenly Father as the Mediator over the New Covenant and our Advocate forever enforcing His will for all who will come to Him in faith; a faith that assures the born again counselee that he has all the necessary power he needs for life and service.

When the power to resist and overcome temptation is

---

[189] Guy P. Duffield and Nathaniel M. Van Cleave (Foundations of Pentecostal Theology; Los Angeles, California; L.I.F.E. Bible College; 1987); Page 253.

experientially realized the bondage of sinful desires and habits will be destroyed and, for the first time, the counselee will be free to personally receive as well as freely express the pure and unconditional love of God, which covers a multitude of sins and ultimately restores broken relationships, both vertically and horizontally. This restoration will then be the motivation that ignites the reparative changes needed in the counselee's life.

Evidences of the New Birth

One aspect of mankind's fallen nature is that, at times we will erect facades by acting like we are something that we honestly, aren't. Unfortunately, this holds true in the Christian counseling setting as well. For this reason there are a few areas that we, as ministers and Christian counselors, can and should monitor in order to honestly evaluate the counselee's confession of salvation.

Now, wait a minute! The Bible says that we are not supposed to judge; now you are saying that we should. Yes, absolutely. While the "judge not" mentality has permeated every cranny and crevice of our world, proper biblical exegesis dictates that we realize it pertains to judging the person's actions; it does not involve condemnation of the individual, but the individual's actions.

Throughout the New Testament, believers are told in one form or another to avoid certain people; these people were always individual's who acted in certain ways or did specific things. Simply put, this meant that the early believers were required to, not judge the person, but the fruit that person was producing. Even Jesus said that you will *know them by their fruit*, (cf. Matthew 7:15-20) which clearly necessitates the act of judging.

Let's stop allowing the god of this world to establish our beliefs, like he did with Adam and Eve, and start standing up to him in the power and wisdom of Christ that now resides in every true believer. We must take back control over our own thoughts; bringing them into subjection to the properly interpreted Word of God. Let's take our God-given authority and *use God's mighty weapons...to knock down the strongholds of human reasoning and to destroy false arguments, capturing all rebellious thoughts and teaching them to obey Christ.* (2 Corinthians 10:4-5)

When we do these things it will become much easier for us as ministers and Christian counselors to lead counselees out of the pits of despair and despondency. Even the crucial "confrontation in love" aspect of counseling that has been missing for far too long will be restored. We must be determined to believe and adhere to all of the Word of God - every book; every chapter; and every verse - or none of it. Either it is all inspired by God or none of it is; let's stop playing god ourselves by trying to decide which parts we will accept as God's truth and which parts we will not.

After expounding with such intensity as to why we should judge fruit, we must also consistently remain cognizant of the fact that an external demonstration of change in a counselee's words or actions does not always equate to true repentance, (i.e. a change of heart, internally). Any legitimate change will have long-lasting and wide-ranging effects. *Billy Sunday used to say, "Religion is not something for your handkerchief but for your backbone." There must be the exercise of the will for repentance to be truly effective. This means an inward turning from sin and a whole-hearted turning to Christ for forgiveness.*[190]

The *inward turning from sin and a whole-hearted turning to Christ for forgiveness* will ultimately produce certain fruit that is common in all who truly make the transition:

1.   The redeemed soul will have freedom from condemnation; from the law of sin and death; and will live and walk in the Spirit (Romans 8:1-13).

2.   Their character traits and attitudes will be reformed and transformed into what the Bible calls the "fruit of the Spirit" (Galatians 5:22-23).

3.   As a result of this reformation and transformation, if one refuses to allow the cares of life to choke it out, the individual will build up others and bear even more fruit (Matthew 7:16-20).

4.   Finally, there will be a desire to quickly repent and ask forgiveness for all unrighteousness when it is realized (1 John 1:7-9).

Arthur W. Pink has well said: "Let us realize that the sinner is not ignorant, needing instruction; he is not weak and in need of invigoration; he is not sick and in need

---

[190] Guy P. Duffield and Nathaniel M. Van Cleave (Foundations of Pentecostal Theology; Los Angeles, California; L.I.F.E. Bible College; 1987); Page 211.

of doctoring. He is dead and needs to be made alive."[191] God has provided for this birthing (or re-birthing) of life to all who will receive it by faith. In His wisdom, God has left the decision to do so up to each individual: if one chooses to ignore or downright refuses to accept the Creator's plan it is neither God's fault nor ours. Once we, as ministers and Christian counselors, present God's plan of salvation to the counselee, the choice is completely and totally theirs.

However, when a counselee believes in their heart that they have been saved, that they have been translated from darkness into the light, there will be corresponding desires to give up worldly things for Christ and wholeheartedly do what is right. And yet, *maintaining our salvation is not a neat balancing act that we must perform as we endeavor to walk a narrow path with a deep chasm on either side. There is a chasm, to be sure; but by faith, obedience, and faithful communion with our Lord we are privileged to walk farther and farther from it as we make our way up the headlands toward the city of God.*[192]

The process of making "our way" is akin to *walking out our own salvation with holy fear and trembling* (Philippians 2:12), which involves sanctification and holiness; the subject of our next chapter.

---

[191] Guy P. Duffield and Nathaniel M. Van Cleave (Foundations of Pentecostal Theology; Los Angeles, California; L.I.F.E. Bible College; 1987); Page 232.
[192] Guy P. Duffield and Nathaniel M. Van Cleave (Foundations of Pentecostal Theology; Los Angeles, California; L.I.F.E. Bible College; 1987); Page 259

Chapter 9 : Counseling's Connection to Sanctification and Holiness

As it is with multiple areas of the Christian's life, sanctification and holiness are akin to a set of tracks that run parallel to one another. Probably one of the most striking things that pertain to these two elements in a believer's life is that, like railroad tracks, if you "lose" one or the other, life will fly off course just like a train attempting to run on one track.

The Bible is the most important "tool" that God has given to keep us running smoothly along as we strive to fulfill His will; not only in the act of salvation (i.e. redemption, justification, regeneration, and adoption) but also in living life here in this world on a day-to-day basis. As ministers and Christian counselors we must forever settle in our hearts and minds that the Bible is the infallible rule of both faith and life. We must come to the conclusion that the Holy Writ of God is *theopnuestos* (God-breathed); that it is fully inspired; that it is without error; and that every word of it, not only those parts we agree with, but also those parts we aren't yet sure that we agree with. We cannot hold any part of in reserve - we believe all of the Word; if we do not, even the parts that we choose to rely on become suspect. This is a reality for every human being that has ever lived - God is the "Great I Am" or He is not; as ministers and Christian counselors, we must choose the former.

Thankfully, for us, that same "Great I Am" does not demand us to have this level of faith from the very instant we accept His free gift of salvation. He does however, expect us to grow into that degree of understanding and faith. To begin the process He provides all new believers with *the measure of faith* (Romans 12:3) and then calls on us to nurture and feed it, causing it to grow and become strong. The Hebrew believers' failure to follow this plan brought about a fairly severe chastening when the author wrote, *for in the time when you should be teachers yourselves, you have need to be taught again the foundational principles of God* (Hebrews 5:12).

God alone has made salvation possible; He is the sole-source of the

Christian's desire to live in a personal and active relationship with Him in Christ. Salvation is totally by His grace - individual intellect, abilities, and wisdom do not gain anyone special favor, only pure and simple faith will do the job: there is nothing we can do to earn what Jesus has already done for us (see chapter 8). Fortunately, at the time salvation occurs there are many other things that happen instantaneously; in the twinkling of an eye. Then, there are other things or areas that transpire on a more gradual basis. Some are sovereign acts of God and God alone, while others employ a reasonable amount of participation by the believer. Sanctification and, by extension, holiness (remember our analogy of the tracks) fall under both categories: they are a sovereign act of God, which also involves individual participation and action.

Prior to proceeding let's take some precautionary measures in hopes that we may avoid any unnecessary confusion, by clearly laying out working definitions of what sanctification and holiness are, biblically speaking. Far too much time is spent in our society trying to make amends because words have such a large variety of meanings, consequently causing unfortunate misunderstandings. And, as if the multiple definition issues weren't enough, ours is a growing and changing language wherein a word, by common usage, continually takes on new connotations - some of which are the exact opposite of our intended use. These are just a few reasons why we need to be on the same page in our understanding of precisely what is being meant when we are discussing a specific topic.

Definitions

Holiness (Holy)

In our modern dictionary we read something along these lines for holiness: the state or quality of being holy. Well, that doesn't really tell us a whole lot so let's look at the word "Holy", which (for our purposes) has three different meanings:

- *Living according to a strict or highly moral religious or spiritual system; saintly: a holy man.*

- *Specified or set apart for a religious purpose.*

- *Regarded or deserving special respect or reverence.[193]*

The final definition will only be realized if we fulfill God's requirements of the first two. Biblically speaking, holiness is fundamentally a separation from what is profane and unclean; to a consecration and dedication in regard to what is pure and undefiled.

In the Vine's dictionary we read that it *denotes the manifestation of the quality of holiness in personal conduct... Believers are to be "perfecting holiness in the fear of God"... Bringing holiness to its predestined end... growing toward perfection in the case of the Christian... Fundamentally...in its moral and spiritual significance,* (it means) *separated from sin and therefore consecrated to God.[194]* There are several pages in Vine's dictionary dedicated to this very word however, this brief snippet more than suffices for our current objective.

In short, holiness signifies a godliness that reveals an internal condition free of moral fault along with a connectedness to the moral perfection of God Himself. To be holy means that one is special and unique, but not in a boastful way or else the holy connection to moral perfection would be lost (even if only temporarily) resulting in the uniqueness becoming marred. Holiness means that one is wholly devoted to God; that he has been and continues to be separated from the world's way of living while being committed to righteousness. Holiness is the absence of sin and wrongdoing and yet, it is much, much more: it also includes the presence of righteousness, purity, and godliness within a person's heart - deep down inside. Holiness includes both internal and external elements.

Sanctification

Sanctification, while being much more than pure holiness, includes holiness. In fact, if all references pertaining to the subject of sanctification, sanctity, holy, pure, clean, etc. in the Bible were added together we would find thousands upon thousands of references pertaining to this subject matter. Clearly it is easy to see that being sanctified is important to our Creator.

---

[193] Philip Babcock Gove (Editor in Chief) (Webster's Third New International Dictionary of the English Language: Unabridged; Springfield, Massachusetts; Merriam-Webster Inc., Publishers; 1993); Page 1081.
[194] W.E. Vine (Vine's Expository Dictionary of Old and New Testament Words; Nashville, Tennessee; Thomas Nelson Publishers; 1997); Pages 555-557.

Just as holy and holiness has a dual meaning sanctification also has a two-part definition. *The Hebrew and Greek words for sanctification mean to make or pronounce clean or holy, morally, physically, and ceremonially; to consecrate, dedicate, hallow; to purify; to set apart from a profane or secular use to a sacred or holy use; to separate from carnal and natural to spiritual purposes; and to venerate or reverence. 1) Separation* **from** *an evil, profane, or secular purpose* **to** *a sacred purpose; to make or to be holy, reverend, sacred, separated, pure, hallowed; to prepare for spiritual and sacred use; to cleanse* **from** *sin and uncleanness and to make free* **from** *manifestations and uses of the natural and carnal life; to make holy anything consecrated to God; the state of being holy and consecrated to God; and the devotion of a person or thing to a particular spiritual exercise and use. 2) Separation, dedication or consecration* **unto God** *this includes any person or material thing that can be given entirely over to God for sacred and spiritual use, anything set apart for service* **unto** *God. Thus, the two-fold meaning of sanctification in one statement is* **any person or thing separated from a profane or secular use, and consecrated unto God to be used wholly for divine and spiritual use, whether sin is involved or not.**[195]

In order for us to have an easy to understand, working definition let's summarize what is said above concerning the two-fold definition of sanctification: the first part equates to the dedication and consecration of some person or thing, setting it aside for a specified and holy purpose: this is commonly referred to as the initial act or positional placement of an object or person into God's service. The second part involves a cleansing and purging of any moral impurities: this part of sanctification is a process that is often called progressive or practical sanctification.

For our purposes we will refer to the former as "Positional Sanctification/ Holiness" and the latter as "Practical Sanctification/Holiness. Additionally, there is a third part of sanctification that we will call "Future Sanctification," which has also been referred to as "complete" sanctification. While we will briefly deal with future sanctification, as ministers and Christian counselors it is important for us to be able to explain to our counselees that, if they have taken care of the positional and practical aspects of sanctification and holiness the final, or future aspect will take care of itself. For now let's turn our attention to the

---

[195] Finis Jennings Dake (God's Plan For Man; Lawrenceville, Georgia; Dake Publishing; 1977); Pages 626-627, emphasis added.

instrument and methods by which sanctification and holiness can be both obtained (positionally) and attained (practically).

A Means To An End

Since the initial act of sanctification is solely the work of our Divine Creator we must understand that He sets the rules and these rules must be followed. There are no shortcuts; no backdoors; no other points of entry. Jesus is the Way, the Truth, and the Life (John 14:6). God has established that there is no other way to the Father than through Jesus - the Only Begotten Son.

All of humanity, by virtue of Adam's fall, are unable to please God. In one sense this is an extremely disheartening reality; yet, all is not lost. God prepared a way - a plan of action - and a method wherein sanctification and holiness can be initiated and followed through to the ultimate completion. This plan involves becoming a disciple of Jesus Christ: salvation and the subsequent supernatural replacement of an old stoney heart with a heart of flesh is the only way to truly be set aside as God's.

For all of our theologian friends (of which I am one) let's not allow division to start here. We do understand that morality is not an issue for sanctification; specific objects as well as individual's have been set apart and consecrated unto God's purposes without ever being born from above. However, as we dispense counsel one of our objectives is to bring them into a place of moral purity in order to see a supernatural transformation now; with an eventual future completion of God's work resulting in eternity in heaven: this should not be debatable.

Since our goal here is to simply introduce appropriate methods and effective measures in the Christian counseling process, at this point, we need to be careful not to infuse confusion pertaining to our subject. We must be able to lay foundational type stones that are correctly placed while at the same time avoiding any distractions to our intended goals.

Now, back to God's plan for replacing a heart of stone with one of flesh. Given the adverse condition of man from birth, what would cause a person to want to turn from their way of life to God's way? Why would anyone opt for a lifestyle in complete conflict with theirs? Well, innate within the heart of every person, there is a void that can only be filled with God's loving kindness. Unbelievers will attempt to fill this emptiness, with every kind of decadence and debauchery attempting to find peace. Eventually, when they hear the Gospel along with the wooing of the Holy Spirit the proverbial scales fall from their eyes and illumination occurs. This is the point where each person that has ever lived will have a choice to make: either accept Jesus, or deny Him.

God sent Jesus into this world where He prayed to the Father that His disciples would be sanctified by the Word, which is truth (John 17:17). When Jesus went to the Cross; died as a propitiation for our sin; was raised from the dead; and exalted to the right hand of the Father in heaven, He set in motion the only way to be positionally sanctified. He then sent the Spirit of Holiness, who we (after salvation) work in unison with toward change. This change provides each believer with the ability to attain a greater level of holiness (i.e. progressive sanctification). Subsequently, as we continue to respond to the Holy Spirit's promptings He produces more and more holiness within us.

In answering the query "How is sanctification effected?" Jay E. Adams writes, *despite views that teach otherwise, the Bible sets forth sanctification as a process (not an act) in which three forces, the Spirit, His Word, and the regenerated saint, all work together to bring about change. It is vital to understand this essential fact and to keep all three of these forces in a harmonious and complimentary relationship.*[196] To which we should be in complete agreement with following the initial act of God, through Jesus wherein the unbeliever, by faith receives their positional or initial sanctification at the time of salvation. Everything that follows involves a harmonious relationship between the believer, the Word, and the Holy Spirit.

Now that we have established a way to an end let's spend a short amount of time discussing God's holiness, the Spirit of Holiness, and the motivation to be holy, prior to addressing the three stages of sanctification in more depth.

---

[196] Jay E. Adams (Growing By Grace; Stanley, North Carolina; Timeless Texts; 2003); Page 24.

God's Holiness

When God says, *be holy for I am holy* (1 Peter 1:16) it is much more than a request for us to be "good" people according to the world's standards; which, in reality are not a standard in any true sense: because what the world declares to be "good" changes with the will of the majority at any given time. The Word tells us that God changes not so He must be the One that establishes our standard for holiness. Since He is our immutable example it would behoove us to take a brief look at Him and His standard of holiness.

When the Bible refers to the holiness of our Triune God (Father, Son and Spirit) it speaks of every aspect of His greatness; His moral perfection; and every other aspect of His attributes. God will never do any thing that falls short of absolute perfection. God; everything He is and everything He does is holy: at every point His character and purity should reassure us and give us confidence to trust Him and take Him at His Word.

When Paul told the Ephesian believers to mimic (imitate) their Heavenly Father as dear children, (Ephesians 5:1) he was calling upon all believers to continually practice a lifestyle of holiness that would ultimately attract an unbeliever's attention and esteem. He places a demand upon us to become like Him. And yet, in all His understanding and wisdom, God did not leave us alone in our struggle to fulfill His command to be holy; this is, at least part of why He has given us His Holy Spirit, or the Spirit of Holiness.

The Spirit of Holiness

*The Good News is about God's Son, Jesus Christ our Lord. As a man, he was born from the family of David. But through the **Spirit of holiness** he was declared to be God's Son with great power by rising from the dead.* (Romans 1:3-4, emphasis added) The New Living Translation says, *He was shown to be the Son of God when he was raised from the dead by the power of the **Holy Spirit**. He is Jesus Christ our Lord* (emphasis added).

The Holy Spirit's designation in the Bible clearly differentiates Him from all other spirits - He is the One sent by Jesus to guide and assist any desirous believer into all holiness. The Greek word is *Paraklesis: a calling alongside to help, to comfort, to give consolation or encouragement. The paraklete is a strengthening presence, one who upholds those appealing for assistance...*[197] This simply means that the Holy Spirit is called alongside to give support. By offering us His support the Spirit of Holiness helps us to develop fruit that the Bible declares brings about perfection. In fact, the Apostle Paul affirmed that when the fruit of the Spirit are fully operating in a believer's life, there is no law that can pronounce judgement against that person. (Galatians 5:22-23)

The holiness of God's people that results from their sanctification by the Holy Spirit must be attributed entirely to Him as He works through His Word. The "fruit" of the Spirit is just that: it is the result of His work.[198] We will refer back to this statement again when we discuss the role of the counselor in the sanctification process. For now let's proceed to the motivation for us to be holy.

Motivation To Be Holy

There are any number of motives that have been enumerated throughout the centuries as to why a believer should desire to live a holy life before God. Some of the more common ones include:

- A desire to please God and express our love for Him.

- An individual's need for maintaining a clear conscience.

- A desire to be used by God in bringing others to Christ.

- Having a desire to receive the covenant blessings of God that are based on obedience.

- A desire to avoid displeasing God.

- A desire to develop a deeper relationship with God as the loving Father.

- A simple wish to do what is right.

While this list is extremely abbreviated, as ministers and Christian

---

[197] Jack W. Hayford (General Editor) (Spirit Filled Life Bible: New King James Version; Nashville, Tennessee; Thomas Nelson Publishers; 1991); Word Wealth, Page 1643.
[198] Jay E. Adams (The Christian Counselor's Manual; Grand Rapids, Michigan; Zondervan; 1973); Page 6.

counselors, we must also realize that many will have a desire to change, but lack the ability to follow through. I have often said that people will figure out a way to do whatever they truly **want** to do. For this reason I personally pray and tell others to pray, asking that God would "make my want to, as big as my desire to." This sounds like a play on words when, in truth it is simply asking the Holy Spirit for help.

Basic to the New Testament concept of motivation is the task of becoming what you are... The Christian life is not static; it is a life of change. The Christian is a pilgrim and a stranger who is on the move. He is traveling to the heavenly city. He has not yet arrived. Change is of the essence to his sanctification... But change is difficult... All change is hard, and there must be powerful motivation to achieve it. Since change comes only gradually and through patient endurance there must be hope... The high calling of the Christian, conferred upon him in Christ by which he is to reckon himself dead to sin but alive to God, is itself a powerful motivation to holy living.[199]

Having a desire to live a holy life before God simply is not enough to do what God commands. The flesh will always be at odds with the Spirit so we must help counselees walk through the development of new patterns of thinking and acting or we will fall back into our old ways of living. Our job in a nutshell is to help the counselee to rethink, causing them to react in a different manner than before. As we renew our minds to the ways of the Lord and replace old ungodly habits with new godly ones we will experience a peace and joy that compels us to continue down the path of sanctification and holiness. Our continued persistence in our progression along this path will result in our growth in conformity to the image of Christ, which should be our hope.

The Process of Sanctification and Holiness

Now that we have, rather superficially, dealt with God's holiness; the Spirit's holiness; and the motivation for a believer's holiness, let's turn our attention to the three stage process of sanctification that we alluded to previously: the positional, practical, and future stages of sanctification and holiness.

---

[199] Jay E. Adams (The Christian Counselor's Manual; Grand Rapids, Michigan; Zondervan; 1973); Pages 161-162.

Positional Sanctification and Holiness

In the New Testament we often see the church being characterized as holy because Jesus cleansed her by the washing of water with the Word (Ephesians 5:26). This "holy" status is one that, as a whole, will not be changed because it is a positional state wherein the conditions are based upon Christ's actions and His holiness. *Jesus was already Perfect... He was specially set apart for the purpose of coming into the world to provide Redemption for mankind. The popular Greek word for "church" is* **ekklesia** *which means "the called out ones." Each member of the Church is especially set apart to bring glory to God. He is sanctified unto Him in this initial* (positional) *sense of the word.*[200]

Additionally, one does not need to read the Bible for very long before they hear of individual's being called saints; or holy in God's sight. Someone once said that when God looks at the believer He sees the blood of Christ and not the sin of the person. Whether one agrees with this statement doctrinally or not is not the point here: positionally speaking, we are sanctified, made holy, and we, as believers, are seated with Christ in heavenly places (Ephesians 2:6).

When an individual, by faith, receives God's free gift of salvation his sins as well as his sin nature are done away with and he is placed, by God Himself, in the position of sainthood. Positional sanctification then, is a part of the regenerative process, which means that a person simply cannot receive one without the other.

Because there is a definitive moral change in our lives at the time of regeneration we can and should consider ourselves dead to sin and alive to God through Christ. (Romans 6:11) We should be able to experience a break from the love and power of sin in our lives. Positionally we are no longer ruled by evil desires and dominated by sinful patterns in our lives. Some have even testified of a supernatural cessation of additions such as alcohol abuse, drug use, gambling, and even smoking cigarettes.

As for me personally, I had to walk out (practical sanctification) my victory over tobacco products, but God supernaturally removed repugnant and vulgar language from my vocabulary. As a matter of fact, at the time of

---

[200] Guy P. Duffield and Nathaniel M. Van Cleave (Foundations of Pentecostal Theology; Los Angeles, California; L.I.F.E. Bible College; 1987); Pages 237-238, emphasis added.

my salvation, I had twelve years of combined military and law enforcement. Using forceful, vulgar language in the performance of my duties often worked in deflating potential volatile situations. On the very day of my being born from above (approximately ten hours later) I found myself in one of those very situations except, when I opened my mouth to release a tirade of vulgarity (in law enforcement it used to be called "Verbal Judo") to take psychological control over a potentially combative person it was as if two things happened simultaneously. First, it felt as though someone was holding my vocal cords preventing the words from being released. And secondly, within a second or two I forgot what I wanted to say; it was as though the profane words had vanished into thin air. God had taken control and every adversarial element of the situation immediately dissipated, and calm ensued.

Paul tells us, as believers in Christ, not to yield our members to sin becoming instruments of wickedness, but we are to yield ourselves to God (Romans 6:12-13). This means that, positionally we have been (past tense) made free from the ruling power of sin. By virtue of the Holy Spirit and regeneration we are seated with Christ in heavenly places (Ephesians 2:6) and sin no longer has any dominion over us.

This is the position we find ourselves in immediately upon accepting God's free gift of salvation by faith. However, *we are not contending that sanctification ends at the new birth, but we must be honest with God and His Word and teach that it begins with the new birth. Men will constantly need deeper works of grace in their lives as they conform to truth and walk in the light.*[201]

As we transition to the next stage or phase of sanctification let's declare that initially and immediately upon salvation *we are... completely sanctified in Christ. His whole righteous life is attributed to us - we are circumcised with Christ, risen with Christ, seated in the heavenlies with Christ. But we do not have all this in daily living in this life. That is why sanctification is taking place - to enable us, day by day, to become in actuality more of what we are reckoned to be in Christ. We must become in ourselves (but not by ourselves) what we already are in Christ. This is quite distinct from self-actualization (becoming what you may be in and by yourself); sanctification is becoming in yourself (by the Spirit's work) what you already are counted*

---

[201] Finis Jennings Dake (God's Plan For Man; Lawrenceville, Georgia; Dake Publishing; 1977); Page 630.

to be in Christ.[202]

This "becoming sanctified" is the topic of our next section or the second stage of sanctification, which we have termed "practical sanctification/holiness".

Practical Sanctification and Holiness

John Wesley once wrote, *How naturally do those who experience such a change (referring to the sanctification in the new birth) imagine that all sin is gone; that it is utterly rooted out of the heart... But it is seldom long before they are undeceived; showing that it was but stunned, not dead. They now feel two principles in themselves, plainly contrary to each other; the flesh lusting against the Spirit; nature opposing the grace of God... When we are born again, then our sanctification, our inward and outward holiness,* **begins***; and thenceforward we are gradually to grow up in Him who is our head.*[203]

What Mr. Wesley was referring to is the act of practical sanctification and holy living. Paul said that the sinful nature, the flesh wants to do evil, which is just the opposite of what the Spirit wants. And the Spirit gives us desires that are the opposite of what the sinful nature or flesh desires. These two forces are constantly fighting each other (Galatians 5:17) so, work out your own salvation with fear and trembling (Philippians 2:12). When an unbeliever surrenders their life to God and is positionally sanctified in Christ there still remains the daily decisions to walk in holiness: to, as an act of free moral agency, remain set apart and morally pure as time progresses. This process is what we call practical sanctification and holiness.

Multiple New Testament scriptures refer to practical sanctification and holiness; many of them deal with daily struggles, personal growth, and the continual pursuit of even deeper holiness. For example: the world of the flesh must be replaced with the fruit of the Spirit (cf. Galatians 5:22-23): ungodliness must be exchanged for godliness, unrighteousness for righteousness, etc. As the believer continues to turn from sin to

---

[202] Jay E. Adams (A Theology of Christian Counseling; Grand Rapids, Michigan; Zondervan; 1979); Page 263.
[203] Finis Jennings Dake (God's Plan For Man; Lawrenceville, Georgia; Dake Publishing; 1977); Pages 640-641, emphasis added.

righteousness in practical ways, sanctification and holiness continues to develop.

According to Peter, God has provided all of the natural and spiritual resources necessary for us to share in His divine nature; promises that helps us escape the world's corruption caused by human desires. (2 Peter 1:4) Unfortunately, accessibility to these promises and the commensurate resources are not sufficient if the individual believer never puts them to use. God has established the standards expected for holy living and, through Jesus, He has revealed that, by His grace, it can be attained. All that is required of the believer is to remain committed and dedicated to the process even when family and friends begin to chide and lecture us for "acting different" or "being strange."

What makes us "act" different is having God's qualities appearing in our life and not our becoming "goofy" or "weird." We must come to the conclusion that sin in our life offends God and separates us from Him, even if only temporarily: this is why the sanctified and holy lifestyle must continue throughout our life.

Since we have had the ruling powers of sin broken over our lives positionally, we need to consider ourselves dead to sin. (Romans 6:11) Practically speaking and by the power of the Holy Spirit working within us, we should continually stand against any temptations and enticements to sin until we acquire the overwhelming victory that is promised to all believer's in Christ. Remember, as believers, we can do all things through Christ, because He gives us the necessary strength. (Philippians 4:13) Sin is no longer our master; even though the enemy is very real and persists in attempting to destroy what God has began

*When Paul talks about the new power over sin that is given to Christians, he does not say that there will be no sin in Christians' lives, but simply tells believers not to let sin "reign" in their bodies nor to "yield" their members so sin (Romans 6:12-13). The very fact that he issues these directions shows his realization that sin will continue to be present in the lives of believers throughout their time on earth. Even James the brother of our Lord could say "**we all make many mistakes**" (James 3:2), and if James himself can say this, then we certainly should be willing to say it as well. Finally, in the same letter in which John declares so frequently that a child of God will not continue in a pattern of sinful behavior, he also says clearly, "**If we say we have no sin in us,***

218

we deceive ourselves, and the truth is not in us (1 John 1:8). Here John explicitly excludes the possibility of being completely free from sin in our lives. In fact, he says that anyone who claims to be free from sin is simply deceiving himself, and the truth is not in him... Therefore, although sanctification will never be completed in this life, we must also emphasize that **sanctification should never stop increasing in this life.**[204]

This is why Peter could tell us to "make every effort" to grow in character traits that enhance our sanctification and holy lifestyle. (2 Peter 1:5) But how are we supposed to honestly be able to make *every effort*? Every effort to true morality can only be attained as the believer responds to God's Word from a wholehearted desire to obey God in covenant faithfulness and by taking every opportunity to act according to God's modus operandi even in the midst of an evil world. In essence this means that we should be striving to become more and more "like" God. Each day we should be working hard to lead a life that reflects God; this involves a renewed willingness to do battle each day against evil and our flesh in order to maintain and, by the grace of God, increase in our level of moral purity.

Everything that we do should contribute toward the goal that lies ahead of every believer; that goal should include hearing a "well done" for living a godly life while here on earth from our Heavenly Father. This requires endurance. Regrettably, *one outstanding failure among Christians* (involves) *a lack of what the Bible calls "endurance." Perhaps endurance is the key to godliness through discipline. No one learns to ice skate, to use a yo-yo, to button shorts, or to drive an automobile unless he persists long enough to do so. He learns by enduring in spite of failures. Through the embarrassments, until the desired behavior becomes a part of him. He trains by practice to do what he wants to learn to do. God says the same is true about godliness.*[205]

Practical sanctification and holiness requires effort, concentration, and self-discipline and as believers we must always be ready and willing to resist every temptation. Mercifully, God does not require us to go through it alone. In reality we can't; only by the power of the Holy Spirit and the

---

[204] Wayne Grudem (Bible Doctrine: Essential Teachings of the Christian Faith; Grand Rapids, Michigan; 1999); Page 330.
[205] Jay E. Adams (A Theology of Christian Counseling; Grand Rapids, Michigan; Zondervan; 1979); Page 244.

Word do we have any real hope of standing fast in the face of overwhelming obstacles. We do have a part in possessing our sanctification and holiness on a practical level but the process is a delicate one. Since all holiness comes from God we are to habitually rely of Him for our moral purification. Unfortunately, like Peter, we have a tendency to take our eyes off Jesus when the storms of life approach, which always leaves us in the precarious predicament of sinking. That is, until we realize what is happening, repent, and re-focus our attention on the One who already has been made sanctification for anyone that will believe. (cf. 1 Corinthians 1:30)

While there are an innumerable amount of issues we could discuss concerning this second stage or phase of sanctification and holiness we must keep in mind that our intentions here are simply to make introductions. In view of this fact we will press on now to the third and final stage or phase of the process; which we have dubbed, "Future Sanctification."

Future Sanctification

I once heard someone say that we are saved; we are being saved; and we will be saved. At the time, while I liked the saying, I really did not understand it. However, like many things in life, we have to grow into it, which is exactly what has occurred with me concerning this statement. I have learned that he was speaking of our sanctification: at the time of the new birth we are sanctified positionally, we have been saved from the penalty of sin. Then, practically speaking, we are being saved because we are in a very real sense "working out our own salvation with fear and trembling" because we have been saved from the power of sin. And finally, we will be saved from the presence of sin as we become partakers of the future sanctification or completion of that which God has began.

In writing to the believers at Philippi, Paul declares that our manner of living is in heaven; from which we eagerly await the Lord Jesus Christ who will **transform our vile body** that it may be conformed to and fashioned after His glorious body. (Philippians 3:20-21, emphasis added)

The essence of these verses declare that there is a future sanctification wherein the level of holiness we can attain will be completed:

we will be given a glorious, undefiled body. This future level of sinless perfection will occur at a time of God's choosing and involves a special work of grace. *This refers to the final act and process of being made holy in body, soul, and spirit, and preserved blameless forever. It is plainly evident that no man that has been made holy here is made absolutely and eternally holy by one act. There must be a process of keeping holy until one is made "whole" in body, soul, and spirit at the rapture and the resurrection and entrance into the eternal state.*[206]

It is sufficient to say that our future sanctification relies completely upon the rapture; our being involved in it; and the capable hands of our Creator as to when it occurs; and while there are endless amounts of time we could spend on the future sanctification of all true believers, we will leave that for a separate study. As ministers and Christian counselors attempting to help and encourage others in overcoming the bumps and bruises and battles of everyday living we will maintain our concentration on the present.

Armed with the knowledge we have of positional and practical sanctification and holiness let us turn our attention to how this information can be used in the counseling setting.

The Counselor's Role

In a previous discussion it was mentioned that in order to help others by rendering assistance or aid the one seeking our counsel does not necessarily need to be born again. We may also be reminded that it is important to show people how much we care before they will care how much we know. Both of these precepts, while being true, do not, indeed cannot be maintained at this point in the counseling process. We need to, with complete sincerity and commitment, agree with others who support Nouthetic Counseling Models concerning positional, practical, and future sanctification and it's relationship to counseling. This model asserts that counseling cannot happen until one is born from above, that any work prior to salvation must be considered as evangelism: this stance must be maintained in order to be scripturally accurate because positional sanctification and holiness, which in the very beginning of the process, is

---

[206] Finis Jennings Dake (God's Plan For Man; Lawrenceville, Georgia; Dake Publishing; 1977); Page 627.

only established at the point of transformation. From this point of view counseling cannot begin until salvation of the counselee has been established.

Previously, in this chapter under the subheading "the Spirit of Holiness" we mentioned that we would follow up on the fact that He, the Holy Spirit, works through His Word; which brings about the "fruit of the Spirit" in a believer's life. Well, true Christian counseling models and methods are simply another aspect of how He works through the Word. The Holy Spirit is our Counselor and must never be overlooked or ignored as we attempt to help others process their lives in light of practical sanctification and holiness on a day-to-day basis.

Since sanctification affects our entire being (intellectually, emotionally, physically, spiritually, and even in our decision-making abilities) as ministers and Christian counselors we must be firmly established in who sets the guidelines of what "holy" is and who declared what is proper for true sanctification. In other words, are we allowed to mix and blend into our process any thing that simply sounds good? The answer to this question is a resounding, NO! God has established the guidelines through His Holy Writ, the Bible, which is powerful and useful for all counseling needs.

Regrettably, far too many have not made full use of what God has provided: the reasons are as wide and varied as there are sessions and our purpose here is not to expose, but to bring clarity in hopes of stopping these corrupt and contaminated counseling models from continuing. *Bruce Narramore* (has) *argued that one reason so many believers have been willing to use Christian counselors is because the church "wasn't stemming the tide [by helping people overcome their troubled lives]*. **What was missing in the church was a practical application of our biblical knowledge to life**... *Too many churches...will not admit that Christians need help. It is as if salvation solves every problem, and sanctification is an idea without practical import in church life. Henry Cloud... decried the deification of willpower in many conservative churches, as if Christians can somehow overcome sin and achieve spiritual maturity by merely choosing to do so. He considered this pull-yourself-up-by-the-bootstraps mentality to be essentially a denial of the gospel, a denial of our need for Christ in an ongoing work of redemptive* *sanctification because we are totally unable to accomplish it ourselves.*[207]

Fulfilling the "what was missing in the church" is the ultimate role of the minister and Christian counselor. Ours is not an end in and of itself, but simply a means of helping others find their true selves in Christ and then walking out their own salvation with fear and trembling. If helping others achieve their role in the Body of Christ is our responsibility, then the goal of all Christian counseling must be the renewal of the image of Christ within the counselee's life; not only from an external or works perspective, but internally as well: as a man thinks in his heart, so is he. (Proverbs 23:7) In order to attain that goal we should be both, capable and willing to assist a counselee in the process of changing from sinful patterns of living into the stature of Christ.

One of the most common misunderstandings that counselees need to be taught is that there is a difference between being tempted to sin and committing the sinful act. Jesus was tempted at all points and yet was found to be absolutely pure - holiness was personified in Him. James tells us that no sin has actually occurred until the Word of God is violated. (cf. James 1:13-16) One of the ploys of the devil is to get believers to follow through on the act after he plants the seed of temptation by deceiving them into believing that the thought is just as bad as the act.

Part of the ministers and Christian counselors role is to teach the counselee that this simply is not true. We must however, be leery of becoming overly legalistic in our demands because a new believer may do many things that a more mature believer would not have the freedom to do. Because each person must walk in the light he has received, (i.e. personal revelation) many young believers will not, as of yet, eliminated some of the old habits; even though the old man is dead, each individual must annihilate or destroy the residual habits of that old man. This is why the strong or mature believer is instructed to walk in love bearing the infirmities of the weaker or less mature brother or sister in the Lord. (Romans 15:1) *A new believer must learn to adjust his ways to the new life and learn to conform to spiritual laws of which he has been in ignorance all his life. Some mistakes in learning will be*

[207] Dr. Timothy Clinton and Dr. George Ohlschlager (Competent Christian Counseling Volume One; Colorado Springs, Colorado; Waterbrook Press; 2002); Page 33, emphasis added.

made, but these are not the same as committing the sin that will damn the soul...[208]

Every counselee has the potential of accepting by faith the free gift of salvation. As ministers and Christian counselors we must not only believe this is true but we must work toward this end. Then, once salvation has been accepted and positional sanctification established, it is time to help them walk it out, practically speaking. Every true believer is indwelt by the Holy Spirit who empowers them to comprehend and follow the Word. Because this is true it becomes our role to train and instruct; encourage and challenge; and at times, chasten and discipline according to God's Word and always in love.

The only way to practical sanctification is to become sanctified and the only way to holiness is to be holy both in, intentions and deeds; for this to happen we must reorient our lives toward God's plan. Day after day we must strive for and seek to annihilate any habits or lifestyle patterns that fail to correspond with the Word of God. This striving and seeking will cause us to consciously monitor both our actions and intentions. Paul tells us to examine ourselves to see if we are remaining faithful. (2 Corinthians 13:5) When we teach our counselees the importance of this scriptural command it requires a commitment to self-discipline and personal integrity because any thing found that is contrary to God's plan must be crucified - put to death. Thus, the end result will be a continual process of setting apart oneself unto God through walking, or at least attempting to walk, in a continual condition of purity.

Sanctification, then, is a significant matter. No counselor can safely fail to understand that his counseling is intended to assist counselees in this process of becoming more thoroughly set apart (sanctified). Anything that does not contribute to growth from sinful thought and behavior to righteous thinking and ways of living has no part in counseling. It is wise for counselors to learn about the definitive (positional) *and the progressive* (practical) *aspects of sanctification so as to be able to call upon counselees to approximate in daily living what they are reckoned to be before God.*[209]

In closing our discussion of the counselor's connection to

---

[208] Finis Jennings Dake (God's Plan For Man; Lawrenceville, Georgia; Dake Publishing; 1977); Page 639.
[209] Jay E. Adams (Growing By Grace; Stanley, North Carolina; Timeless Texts; 2003); Page 10.

sanctification and holiness we must say that concentration, effort, and self-discipline are required of every believer. Additionally, we need to understand there is a delicate balance that needs to be maintained between man's responsibilities and God's work. God is the Sanctifier while we are the free moral agents who simply opt to agree with and obey His plans and instructions, and the two must never be switched.

In our next, and final chapter, we will discuss various ancillary issues and a few warnings for every minister and Christian counselor. These areas are necessary for the every day operations environment; they need to be in place for the safety and security of both the session leader and the one seeking assistance.

Chapter 10: Additional Issues in Counseling

The Counselor's Mantle

"And it came to pass, when the LORD was about to take up Elijah into heaven by a whirlwind, that Elijah went with Elisha from Gilgal. Then Elijah said to Elisha, "Stay here, please, for the LORD has sent me on to Bethel." But Elisha said, " As the LORD lives, and as your soul lives, I will not leave you!" So they went down to Bethel. Now the sons of the prophets who were at Bethel came out to Elisha, and said to him, "Do you know that the LORD will take away your master from over you today?" And he said, "Yes, I know; keep silent!" Then Elijah said to him, "Elisha, stay here, please, for the LORD has sent me on to Jericho." But he said, " As the LORD lives, and as your soul lives, I will not leave you!" So they came to Jericho. Now the sons of the prophets who were at Jericho came to Elisha and said to him, "Do you know that the LORD will take away your master from over you today?" So he answered, "Yes, I know; keep silent!" Then Elijah said to him, "Stay here, please, for the LORD has sent me on to the Jordan." But he said, " As the LORD lives, and as your soul lives, I will not leave you!" So the two of them went on. And fifty men of the sons of the prophets went and stood facing them at a distance, while the two of them stood by the Jordan. Now Elijah took his mantle, rolled it up, and struck the water; and it was divided this way and that, so that the two of them crossed over on dry ground. And so it was, when they had crossed over, that Elijah said to Elisha, "Ask! What may I do for you, before I am taken away from you?" Elisha said, "Please let a double portion of your spirit be upon me." So he said, "You have asked a hard thing. Nevertheless, if you see me when I am taken from you, it shall be so for you; but if not, it shall not be so. " Then it happened, as they continued on and talked, that suddenly a chariot of fire appeared with horses of fire, and separated the two of them; and Elijah went up by a whirlwind into heaven. And Elisha saw it, and he cried out, "My father, my father, the chariot of Israel and its horsemen!" So he saw him no more. And he took hold of his own clothes and tore them into two pieces. He also took up the mantle of Elijah that had fallen from him, and went back and stood by the bank of the Jordan. **Then he took the mantle of Elijah that had fallen from him, and struck the water, and said, "Where is the LORD God of Elijah?" And when he also had struck the water, it was divided this way and that; and Elisha crossed over.** *Now when the sons of the prophets who were from Jericho saw him, they said, "The spirit of Elijah rests*

on Elisha." And they came to meet him, and bowed to the ground before him." (2 Kings 2:1-15 NKJV, emphasis added.)

According to Strong's the word *"mantle" is something ample; a garment,* **glory**, *godly, mantle; robe.*[210] It also has associated with it the words splendor, powerful, mighty, mightier, excellent, glories, and to be great. Our modern dictionary adds to this by defining a mantle as: *1...b: a mantle regarded as a symbol of preeminence or authority... 2a: something that covers, enfolds, or envelops... mantle... to become coated with a coating.*[211]

It is easy to conclude that Elijah's mantle was more than a literal cloak. Even though it was a "cloak", it also represented an anointing which allowed for Elisha to continue to walk in the same Spirit that Elijah had walked. In fact, in verse fifteen the sons of the prophet said, *"The spirit of Elijah rests on Elisha"*. When Elisha asked Elijah for a double portion (verse 9) of the same spirit that was on Elijah he was actually asking for the privilege commonly reserved for the firstborn. Elisha was asking for the spiritual inheritance of the anointing which had been upon Elijah for years.

Then, when Elijah was taken into heaven in a chariot of fire by a whirlwind, Elisha was granted the mantle that was left behind: a physical mantle that covered his body. But, perhaps more importantly, a spiritual mantle that was endued with glory, power, and might: one that revealed the authority of God upon this earth through might and demonstration.

In the New Testament we deal with gifts and callings (Romans 11:29). The Apostle Paul tells us that if any one is in Christ, that person is a new creation; old things have passed away; behold, all things have become new (2 Corinthians 5:17) and as such we are now **ambassadors** for Christ (2 Corinthians 5:20). An ambassador is the representative of a ruling authority. People that are usually chosen from the ranks of the mature and experienced. Caring for and counseling those individuals that are hurting is a sacred trust given to those who have been proven to be mature in Christ.

So, what does all this mean for ministers and Christian counselors? It means that we have the privilege and duty to nurture as well as edify

---

[210] James Strong; (Strong's Exhaustive Concordance of the Bible; Nashville, Tennessee; Thomas Nelson Publishers; 1990); page 9.
[211] Philip Babcock Gove (Editor in Chief); (Webster's Third New International Dictionary of the English Language: Unabridged; Springfield, Massachusetts; Merriam-Webster Inc., Publishers; 1993); page 1378.

those individuals who choose to seek our guidance: counsel. As ambassadors we have no right or authority to do or say anything that is contrary to the will of the One who sent us. If we are truly gifted with His mantle and called upon to be Christ's representative in the counseling setting we have no other recourse than to be faithful in re-presenting God's will and plans. Ambassadors are typically viewed as people with high character. Someone who refuses to become distracted by or entangled with self-serving desires or anything else that might impede or obstruct them from their predetermined course.

Ministers and Christian counselors are to be in service to the Kingdom of God by serving God's children when they come to us for assistance and/or advise. It is a high calling to minister to and provide care for others when there is a need: to make a positive difference in the lives of those who are hurting. We are living in a time where hearts have become jaded and hard; times where the lines between good and evil are being clearly drawn; a time where wrong is becoming accepted and even defended.

As ministers and Christian counselors we need to "keep it real" while being able to express the unconditional love of God. True healing and spiritual transformation simply cannot take place apart from God's love and grace. Because many who will come to us for help may not believe in God's existence or that, if He does exist, He really doesn't care about them or their life, we will need to break through these false beliefs before any true progress can be accomplished.

As ambassadors for Christ who wear the mantle of His authority, we are covered with a coating that empowers us to demonstrate the affirmation of life while lifting up human dignity and encouraging those seeking help to step out in faith, believing that God not only exists, but that He cares for and rewards those who diligently seek Him (Hebrews 11:6).

Concerning the *call to care* and the mantle that God places upon ministers and Christian counselors one author writes, *Are you called to Christian counseling? Are you called by God to lead others into a life-changing encounter with the living God? Just as God calls us and uses us to help others enter into a unique healing encounter with Him, Jesus used Philip to draw his skeptical friend into a life-*

changing encounter with Jesus Himself (cf. John 1:43-50).[212]

A simple and easy study of God's Word will reveal many things about the minister and Christian counselor's mantle. For example, "*Where there is no counsel, the people fall...*" (Proverbs 11:14a). "*Without counsel purposes and plans go awry and become frustrated.*" (Proverbs 15:22).

"*You did not choose me; I chose you. And I gave you this work: to go and produce fruit, fruit that will last. Then the Father will give you anything you ask for in my name.*" (John 15:16)

"*But the Lord said to him, "Go, for he is a chosen vessel of Mine to bear My name before Gentiles, kings, and the children of Israel.*" (Acts 9:15)

"*Then suddenly a man appeared who was sent from God, a messenger named John.*" (John 1:6)

"*Come to me and listen to this. From the beginning I have spoken openly. From the time it began, I was there." Now, the Lord GOD has sent me with his Spirit.*" (Isaiah 48:16)

The above verses reveal that God has chosen to use His ambassadors (i.e. those who have been cloaked with His mantle of authority) as instruments and divine messengers to accomplish His purposes. In Isaiah God asks, "*Whom shall I send, and who will go for Me?*" (Isaiah 6:8). By this we know that it is God's desire to send people to carry His message of hope to a lost and desperate world. People are still hurting, they are still searching for and frantically seeking hope. If there was ever a time for wise counsel, for godly leadership, and true biblical direction, it is now.

The counselor's mantle must include, in addition to the covering and authority, wise counsel. To biblically counsel means to: '*etsah (ayst-ah): Strong's #6098: Advice, plan; counsel; purpose. This noun comes from the verb ya'ats, "to counsel, to advise." 'Etsah occurs about 85 times, referring to both the Lord's counsel...and the counsel of a true friend, or group of wise persons...*[213]

In essence, this is what Jesus did when the scribes and Pharisees

---

[212] Tim Clinton, Archibald Hart, George Ohlschlager; (Caring For People God's Way; Nashville Tennessee; Thomas Nelson Publishers; 2005); page 14.

[213] Jack W. Hayford (General Editor); (Spirit Filled Life Bible: New King James Version; Nashville, Tennessee; Thomas Nelson Publishers; 1991); Word Wealth; page 1370.

brought before Him the woman who had been caught in adultery (cf. John 8:3-11). Jesus never belittled or discounted her for her sin. He expressed grace and love; He extended to her the counsel of peace when He said, *go and sin no more*. The counsel of peace results in inner tranquility and reconciliation, which is exactly what we, as ambassadors for Christ are supposed to be involved in: the ministry of reconciliation (cf. 2 Corinthians 5:18).

Within this ministry of reconciliation we have been entrusted to faithfully represent the Kingdom and principles of a sovereign God. As we do so it authenticates the mantle God has placed on us as we represent and speak on behalf of the King of kings to a hurting world that simply needs to see and experience the unconditional love of God in operation.

In a sense much like Paul's words in 1 Corinthians 4:1, "Let a man so consider us, as servants of Christ and stewards of the mysteries of God," we often assent in Christian counseling that "God never wastes a wound." Although He is not the author of evil or sorrow, He is wise to use every kind of wrong suffered and dream dashed to reach out to us to grab hold of His healing hand. He is the "God of all comfort, who comforts us in all our tribulation, that we may be able to comfort those in any trouble, with the comfort with which we are comforted by God" (2 Corinthians 1:3b-4). What a glorious circle of care! God comforts us, enabling us to turn and comfort others with the same care given by God, enabling both to worship God and give to others again. We are His agents, His regents, His care-giving disciples given to a call to "bear one another's burdens, and so fulfill the law of Christ (Galatians 6:2).[214]

This fulfilling of "the law of Christ" is love; unconditional and uncompromising "agape": love. Unfortunately, we still have an enemy that has secreted himself away in the counseling process and, at times, has caused grave damage to all involved in the restorative process. This is one of the primary reasons why we now have in place ethical guidelines and legal issues to consider, which is the topic of our next section.

Ethics and Legal Considerations

One of the primary roles of most ministers, especially Pastors, is that of a counselor. Consequently, this very same function or role is also one of the areas that can cause the most destruction to a minister, Christian

---

[214] Tim Clinton, Archibald Hart, George Ohlschlager; (Caring For People God's Way; Nashville Tennessee; Thomas Nelson Publishers; 2005); pages 14-15.

counselor, the counselee, and even, the local congregation. The era in which we live, tort and legal actions have dealt a financial death blow to many churches. While the financial devastation can be horrific is seems almost disrespectful to even mention it when we take into consideration the emotional, physical, familial, and spiritual damages that can occur if proper ethical guidelines are not adhered to.

L. Ronald Brushwyler, D.Min. writes, *like pastoral care professional counseling (or professional counseling by a pastor) is serious business with significant clinical responsibilities given by our cultural climate today. Legally, professional counseling is no longer regarded a casual activity. Pastors who engage in professional counseling activities are not free to simply dabble with some tools and techniques under the umbrella of their ordination. When they move away from the ancient activities of pastoral care and engage in professional counseling methods, they are then held to the specific standards of the counseling profession, regardless of whether the are, in fact, licensed professionals. Before the law they will not find the privilege or protection they have within the ancient practice of pastoral care. Several protective legal guidelines for the practice of ministry* (especially as it pertains to the counseling setting) *includes:*

- *Be clear about the expertise offered. Refer to your activities in unambiguously religious terms, not professional counseling terms. Unless you are trained and are willing to adhere to all of the professional standards of licensed professional counselors, stay with practices that you identify as pastoral care. If you hold yourself out as a "professional" or "psychological" counselor, the law will treat you as one.*

- *Do not assume broader duties which are not part of your competence or calling* (knowing your limitations will be addressed later in this chapter).

- *Adopt, in conversation with your leaders, policies and guidelines for pastoral care practice.*

- *Determine appropriate physical settings and circumstances of meeting for pastoral care.*

- *Engage in regular peer review or supervision to maintain clarity in your pastoral practice.*

- *Maintain a list/network of* (Christian) *counseling professionals to whom you can refer persons with chronic or more serious emotional/mental difficulties.* (Once again, know your limitations.)[215]

God is our Mighty Counselor, Jesus is our Wonderful Counselor, and the Holy Spirit is our Counselor, Comforter, and Guide. As mature believers in Christ, ministers and Christian counselors are exhorted to encourage others, to warn the idle, and help the weak (cf. 1 Thessalonians 5:11-14). Most individuals who seek out ministers and Christian counselors believe that God is the Author of all truth and that the Bible is the authoritative guide to any effective counseling model. Sound counseling techniques, when they are specifically founded upon and supported by properly interpreted Scriptures, should be used to promote change and wholeness in the counselee. Two of the most common areas that determine effective transformation in the counselees life, which are clearly addressed in the Word of God are: 1) Personal accountability and responsibility for their behavior; and 2) changing their thought or cognitive processes to coincide with Scriptural truths.

In other words, a minister or Christian counselor may be doing their best in every way at dealing with someone's thinking or behavioral issues when, due to a lack of training or knowledge, they unintentionally create a situation that results in harming the counselee. In todays litigious society these occasions, far too often, end up in the courts and on the front page of every area newspaper. This is one of the primary reasons many pastors have completely done away with counseling as a part of their normal duties.

However, the love and compassion for others that God has placed in the heart of pastors and ministers will cause them to have an overwhelming desire to help the hurting. So, one of the questions that all pastors and ministers need to ask themselves (Christian counselors, not so much because they have already accepted the role by virtue of their very title) is: "Do I counsel anyone?"

This query may sound both cynical and comical at the same time. Unfortunately, it needs to be consciously considered and answered before

---

[215] L. Ronald Brushwyler, D.Min; (Pastoral Care vs. Professional Counseling: Discerning the Difference; Westchester, Illinois; The Midwest Ministry Development Service; 1999) pages 2-3.

proceeding any further. Some have chosen to not provide any counsel, advice, or guidance to anyone stating that their only job is to expound upon Scripture and administer the sacraments. Others have opted for a middle of the road approach wherein they have elected to conduct pre-marital counseling, some light financial counseling, direction and guidance concerning giftings and callings, etc. While a few will dive headlong into any topic at any time in an attempt to relieve or totally alleviate an individual's pain.

Often pastors, ministers, and church leadership will opt for counseling, stating, in essence, that it is a part of the disciple making process, that all believers are commanded to do as part of the Great Commission even though they will choose to use different terminology. Language that avoids the use of "professional" counseling terms: for example, in lieu of using the term "counsel" (and all of its derivatives) they will elect for more generalized terminology, such as "life coach" or "helper".

You may be asking, "Are you trying to instill fear in me so that I'll stop counseling others?" Absolutely not. What I am attempting to explain is the current environment wherein we live. And that, by choosing to use the terminology of "counsel", "counselor", or "counseling" it may be misconstrued as inferring a level of competency that we may not be able to deliver. If this occurs it may result in grave damage being done to all parties involved.

What I am abdicating is to help reduce the potential for any confusion or inadvertently misrepresenting our competency levels and abilities is to simply use alternative terminology. In a language such as ours, one that is ever-changing and evolving, it is crucial that we use terminology apropos to effectively communicate our ideas, emotions, dreams, intentions, etc. Any failure in effective communication can, and in all likelihood will, create confusion or strife. Confusion may, at the very least, slow the healing process or, at worst, destroy the relationship between all parties involved, resulting in a total suspension of the counseling process or even worse. With these thoughts in mind I would simply suggest that you seriously consider and make your decisions fully aware of the possible ramifications to your calling, the one seeking assistance, and ultimately, to the body of Christ.

Currently, all fifty states have laws that govern "counselors". Some are extremely restrictive while others are more liberal, but all fifty states have statutes in place that defines what is involved in the "practice of psychology". Most of these state's legislated definitions involve comments like; rending or giving service wherein the influencing of behavior are included; espousing principles that pertain to perception, motivation, thinking, emotions, or interpersonal relationships; and where any counseling or behavioral modification methods or techniques are used.

These are but a few of the statements made in the wide ranging and varied legal definitions being employed today. As one can easily deduce from the examples I have given, ministers and Christian counselors must be aware of the potential problems/issues that can arise. One thing is absolutely certain, no matter what terminology one chooses to employ we must know our limitations.

Know Your Limitations

Before I ever accepted the call of God to be a Pastor I had faithfully served under a man of God that taught me many valuable lessons. I had successfully completed a two-year course of Bible study and had earned a Bachelor of Theology Degree. I also had in excess of twenty years of experience in law enforcement, dealing with untold numbers of varying situations. So I felt "ready" when I began pastoring. However, it wasn't very long before I realized that I was completely unprepared to deal with and handle many of the personal issues that the members of my congregation brought to me. In other words, I quickly became aware of my limitations and, as a result, I concluded that I was grossly inadequate.

This honest evaluation of my abilities and limitations caused me to return to academia where I was introduced to the American Association of Christian Counselors (AACC) and Light University. Subsequently, I have taken more than one hundred and fifty classes pertaining to various issues that nearly every believer will have to deal with at one point or another in their life.

Unfortunately, much of the ministerial counseling that occurs involves ministers who have very little, if any, formalized training in the counseling arena and some who have received no higher education of any kind, including theological. We must all be aware of our limitations, and even more so when a lack of education or understanding is the case. A minister's desire to help frequently gets in the way of prudence. This can ultimately cause us to end up stepping outside the boundaries of our abilities, if we aren't careful. When this takes place, we can end up initiating a chain of events that end up hurting those same people we desire to help. This can negatively impact the one seeking relief; their family; ourselves personally; and even our ministry. All of this devastation and destruction because we simply tried to help someone without either recognizing, or ignoring our own limitations.

Dr. Brushwyler writes, *many persons today continue to turn to their pastors as a primary resource in times of crisis. Pastors are usually more immediately and directly accessible than some other professionals, do not charge fees, and are often known and trusted within a community. They are also generalists who have some familiarity with a broad spectrum of experiences. Consequently, parishioners and community residents commonly look to pastors for assistance with a wide range of needs, including counseling... Pastoral care is regarded as a primary function of ministry by many ministers themselves as well as a majority of parishioners... Some pastors are members* (of organizations)*...which has developed educational and training standards along with a carefully formulated Code of Ethics...* (Dr. Brushwyler continues) *however most pastors do not meet these educational or training standards... There is an inherent imbalance of power which some, particularly pastors, are uncomfortable acknowledging, but which exists whenever a person in distress seeks succor from one viewed as more knowledgeable. Healing is certainly a central focus in any such helping relationship. Also,* **boundary issues must be attended to in order to create the safest possible atmosphere** *in which a parishioner or counselee can process his or her pain.*[216]

Knowing your limitations and consciously restricting yourself within those boundaries are crucial to the effectual conclusion of the counseling process. Once you have bumped up against your limitations or boundaries don't simply continue on "a wing and a prayer". This is where ministers and Christian counselors alike end up getting into trouble and inadvertently causing harm. This is one of the primary reasons that we need to be held accountable and responsible to other, more qualified or mature ministers and Christian counselors.

---

[216] L. Ronald Brushwyler, D.Min; (Pastoral Care vs. Professional Counseling: Discerning the Difference; Westchester, Illinois; The Midwest Ministry Development Service; 1999); pages 1-2, emphasis added.

Responsibility and Accountability

Everyone who has ever lived, whether they realize it or not; whether they want to admit it or not; whether they accept it or not, will be held accountable for their own life and actions. Paul said, *each of us will have to answer to God* (Romans 14:12 NCV)

The sobering words of this verse describe a day when each individual will stand alone before God almighty to "give account". At that moment, there will be no excuses, no hidden agendas, no chance to lie and get away with it. Each person is ultimately accountable to Christ, not others. The context of this verse speaks of diversity in the Christian fellowship, encouraging believers to allow for differences of opinion in matters that do not conflict with God's Word. Elsewhere Paul encourages believers in this diversity saying, "work out your own salvation with fear and trembling" (Philippians 2:12). We must each seek to grow in our faith, on our own before God. **Accountability to others can help this process**, *but ultimately we will be accountable to God for how we have lived. Follow God's Word - it is a sure guide.*[217]

All people, including ministers and Christian counselors, need someone in their life that they can be completely honest and totally transparent with; someone they can openly share their deepest thoughts, hurts, and feelings with; someone with whom they can discuss their likes and dislikes without being judged or condemned.

The Word tells us to examine, test, and evaluate ourselves to determine whether we are holding fast to our faith and showing the proper fruits of it (cf. 2 Corinthians 13:5). By honestly evaluating every aspect of our life we are taking the first step toward being a responsible believer. Unfortunately, many will evaluate their life without doing anything to bring about necessary change in the areas they find deficient or in error.

Personal responsibility and accountability builds a bridge between what the Word says and the practice of its principles in our daily lives. One of the primary means of remaining accountable is to find others in whom you trust enough to voluntarily become accountable. As we have already covered, every person, believers and non-believers alike, will ultimately be held accountable by God. However, here on this earth, in our own lifetime, as ministers and Christian counselors we have been given the task of

---

[217] Tim Clinton (Executive Editor); (The Soul Care Bible; Nashville, Tennessee; Thomas Nelson Publishers; 2001); page 1487, emphasis added.

helping care for the souls of others.

I know of no minister or Christian counselor that simply wakes up one morning and says, "today, I think I'll destroy someone's life". No one who loves others as Christ loves the Church willingly causes hurt or pain to others. But it does happen and is often brought about because the minister or counselor has failed to be held accountable by another. In short, everyone needs an accountability partner or group of partners.

Accountability requires self-evaluation, pure motives, and the absence of hypocritical judgement. People must not hold someone else accountable to a standard they are not willing to meet themselves. Accountability partners should be maturing Christians who have the desire and the time to invest in relationships with others. They must be able to keep reasonable confidences and be concerned enough with others' personal growth that they can be tough when it is needed.[218]

Jesus came as a man. He served and set the right example for all of humanity to follow. As minister and Christian counselors we are compelled to lead by example. The Apostle Paul said, *imitate me as I also imitate Christ* (1 Corinthians 11:1). We need to echo these same sentiments. To help us ensure that we are "imitating Christ" we need to be submitting ourselves to others who are more mature and more experienced in the counseling process.

Concerning accountability and oversight Dr. Tim Clinton and Dr. Eric T. Scalise write, *True oversight - an invitation to accept practical and clinical supervision - along with the freedom to allow others to give honest feedback are the marks of an ethically-oriented counselor, as well as one who is humble enough to value such a process. Whether we are discussing issues of confidentiality, consent, or competence, we must continue honing our skills and overall awareness level and should do so with the input of our colleagues and peers. Isolation leading to closed ears, a closed mind, and a closed spirit is the mortal enemy of ethical practice and results in unnecessary risk taking. Accountability is a lost spiritual discipline for many and, yet, one day each of us will stand before the throne of God and give an account for our stewardship. As (ministers and) Christian counselors, we have been tasked with not crossing a line that would violate the tenants of compassionate and professional caregiving. God wants us to make a*

---

[218] Tim Clinton (Executive Editor); (The Soul Care Bible; Nashville, Tennessee; Thomas Nelson Publishers; 2001); page 966.

positive eternal difference in the lives of those He brings to us.[219]

Opposite Sex Counseling

At the outset of this topic we are compelled to reiterate the realities of the times in which we live: ours is a litigious society where both criminal and civil charges may be brought solely on appearances. We live in a time where a person is no longer innocent until proven guilty; but guilty based on presumption and emotions rather than upon reality and produced facts. In the courts of public opinion a minister and Christian counselor may be convicted, demoralized, and publicly humiliated simply by trying to help someone. Unfortunately, even when the allegations have been proven to be false, one may never fully recover personally and professionally because there will always be a certain segment of society that believes the accusations to be true.

For this reason Paul said to *abstain from all* **appearance** *of evil* (cf. 1 Thessalonians 5:22). By following this primary rule in our lives we will reveal a good reputation even with unbelievers. For this reason I strongly urge ministers and Christian counselors to never go behind closed doors when counseling individuals of the opposite sex.

There will frequently arise the need for counseling with members of the opposite sex, however, there should always be rigid guidelines in place and followed when this occurs. Personally, I will never meet with a child or a female counselee without the presence of another female (preferably non-related) being present. In rare cases where the female counselee does not want anyone else to "know" what is being addressed I will, if possible refer. If the situation is such that referral is not an option I will leave the door wide open and have another female within range of hearing any raised voices. This helps protect all parties involved while still promoting confidentiality.

If the individual seeking relief will not agree with these rigid, non-negotiable guidelines I simply refer them to someone else, usually another qualified minister or Christian counselor of the same sex as the individual seeking relief. While this is one of the few areas where professional, ministerial, and Christian counseling models nearly all agree the next area

---

[219] Tim Clinton, Eric Scalise; (Ambassadors of Reconciliation: Ethics in Christian Caregiving: Christian Counseling Today; Volume 17, number 3); page 28.

up for discussion widely varies.

Transference and Counter-transference

The phenomenon frequently referred to as "transference" and "counter-transference" often involves a transferring of emotional attachments and/or feelings from one to another. With transference it involves the counselee projecting his/her past onto the minister or Christian counselor; while counter-transference is based on the counselor's projecting their past onto the current counselee.

In short, we may conclude that the emotional attachments being projected has to do with the directional flow of the emotions. Those from the counselee to the counselor are transference; those emotions deriving from the counselor and being projected onto the counselee are counter-transference.

While there are varying levels and types of transference and counter-transference they can all be traced back to Sigmund Freud where he espoused that external pressures may have been perpetrated or reinforced by parents, siblings, grandparents, etc. All of these "external" pressures, which have now been internalized, come to the surface when given a specific set of circumstances (i.e. phrases, scents, looks, etc.) and are projected into the current situation. One who prescribes to Freud's methodologies may then deduce and declare that it is not the counselees fault. That he/she cannot be held accountable for what society has forced upon them. This conclusion is simply untrue because each and every person that has ever lived will give an account of themselves to God (cf. Romans 4:12).

Possible examples of a counselee exhibiting transference might include: displaying a strong sexual attraction, it may involve unnecessary anger, it may even result in a premature termination of the counseling process.

Some believe that it should be left up to the individual minister or Christian counselor as to whether transference/counter-transference will be helpful or detrimental to the counseling process. However, I tend to agree with Jay E. Adams when he writes, *by "transference" Rogerians and other Freudians mean that clients frequently redirect their feeling (often negative) for one person to another (in this case the counselor). Hatred for a father may be transferred to the counselor. Transference is encouraged by many as a useful technique in counseling. But is transference a technique that Christians may use? No. When counselors encourage or allow clients to transfer feelings of hatred and resentment to themselves, they thereby encourage clients to perpetuate and multiply their sin and guilt. In contrast, nouthetic techniques call for the loving rebuke of sinful attitudes and actions, even when directed toward the counselor. Instead of adopting reflective methods which encourage transference, the nouthetic counselor considers incidents of transference a nouthetic opportunity to put an end to such transference. He will therefore employ methods appropriate to bringing about repentance and reconciliation rather than the acceptance of sinful feelings. He points out to the client that his negative transference is one evidence that he has been using wrong methods of handling his problems. Whenever a client transfers strong feelings of antipathy toward his counselor, for instance, the counselor should seize upon the opportunity to observe that such behavior may be one instance of underlying patterns which in the past have gotten the client into difficulty....*

The counselor, by capitalizing upon this instance of the client's sinful behavior, already has begun to help him by not allowing sin to go unchallenged. Because he handles sin at this level, he is able to show concretely how sinful behavior brings difficulty into the counslee's life on many other levels, as well.

It is impossible to destroy the foundation and preserve the superstructure. Because non-biblical systems rest upon non-biblical presuppositions, it is impossible to reject the presuppositions and adopt the techniques which grow out of and are appropriate to those presuppositions. Rogerian "acceptance" and Freudian "transference" techniques fail because of the fallacies of the Rogerian philosophy of autonomy and the Freudian ethic of irresponsibility upon which they rest.

One specific objection to the use of transference as a tool in counseling is that such usage encourages clients to sin against another and, thus, adds to their guilt. Corollaries to that basic objection are: first, that counselors become a party to the client's sin, so that counselor and counselee both sin in employing such transference. Secondly, sin is condoned. Even if the counselor simply sits back in an accepting manner without making nouthetic responses to sinful attitudes or statements about sin, he has become a party to condoning that sin, in the eyes of many clients. Acceptance of sin is sin. Thirdly, to agree to use transference is to agree that the ends justify the means.

Of course, one might ask, does transference really help? The answer again is, no. Sinful attitudes and behavior are never helpful, for they violate God's law. And it is a fundamental Christian assumption that any practice which is contrary to God's law will harm clients. Thus Christians must look upon the transference and all other such eclectic borrowings as counterproductive.[220]

While one may extrapolate a multitude of pro's and con's in connection to the employment and use of transference/counter-transference techniques I am compelled by the Word of God and my conscience to refuse any technique or methodology that runs contrary to Scripture, which these techniques definitely do. Nowhere in Scripture are we allowed to "blame-shift" or to mistreat someone on the basis of how others have treated us. We are, from the Garden of Eden to the Great White Throne, instructed to accept personal responsibility for our own actions and reactions while extending forgiveness to others just as Jesus has toward us.

Data Gathering, Record Keeping, and Confidentiality

Our final topics under consideration are possibly some of the most crucial when considering the effectiveness and successful conclusion of any series of counseling sessions. As ministers and Christian counselors we need to understand that, while I have opted to save these areas until the end, they must be followed and adhered to at every stage or step of the process. Failure to do so can cause grave damage to successfully helping others and possibly destroy forever the minister's or Christian counselor's reputation and ability to help anyone ever again: it is so important that failing to follow these simple guidelines could ultimately cause you to end up in litigation and possibly even criminal prosecution.

Information and Data Gathering

When a potential counselee makes an initial contact with the minister or Christian counselor the information and data gathering process begins. We collect large amounts of personal data about the counselee (i.e. name, date of birth, marital status, sex, etc.). We then expand upon our data gathering process by inquiring as to their needs, concerns, and expectations. Then, if we choose to enter into a counselor/counselee relationship even more data - potentially very sensitive information - will be collected and documented.

The following three recommendations are offered as minimal starting points for the development of pastoral record-keeping procedures. First, basic demographic data

---

[220] Jay E. Adams; (Competent To Counsel; Grand Rapids, Michigan; Zondervan; 1970); pages 101-103.

should be gathered along with dates of contact. Next, include a brief and succinct statement of the general nature of the request. Third, recommendations directly presented are noted. If referral to another helper is necessary, provide a list of credible resources so that the client can make an informed choice.[221]

Today a minister or Christian counselor may be tempted to look at the internet for help and guidance concerning certain situations/issues. To this temptation, I simply say, beware. Unfortunately, there is little, if any, oversight and supervision concerning the gathered information and how to use it. So, if you do opt for internet information gathering, ensure that you are using a site that maintains their credibility through extremely high standards, such as aacc.net or nouthetic.org.

There also seems to be an infinite number of tests, questionnaires, and assessment techniques available to anyone conducting a simple search of the worldwide web. I would also warn the minister or Christian counselor to be extremely careful of using most of them. The reason is not necessarily the fact that you may gather more information than is needed for your current purposes, although that is a definite possibility; one for which you could be held accountable if the information should unintentionally be disseminated. The primary reason I do not recommend the use of these items is that, in many cases, they are designed for licensed professional psychologists and require a specific set of skills to properly employ, evaluate, and interpret. Skills that ministers and Christian counselors normally do not possess.

Ministers and *Christian counselors do clinical evaluations of clients only in the context of professional relations, in the best interests of the clients, and* **with the proper training and supervision**. (Ministers and) *Christian counselors avoid (1) incompetent and inaccurate evaluations; (2) clinically unnecessary and excessively expensive testing; and (3) unauthorized practice of testing and evaluation that is the province of another clinical or counseling discipline. Referral and consultation are used when evaluation is desired or necessary beyond the competence and/or role of the* (minister or Christian) *counselor.*[222]

---

[221] Dr. Tim Clinton, Dr. Ron Hawkins; (The Popular Encyclopedia of Christian Counseling; Eugene, Oregon; Harvest House Publishers; 2011); page 518.
[222] Dr. Timothy Clinton and Dr. George Ohlschlager; (Competent Christian Counseling Volume One; Colorado Springs, Colorado; Waterbrook Press; 2002); page 281, emphasis added.

Since we rarely have divine revelation or concrete knowledge of what has occurred to bring an individual to us for help it is crucial that our information and data gathering be accurate and recorded in proper perspective without any exaggerations, elaborations, or expansion. At this stage in the process we simply desire to acquire a solid foundation that we can reference and draw from in the future.

As we continue to gather information concerning the counselee's concerns we should be considering how we can interpret the data within Scriptural categories and biblical conclusions. The counselee should not be allowed to continue to shift the blame for their actions or lack thereof to others. In nearly every modern-day model for counseling blame-shifting is commonplace and is, in reality, acceptable because telling someone they are "wrong" or that the problems they are experiencing is a direct result of "sin" is an absolute no-no. In fact these techniques require a counselor to remain neutral when dealing with ethical issues.

Unfortunately, more often than not, remaining "neutral" simply allows for an indiscriminate number of sessions with little or no progress in the healing process. Concerning this very issue Adams writes, *as Menninger has noted...all sorts of people carry loads of guilt around because modern constructs of human problems do not allow for the concept of sin and thus do not allow for forgiveness. The cruelest thing a counselor can do is to consign a guilty person to a state of non-forgiveness by eliminating the biblical constructs of lawbreaking and sin. Forgiveness is exactly what the person needs. Reaching the conclusion that a counselee has sinned, the counselor can point to forgiveness in Christ through His substitutionary, penal, and sacrificial death on the cross... The kindest move on the part of any counselor is to label what is truly sin, "sin". There is forgiveness for sin, not for "neurosis" or an "emotional problem"! There is really no solution to problems described by labels that mask the very root of the problems.*[223]

I could continue along these lines, however, this is merely an introduction and as such, we need to move on. If you will recall, at the outset of this section we discussed limiting our information and data gathering to only what we need to effectively help those who come to us for assistance. This next topic will help to clear up why we don't want to gather inordinate amounts of personal information.

---

[223] Jay E. Adams; (How To Help People Change; Grand Rapids, Michigan; Zondervan; 1986); pages 120-121.

Record Keeping

In today's ever-changing and expanding environment a ministers' and Christian counselor's responsibilities have became more significant. Accurate documentation of session conversations and recommendations are crucial for the benefit of all parties involved.

With the *expanding use of services, greater consumer awareness, increasing litigation issues, professionalization or practice, and the growing severity of client problems all demand a greater degree of competence and quality in our counseling work. In the past, much Christian counseling has been legitimately criticized as being unprofessional and unbusinesslike. For many counselors, the fear of being seen as secular and mercenary by the church made it difficult to combine professionalism and good business practice with the call to a people-helping ministry that brought us into this field. However, there is nothing spiritual about sloppy work. The ambiguity involved in helping individuals in a spiritual context is not a valid excuse for not articulating the counseling process or meeting appropriate professional standards.*[224]

I spent over three decades in law enforcement at one level or another and the one inviolable and protected rule was: **no job is done until the paperwork is completed**. This same rule applies to ministers and Christian counselors where counseling is concerned. Documentation of all client interactions is mandatory! This documentation should be of sufficient detail to reveal the quality, effectiveness, and legality of services rendered.

Stephen P. Greggo does an outstanding job of explaining the necessity for proper record keeping in the following, rather lengthy, treatise: *Routine documentation is an expectation of state boards, which issue licenses, as well as professional guilds, which establish ethical codes and standards of care. Third-party payers, generally insurance companies, anticipate that the client treatment record will plainly show that any treatment provided was medically necessary to address the symptoms and diagnosis that fit established criteria for an actual condition. The paper or electronic record kept by helping professionals will include documents that relate to the following aspects of care:*

- *evidence of informed consent*

- *permission to release information or make recordings*

---

[224] Dr. Timothy Clinton and Dr. George Ohlschlager; (Competent Christian Counseling Volume One; Colorado Springs, Colorado; Waterbrook Press; 2002); page 325.

- *initial assessment details and diagnosis*

- *treatment plans directly linked to presenting concerns and identified medical issues*

- *intervention procedures*

- *status updates and ongoing progress*

- *outside referrals, consultations, and supervision*

- *termination summaries describing outcomes and recommendations for aftercare.*

This list represents the main categories of documentation, but it is not a comprehensive checklist. There are substantial details in each category. Consult a reputable source for a thorough explanation... Once a comprehensive record exists, there are definite expectations for securely storing, sharing, transmitting, transferring, and disposing of records.

Expectations for routine progress notes have changed considerably in recent years. The bar is high. Notes should be legible and consistently cover all essential aspects of the entire episode of treatment. Clinicians are advised to stay current on standards and not slip into careless habits... Spiritual formation activities included in sessions should be documented in a manner that transparently indicates the relationship between the client's request, presenting concern, plain and fully informed consent, and receptivity...

All discussion of documentation can provoke anxiety about potential liability and possible repercussions... The practice of record keeping is not the price one pays to enjoy the privilege of client relationships. Instead, it is a central method to advance quality care for valued counselees.

Pastoral or lay counselors may not hold credentials or association memberships that obligate direct adherence to an explicit secular code of professional ethics. There may be no financial arrangements that determine documentation duties to outsider payers or clients. Nonetheless, it is reasonable to predict that if client assistance is offered under the designation of counseling or if pastoral care procedures substantially resemble this professionally regulated service, essential features of generally accepted requirements should inform customary documentation practice in this area. Most lay counseling ministries are presented to constituents as a method to extend the impact of the pastoral staff. Therefore, procedures and training instituted to promote excellence in soul care should include specific and explicit expectations for record keeping as well as secure access. Policies for supervisory oversight of the counselors should be transparent to counselees...

The Gospel of Matthew records a memorable occasion when the Pharisees set out to entrap Jesus into making a statement regarding civil disobedience in the matter of paying taxes to Rome (Mt. 22:15-22). Jesus refused to be cornered and asserted that in matters of ethical practice, Christ's followers respect civil authority and honor God. Service to the Lord does not excuse disobedience to standard laws and expectations. When it comes to the complexities of helping people, Christians have to evaluate worldview, cultural, governmental, and professional expectations in light of a full range of biblical instruction. Record keeping and documentation in counseling demonstrates the use of customary procedures and delivery of quality care. In services that are uniquely Christian, there is no theological rationale to reject these currently respected standards of care. Instead, good documentation helps to focus the caregiver's plans, increases effectiveness, and may provide important information needed in the future.[225]

In closing this subsection let me also include that a minister or Christian counselor may also request that a counselee start a "Homework Book" where they can record their understanding of what is happening along with potential ways of dealing with their issues. (I recommend either an inexpensive spiral or composition notebook.) When an individual is asked to put their thoughts into a written format it often helps them to clearly articulate what they are feeling and ideas of how to aid in their healing process.

By proposing possible solutions they will oftentimes be able to "see" for themselves what is occurring. Whether the counselee begins to discern or grasp the issues involved in the process or not, copies of the counselee's homework notes should become a part of the data gathering and record keeping process.

I use this technique to help avoid potential misunderstandings and/or confusion as the process progresses. It can also be used as a means of a written agreement as to what the counselee expects from the minister or Christian counselor. Additionally, if there needs to be a change of direction later on in the process, the original counselee's work can become the basis for change rather than having to start at the beginning again.

Christian counselors maintain appropriate documentation of their counseling

---

[225] Dr. Tim Clinton, Dr. Ron Hawkins; (The Popular Encyclopedia of Christian Counseling; Eugene, Oregon; Harvest House Publishers; 2011); pages 517-518.

activities, adequate for competent recall of prior sessions and the provision of later services by oneself or others... Records of professional activities will be created, maintained, stored, and disposed of in accordance with the law and ethical duties of the counselor, especially maintaining client confidentiality.[226] This leads us to our next area of consideration: client confidentiality.

Confidentiality

Confidentiality is a foundational ethical issue. It is absolutely crucial and involves various areas of the process that cannot be violated. Confidentiality statements should be clearly addressed from the outset and adhered to throughout the entire process with very few exceptions. Some of the exceptions to the rules of confidentiality include: disclosure of child or elder abuse, intent to commit harm to self or others, written authorization by a parent or legal guardian, drug and/or alcohol therapy for children under a certain age (refer to your state laws for specific ages), group counseling settings whether it includes families or groups of other individuals (e.g AA or NA), and a host of other situations that may arise either ethically or legally.

With regard to confidentiality, it is wise to follow the legal and ethical standards of professional counselors and to require that lay helpers report child or elder abuse and the potential danger to the client or to others as they constitute the legal limits to confidentiality. Such limits to confidentiality should be disclosed to clients **at the beginning of the first session.**[227]

Since written documentation is necessary for the protection of all parties involved, the protection and confidential storage of these documents is crucial. George Ohlschlager writes, *Christian counselors will preserve, store, and transfer written records of client communications in a way that protects client confidentiality and privacy rights. This requires, at minimum, keeping records files in a locked storage with access given only to those persons with a direct professional interest in the materials... Christian counselor's take special precautions to protect client privacy rights with records stored and transferred by electronic means. This requires, at minimum, use of password entry into all electronic client files and/or coded files that do not use client*

---

[226] Dr. Timothy Clinton and Dr. George Ohlschlager; (Competent Christian Counseling Volume One; Colorado Springs, Colorado; Waterbrook Press; 2002); page 281.
[227] Dr. Timothy Clinton and Dr. George Ohlschlager; (Competent Christian Counseling Volume One; Colorado Springs, Colorado; Waterbrook Press; 2002); page 434, emphasis added.

names or easy identifiers. Client information transferred electronically - FAX, e-mail, or other computerized network transfer - shall be done only after the counselor determines that the process of transmission and reception of data is reasonably protected from interception and unauthorized disclosures...

Christian counselors hear the most private and sensitive details of client lives - information that must be zealously guarded from public disclosure. Rapidly expanding and interlocking electronic information networks are increasingly threatening client privacy rights. Though federal and state laws exist to protect client privacy, these laws are weak, are routinely violated at many levels, and the record of privacy rights enforcement is dismal. Accordingly, Christian counselors are called to wisely protect and assertively advocate for privacy protection on behalf of our clients against the pervasive intrusion of personal, corporate, governmental, even religious powers.[228]

In closing this chapter I wish to leave you with further assistance concerning session documentation. The old adage that "no job is complete until the paperwork is completed" is true. There are numerous resources available to assist you with the proper documentation of the counseling process from beginning to end. Some resources that may help you in getting started include the books:

- Shepherding God's Flock: A Handbook on Pastoral Ministry, Counseling, and Leadership by Jay E. Adams

- The Christian Counselor's Casebook: Applying the Principles of Nouthetic Counseling by Jay E. Adams

- Advanced Triage Counseling: Counseling That Heals Teenagers and Parents by Sara Trollinger, D.D.

- Caring For People God's Way: Personal and Emotional Issues, Addictions, Grief, and Trauma by Tim Clinton, Archibald Hart, and George Ohlschlager

In conclusion ministers and Christian counselors speak the truth found in the Word of God in a loving but firm manner, using terminology that everyone involved in the process can understand. We must maintain the fair, unbiased, and effective role of leadership throughout the entire

---

[228]Dr. Tim Clinton, Dr. Ron Hawkins; (The Popular Encyclopedia of Christian Counseling; Eugene, Oregon; Harvest House Publishers; 2011); page 516.

process. Failing to complete proper documentation, from beginning to end, is tantamount to failure, especially where legalities and the legal system come in to play. Always remember that, as far as the court system is concerned: if it's not documented, it did not happen.

Prologue to Appendixes

Each of the following appendixes have been graciously provided as a part of this book by a personal friend that has family counseling agencies. Both the founder and lead practitioner of these agencies have given their permission for anyone that legally obtains this work to use as is, or to make any changes they deem necessary for their personal use.

No copyright infringement and no liability will be raised or challenged if you opt to utilize (in part or in full) the following documentation/appendixes.

Nor will the author, publisher, or originating family counseling practice be held accountable, liable, or responsible should you choose to utilize (in part or in full) any of the following documentation/appendixes.

Appendix #1: Notice of Privacy Practices: Policy

Notice of Privacy Practices: Policy

Effective: (enter your effective date here)

This Notice describes how Medical Information about you may be used and disclosed and how you can get access to this information. Please review this notice carefully.

Your health record contains personal information about you and your health. This information about you that may identify you and that relates to your past, present or future physical or mental health or condition and related health care services is referred to as Protected Health Information ("PHI"). This Notice of Privacy Practices describes how "Your Name Here" Counseling may use and disclose your PHI in accordance with applicable law and the ACA Code of Ethics. It also describes your rights regarding how you may gain access to and control your PHI.

Under the Health Insurance Portability and Accountability Act of 1996 ("HIPAA"), "Your Name Here" Counseling is required to maintain the privacy of PHI and to provide you with notice of our legal duties and privacy practices with respect to PHI. "Your Name Here" Counseling is required to abide by the terms of this Notice of Privacy Practices. We reserve the right to change the terms of this Notice of Privacy Practices at any time. Any new Notice of Privacy Practices will be effective for all PHI that we maintain at that time. "Your Name Here" Counseling will provide you with a copy of the revised Notice of Privacy Practices by sending a copy to you in the mail upon request or providing one to you at your next appointment.

How "Your Name Here" Counseling may use and disclose Health Information about you.

For Treatment: Your PHI may be used and disclosed by those who are involved in your care for the purpose of providing, coordinating, or managing your health care treatment and related services. This includes consultation with clinical supervisors or other treatment team members. We may disclose PHI to any other consultant only with your authorization.

For Payment: We may use and disclose PHI so that we can receive payment for the treatment services provided to you. This will only be done with your authorization. Examples of payment-related activities are: making a determination of eligibility or coverage for insurance benefits, processing claims with your insurance company, reviewing services provided to you to determine medical necessity, or undertaking utilization review activities. If it becomes necessary to use collection processes due to lack of payment for services, we will only disclose the minimum amount of PHI necessary for purposes of collection.

For Health Care Operations: We may use or disclose, as needed, your PHI in order to support our business activities including, but not limited to, quality assessment activities, licensing and conducting or arranging for other business activities. For example, we may share your PHI with third parties that perform various business activities (e.g., billing or typing services) provided we have a written contract with the business that requires it to safeguard, the privacy of your PHI. For training or teaching purposes PHI will be disclosed only with your authorization. We may use PHI to contact you to provide appointment reminders or information about treatment alternatives or other health-related benefits and services.

Required by Law: Under the law, we must make disclosures of your PHI to you upon your request. In addition, we must make disclosures to the Secretary of the Department of Health and Human Services for the purpose of investigating or determining our compliance with the requirements of the Privacy Rule.

Without Authorization: Applicable law and ethical standards permit us to disclose information about you without your authorization only in a limited number of other situations. The types of uses and disclosures that may be made without your authorization are those that are:

- Required by Law, such as the mandatory reporting of child abuse or neglect or elder abuse, or mandatory government agency audits or investigations (such as the social work licensing board or the health department).

- Required by Court Order.

- Necessary to prevent or lessen a serious and imminent threat to the health or safety of a person or the public. If information is disclosed to prevent or lessen a serious threat it will be disclosed to a person or persons reasonably able to prevent or lessen the threat, including the target of the threat.

Verbal Permission: We may use or disclose your information to family members that are directly involved in your treatment with your verbal permission.

With Authorization: Uses and disclosures not specifically permitted by applicable law will be made only with your written authorization, which may be revoked.

Your Rights Regarding Your PHI

You have the following rights regarding PHI we maintain about you. To exercise any of these rights, please submit your request in writing to: (Enter your information here)

- Right of Access to Inspect and Copy. You have the right, which may be restricted only in exceptional circumstances, to inspect and copy PHI that may be used to make decisions about your care. Your right to inspect and copy PHI will be restricted only in those situations where there is compelling evidence that access would cause serious harm to you. We may charge a reasonable, cost-based fee for copies.

- Right to Amend. If you feel that the PHI "Your Name Here" Counseling have about you is incorrect or incomplete, you may ask us to amend the information although we are not required to agree to the amendment.

- Right to an Accounting of Disclosures. You have the right to request an accounting of certain disclosures that we make of your PHI. We may charge you a reasonable fee if you request more than one accounting in any 12 month period.

- Right to Request Restrictions. You have the right to request a restriction or limitation on the use or disclosure of your PHI for treatment, payment, or health care operations. We are not required to agree to your request.

- Right to Request Confidential Communication. You have the right to request that we communicate with you about medical matters in a certain way or at a certain location.

- Right to a Copy of this Notice. You have the right to a copy of this notice.

Complaints

If you believe we have violated your privacy rights, you have the right to file a complaint in writing with "Your Name Here" Counseling. At (enter your information here). We will not retaliate against you for filing a complaint.

The effective date of this notice is _____.

Appendix #2: Notice of Privacy Practices: Signature Confirmation

Notice of Privacy Practices: Signature Confirmation

Receipt and Acknowledgment of Notice

Counselee Name:

_____

Date of Birth: _____/_____/_____

Social Security Number: _____-_____-_____

I hereby acknowledge that I have received and have been given an opportunity to read a copy of "Your Name Here" Counseling: Notice of Privacy Practices. I understand that if I have any questions regarding the notice or my privacy rights, I can contact "Your Name Here" Counseling at (enter your phone number here) or at (enter your email information here)

Counselee Signature:

_____ Date

: _____/_____/_____

Parent, Guardian or Personal Representative Signature*:

_____

Date: _____/_____/_____

*If you are signing as a personal representative of an individual, please describe your legal authority to act for this individual (power of attorney, healthcare surrogate, etc.)

_____Counselee Refuses to Acknowledge Receipt

Signature of Witness: _____ Date: _____/_____/_____

Appendix #3: Authorization for Release of Confidential Health Information

Authorization for Release of Confidential Health Information

I, _____ hereby authorize "Your Name Here" to release

to/secure from

_____   _____

(Name of Health Care Facility, Physician, Agency, etc.)   (Street Address, City, State, and ZIP Code)

the following information contained in the client record of_____

(Counselee's Name)

Born: _____/_____/_____
(MM/DD/YYYY)

To be disclosed, the following items must specifically be checked:

O Account Information   O Treatment Summary
O Office Psychotherapy Notes   O Verbal Discussion of Case
O Psychological Testing Report   O Other (specify):

_____

The purpose(s) of the authorization is (are):

O At the request of the individual   O Coordination of Mental Health
Health
                    Treatment

259

O Payment of Account   O Other (specify): _____

I understand that the practice may not condition treatment on whether I sign this authorization. I understand that information used or disclosed pursuant to this authorization may be subject to redisclosure by the recipient and may no longer be protected by law.

I understand that I may be responsible for the cost of medical record copying service.

I understand that this authorization is valid until it expires, unless revoked before that. I understand that I may revoke this authorization at any time by giving written notice to the practice of my desire to do so. I also understand that I will not be able to revoke this authorization in cases where the therapist has already relied on it to use or disclose my health information. Written revocation must be sent to the practice. Absent such written revocation, this Authorization for Release of Confidential Health Information will terminate on _____.

(Date)

Date: ____/____/____

_____

Counselee's Signature**

_____   _____

_____

Signature of Witness   Signature of
Parent or Guardian

**Counselee signature is required in addition to the parent or guardian signature for clients ages 12-17.

Appendix #4: Counselee Agreement/Informed Consent

Counselee Agreement/Informed Consent

Services Offered:

Our services are typically offered on a once-per-week basis. Although there are many definitions and philosophies of coaching, and each of our coaches will offer their own unique approach in unison with your goals, desires and preferences, the following is a brief description of (Your Name Here's - YNH) philosophy of the services we provide:

Coaching in its broadest definition is about growth. It is about living more authentically and autonomously by removing defenses and other "survival" responses that were developed during one's life, most often in childhood. One goal is to replace these functional, yet no longer appropriate, patterns with responses that are more congruent with the individuals' present life and social environment. During the initial stages of coaching, an understanding of the process and a beginning awareness of the underlying issues take place.

During the intermediate stages of the process, the initial awareness and understanding progress to a more active status, in which old patterns begin to be replaced with more appropriate, healthy responses. Functionality increases, while negative emotional responses and behaviors decrease.

A counselee becomes increasingly able to continue the growth process on their own designates the final stages of therapy. They in essence, and again to varying degrees, become their own coach. The safety and support of the coaching medium has been replaced with an internal autonomy and authenticity, allowing them to face their own issues, and adjust their own course as necessary and desired.

Confidentiality:

I understand that (Your State here) state law requires that information provided to mental health practitioners, which includes coaches, remain confidential, and makes every effort to ensure confidentiality is maintained with respect to all aspects of the process. As an (YNH) counselee, you agree to the following exceptions to confidentiality, in which case information may be disclosed to the appropriate authorities/agencies/individuals:

- If your coach has reason to believe that you may harm yourself or others.
- If your coach has reason to believe that you are involved in or have knowledge of abuse or neglect of a child; or abuse, neglect, or exploitation of a person who is elderly or has a disability.
- Ordered disclosure by state or federal courts.

In addition, (YNH) requires disclosure of information in the following circumstances:

- A signed release form granting permission to designated third parties to receive information (as needed).
- Discussion of issues with another coach or coach leader, as well as anonymous discussion with peer therapists at (YNH).
- In the case of minors, parents or legal guardians have access to their child's records, unless emancipated.

In the rare case that emails or text messages are exchanged between coach and counselee with any coaching related discussions, confidentiality is not guaranteed but will be protected to the best of our ability.

Appointment Scheduling/Attendance/Cancellation:

The primary service offered by (YNH) is weekly coaching. The time and day of your appointment should be coordinated with your coach.

Regular sessions promotes faster healing and progress, so it is important that you attend your scheduled coaching sessions consistently. The agency policies are outlined below.

- If I cannot attend a session, I agree to notify my coach at least 24 hours in advance whenever possible.
- I understand that I will be charged for any session cancelled with less than 24-hours notice.

- Your coach reserves the right to transfer/terminate services at any time, for any reason they consider appropriate.

There are policies/procedures in place allowing for exceptions to the above policy. Please discuss any concerns or special circumstances you may have with your coach. Please note that exceptions to the above attendance policy do not necessarily relieve responsibility for payment of those sessions.

If your coach is involved in an emergency, please be aware that another coach at "Your Name Here" will contact you to make future arrangements.

Length and number of sessions:

Sessions typically last 50 minutes. (Some insurance carriers state a 45 minute limit). They are expected to begin promptly, and end at the scheduled time. Although it is understood that there may be instances when you arrive late for a session, late arrival will not extend the scheduled ending time for the session. Your coach is also expected to be on time, and will offer appropriate remedy if late, such as making the time up, prorating the fee, etc. The total number of sessions is dependent on a number of factors including your goals, timeframe, rate of progress, etc. It should be noted again that progress resulting in lasting change is often a long-term process, lasting several months or longer. Please discuss any issues/concerns you have with your coach so that an appropriate treatment plan can be formulated which will best suit your needs/desires.

Fee/Payment:

- Payment (co-pay, deductible, or out of pocket expenditure) is due at the time of service delivery.
- I agree to pay a $??.?? service charge for each check that is returned to (YNH).
- Out of pocket session fee is $ (enter your fees here)/hour. If paid in cash a 10% discount is given.
- If my coach is called to court or an attorney's office I agree to pay $ (enter your fees here) per session the coach has to be unavailable to other clients plus mileage and parking. This is to be paid before service is rendered.
- If records are requested by myself, an attorney, or anyone on my (or my child's behalf) I agree to pay $.??o per page.

Risks of Coaching:

There are certain risks associated with the counseling process that should be understand before work progresses. These risks are sometimes associated with lack of knowledge regarding the coaching process, while most, when experienced, are direct consequences of positive growth/movement. Some of the more common risks that you should be aware of are:

- Long-lasting psychological change often requires a significant investment of time, often longer than the initial perception.
- Counselee's often experience deterioration in emotional and psychological stability at different times during the process. This often occurs during the beginning stages, but may occur at any point, often brought on by an awareness of previously unconscious, emotionally-laden material.
- Relationships are often affected as a result. Significant relationships will often experience varying degrees of tension. This is often the most prevalent within family relationships, but may extend beyond into one's social and professional life.

Relationship:

The relationship between coach and counselee is the container through which change can take place. As such, it is often one in which close emotional bonds develop. It is also a professional relationship, in which appropriate boundaries must be maintained. For the most part, the professional relationship both begins and ends at the office. Although this is sometimes difficult to understand, it is a necessary requirement for proper maintenance of the coaching environment. As such, your coach cannot be expected to be involved in a social relationship or friendship of any kind that exists outside of the session arena.

Therapist Orientation and Credentials:

There are many different approaches to the coaching process. Your coach will work with you to provide you with the most appropriate interventions for your particular issue(s)/goals. Please discuss any concerns or questions you have regarding your desired results with your coach at any time during the process.

Confidentiality With Regard To Minors:

The parents or legal guardians of (YNH) clients under the age of 18 have the right to access their child's records. The exception to this is in the case of an emancipated minor. A minor is emancipated if he or she is on active duty with the armed services, is married, or is 16 years of age or older and resides separate and apart from his/her parents, managing conservator, or guardian and manages his/her own financial affairs. Your child's coach will discuss with you the limitations, procedures, and implications with regard to your child's records and progress.

Termination of the Process:

Each individual coach reserves the right to terminate sessions at their discretion. Reasons for termination include, but are not limited to, untimely payment of fees, failure to comply with treatment recommendations, conflicts of interest, failure to participate, the counselee's needs are outside of the coaches scope of competence or practice, or the client is not making adequate progress. The counselee (or the parents, if the client is a minor) has the right to terminate the process at his/her discretion. Upon either party's decision to terminate, the coach will generally recommend that the counselee participate in at least one, or possibly more, termination sessions. These sessions are intended to facilitate a positive termination experience and give both parties an opportunity to reflect on the work that has been done. The coach will also attempt to ensure a smooth transition to another by offering referrals.

Grievance/Complaint:

I understand that I have the right to file a confidential grievance if I have an unresolved concern regarding my coaching process, or any issue involving any representative of (YNH). Any grievance should be in written form and addressed to:

(Enter your information here.)

After Hours Policy/Procedure:

If you need to contact your coach at any time, you may do so by leaving a message on their confidential voice mailbox at (YNH). If needed, you should discuss other alternative means of contact with your therapist. *__If you are in crisis, please call 911.__* (YNH) is not a crisis facility and will not be held responsible for any damages occurring as a result of unmet crisis or acute care needs. Your coach may not be available to respond to emergency situations. *__If you need immediate assistance, please call 911.__*

Appendix #5: Counselee Agreement/Informed Consent Signature Page

Counselee Agreement/Informed Consent Signature Page

I have read and received a copy of the counselee agreement and informed consent. I had the opportunity to ask questions about the agreement/informed consent before signing.

_____

    _____

Client   Date

_____

    _____

Parent / Guardian   Date

Bibliography

1. Jay E. Adams; The Christain Counselor's Manual; Grand Rapids, Michigan; Zondervan; 1973.
2. Jay E. Adams; Competent To Counsel; Grand Rapids, Michigan; Zondervan; 1970.
3. Jay E. Adams; Growing By Grace; Stanley, North Carolina; Timeless Texts; 2003.
4. Jay E. Adams; How To Help People Change; Grand Rapids, Michigan; Zondervan; 1986.
5. Jay E. Adams; Shepherding God's Flock; Grand Rapids, Michigan; Zondervan; 1075.
6. Jay E. Adams; A Theology of Christian Counseling; Grand Rapids, Michigan; Zondervan; 1979.
7. Dr. Timothy Clinton and Dr. George Ohlschlager; Competent Christian Counseling Volume One; Colorado Springs, Colorado; Waterbrook Press; 2002.
8. Finis Jennings Dake; God's Plan For Man; Lawrenceville, Georgia; Dake Publishing; 1977.
9. Guy P. Duffield and Nathaniel M. Van Cleave; Foundations of Pentecostal Theology; Los Angeles, California; L.I.F.E. Bible College; 1987.
10. Philip Babcock Gove (Editor in Chief); Webster's Third New International Dictionary of the English Language: Unabridged; Springfield, Massachusetts; Merriam-Webster Inc., Publishers; 1993.
11. Wayne Grudem; Bible Doctrine: Essential Teachings of the Christian Faith; Grand Rapids, Michigan; 1999.
12. David Hansen; The Art of Pastoring; Downers Grove, Illinois; Inter Varsity Press; 1994
13. Jack W. Hayford (General Editor); Spirit Filled Life Bible: New King James Version; Nashville, Tennessee; Thomas Nelson Publishers; 1991.

14. Dr. Robert L. Reymond; A New Systematic Theology of the Christian Faith; Nashville, Tennessee; Thomas Nelson Publishers; 1998.
15. Oral Roberts; The New Testament Comes Alive Volume Three; Nashville, Tennessee; Parthenon Press; 1984.
16. Dr. William Smith; Smith's Bible Dictionary; Philadelphia, Pennsylvania; A.J. Holman Company; Original copyright 1863, current copy has no date included.
17. James Strong; Strong's Exhaustive Concordance of the Bible; Nashville, Tennessee; Thomas Nelson Publishers; 1990.
18. W.E. Vine; Vine's Expository Dictionary of Old and New Testament Words; Nashville, Tennessee; Thomas Nelson Publishers; 1997.
19. http://www.iep.utm.edu/Freud; August 2011.
20. Logos Library System; http://www.logos.com; King James Bible Commentary; January 2012.
21. http://www.nanc.org; August 2011.
22. http://www.newworldencyclopedia.org; August 2011.
23. http://www.sntp.net; August 2011.
24. http://www.webspace.ship.edu; August 2011.
25. http://en.wikipedia.ore/wiki/Orval_Hobart_Mowrer; August 2011.
26. Tim Clinton, Archibald Hart, George Ohlschlager; Caring For People God's Way; Nashville Tennessee; Thomas Nelson Publishers; 2005.
27. L. Ronald Brushwyler, D.Min; Pastoral Care vs. Professional Counseling: Discerning the Difference; Westchester, Illinois; The Midwest Ministry Development Service; 1999.
28. Tim Clinton (Executive Editor); The Soul Care Bible; Nashville, Tennessee; Thomas Nelson Publishers; 2001.
29. Tim Clinton, Eric Scalise; Ambassadors of Reconciliation: Ethics in Christian Caregiving: Christian Counseling Today; Volume 17, number 3.
30. Dr. Tim Clinton, Dr. Ron Hawkins; The Popular Encyclopedia of Christian Counseling; Eugene, Oregon; Harvest House Publishers; 2011.

Made in the USA
Monee, IL
21 July 2020